ANTHROPOLOGY AND MIGRATION

ANTHROPOLOGY AND MIGRATION

Essays on Transnationalism, Ethnicity, and Identity

Caroline Brettell

A Division of Rowman & Littlefield Publishers, Inc.
Walnut Creek • Lanham • New York • Oxford

AltaMira Press
A Division of Rowman & Littlefield Publishers, Inc.
1630 North Main Street, #367
Walnut Creek, CA 94596
www.altamirapress.com

Rowman & Littlefield Publishers, Inc.
A Member of the Rowman & Littlefield Publishing Group
4501 Forbes Boulevard, Suite 200
Lanham, Maryland 20706

PO Box 317
Oxford
OX2 9RU, UK

British Library Cataloguing in Publication Information Available

Library of Congress Cataloging-in-Publication Data

Brettell, Caroline.
  Anthropology and migration : essays on transnationalism, ethnicity, and
identity / Caroline Brettell.
    p. cm.
Includes bibliographical references and index.
  ISBN 0-7591-0319-4 (alk. paper) — ISBN 0-7591-0320-8 (pbk. : alk. paper)
  1. Portuguese—Foreign countries—History. 2. Portugal—Emigration and
immigration—Social aspects. 3. Return migration—Portugal—History. 4.
Identity (Psychology)—Portugal. 5. Ethnicity—Portugal. I. Title.
  DP534.5.B74 2003
  305.86'9'009—dc21

                    2003006176

Printed in the United States of America

∞™ The paper used in this publication meets the minimum requirements of
American National Standard for Information Sciences—Permanence of Paper
for Printed Library Materials, ANSI/NISO Z39.48-1992.

Contents

v

List of Tables

Introduction

Anthropology, Migration, and the Portuguese Diaspora

Anthropology, as a discipline, came relatively late to the study of migration as a social, political, economic, and cultural process. Indeed, anthropologists often chose not to write about it, even when it was happening right in front of them, because it did not fit the timeless and bounded idea of culture that framed their analyses. For example, while it has been estimated that approximately 52 percent of the Chambri (Tchambuli) men between the ages of fifteen and forty-five were working as migrant laborers and therefore absent from the Papua New Guinea village where Margaret Mead was living in 1933, she "did not take these articulations with the larger system into consideration" (Gewertz and Errington 1991, 87). Similarly, although George Foster (1967) acknowledged that some residents of the Mexican village of Tzintzuntzan, where he carried out field research in the mid-1940s, were involved in the *bracero* program, he leaves the significant impact of migration out of his model of the "image of limited good."

However, by the late 1950s and early 1960s, it became apparent to many anthropologists that migration should receive more systematic attention as a topic for research. Initially the emphasis was on rural–urban migration, the demographic factor that most contributed to the exponential growth of cities such as Mexico City, Cairo, Jakarta, Lagos, Nairobi, Lima, São Paolo, and Rio de Janeiro. Migration was a manifestation of a pervasive transformation from a rural agrarian base to an urban industrial base in the economies of most developing countries (Safa 1975). In the emerging cities of South and Southeast Asia, Africa, and Central and South America, rural villagers were finding employment as unskilled or semiskilled workers and were living in neighborhoods with people of their own ethnic group or home community. Interest in migrants and migration grew in conjunction with the growth of both peasant studies and urban anthropology, as anthropologists began to focus on "peasants" or "tribesmen" in cities (Butterworth 1962; Gutkind 1965; Kemper 1977; Mangin 1970; Mayer 1961; Plotnicov 1967; Whiteford 1976; see also Brettell 2000). Eventually anthropologists also began to study those peasants and tribesmen who found their way to the cities of the developed world (Deshen and Shokeid 1974; Foner 1979; Helweg 1979; Philpott 1973; Watson 1975). The number of ethnographic monographs on these particular migration streams increased significantly during the 1980s and 1990s, as migration was established as a central topic in anthropological research (for example, Bhachu 1985; Burns 1993; Carter 1997; Gilad 1989; González 1992; Gmelch 1992; Klaver 1997; Werbner 1990).

Today anthropologists can hardly avoid some consideration of migrants and the migratory process. It has been estimated that in 1990 120 million people were living outside their country of birth or citizenship, and that by 2000 this figure had risen to 160 million (Martin and Widgren 2002). Anthropologists have not only continued to examine the impact of out-migration on sending communities, they have also increasingly turned their attention to the study of immigrant populations in the United States (for example, Chavez 1992; Gold 1995; Glick Schiller and Fouron 2001; Grasmuck and Pessar 1991; Khandelwal 2002; Lessinger 1995; Mahler 1995; Margolis 1994; Stepick 1998).

The breadth of geographical coverage over several decades has also generated a breadth of conceptual and analytical insights. This book is about some of the theoretical contributions made by anthropology as it has increasingly engaged with the subject of migration. It addresses the question of varying units of analysis, something that has become particularly challenging to anthropologists as they have tried to merge micro and macro perspectives. It examines the concept of transnationalism, a concept that has transformed how we understand the process of immigrant incorporation by offering an alternative model to the older assimilation model. It explores the insertion of immigrant populations in cities and questions of ethnicity and ethnic identity. And finally it tackles the relationship between gender and migration, a topic to which anthropology has made extremely important empirical and theoretical contributions.

I examine these conceptual and theoretical questions in the anthropology of migration through the lens of a particular immigrant experience with which I have been working for more than thirty years, that of the Portuguese. I do so for three reasons: because I believe there is much to learn from this particular case, because there is great historical depth to the Portuguese experience with migration, and because I believe fundamentally in the significance of cross-cultural comparison to the anthropological enterprise. I bring together a series of essays about the Portuguese experience in order to address similarities and differences across both space and time in the migration process.

My interest in Portuguese migrants dates back to the summer of 1971. I was invited by the chair of the department of anthropology at Brown University to spend two months working on a project funded by the National Institutes of Mental Health on immigrants in the Providence area. I had just completed a year studying the Portuguese language to fulfill the requirements for a major in Latin American studies at Yale University. I could not have been more amazed, upon my arrival in Providence, to discover a large community of Portuguese immigrants (largely from the Azores and the Cape Verde Islands) in East Providence and in Fall River and New Bedford, Massachusetts. My earliest field research involved attending several of the summer festivals sponsored by the Portuguese and other immigrant populations in Rhode Island. I recorded the following observations in my field notes for the Feast of Santo Cristo of June 27, 1971.

> Two masses were held, both a high mass and a low mass. Portuguese was definitely the predominant spoken language in and around the church, although the masses were given in English. At 2:30 the streets were very crowded and over the P.A. instructions were given on the arrangements for the procession. Among the clubs that arrived were the Portuguese American Athletic Club (founded 1901), the Banda Recreativa de Rosário of Providence, the Associação Académica (founded 1962), the Banda da Nossa Senhora da Luz of Fall River (founded 1909), and the Açoriano Band of Fall River. . . . Each group had an organizational banner but carried as well both the American and Portuguese flags. . . . The procession began. The bells of the church rang as those carrying reliquaries appeared out of the church door. They were followed by a number of men carrying the special *altar* that had been placed in the front left corner of the church for the two masses. It was florally decorated and had a large wooden statue of Santo Cristo in the center. The *altar* was followed by about fifty elderly ladies carrying candles and wearing lace coverings on their heads. They were followed, in turn, by the Fall River bishop general of the Knights of Columbus. After them came the three officiating priests, in their vestments and under a canopy. The procession took about one hour and twenty minutes to make its full circuit back to the church. As the priests passed, people kneeled and crossed themselves. Upon the conclusion of the procession there was an *arraial*—concerts, auctions, and a sale of Portuguese and American foods until 11:30 p.m. The foods were Portuguese stew, favas, chouriço, corn, and Quahogs.

The roots of the Portuguese immigrant communities in southeastern New England can be traced to the early nineteenth century. Whaling boats picked up crews in the Cape Verde and Azorean Islands and deposited them in the vicinity of New Bedford, Massachusetts, for short periods of time as they reoutfitted for a new voyage (Halter 1993; Williams 1982). Many of these mariners remained in New England after the decline of the whaling industry, settling in Providence and New Bedford and sending for family members (Baxter et al. 1985). Later in the nineteenth century it was the textile mills that attracted Portuguese immigrants as they attracted other immigrants.

> The rivers and streams that dropped down out of the Massachusetts hinterland to the sea were impossible to navigate, but an excellent source of cheap power. These streams were harnessed, up and down the coast, to drive the machinery of industry development. Cotton mills, where raw fibers were converted into finished materials, sprang into life all along this fall line in the early 1800s. The first cotton mill in Fall River, a port town fourteen miles west of New Bedford and eighteen miles southwest of Providence, began production in 1813; sixty years later the textile mills in Fall River were employing in excess of ten thousand workers. New Bedford, although preoccupied with whaling, eventually perceived the advantages of a more assured industrial base, and its first cotton mill went into operation in 1849; others followed, and by 1870 the city's four mills provided jobs for about two thousand industrial workers. (Williams 1982, 12)

The 1870 census reported 8,971 Portuguese in the United States, of which 257 were "colored" and undoubtedly Cape Verdean. Thirty-six percent of these Portuguese natives lived in the four New England states of Massachusetts (2,555), Connecticut (221), Rhode Island (189), and New York (334); forty percent (3,435) resided in California (Williams 1982, 13). The 1880 U.S. Census counted 15,650 Portuguese-born residents in the continental United States; by 1900 the number was 40,431, and by 1920 114,321. In 1900, 63.5 percent of the foreign-born Portuguese of Massachusetts were concentrated in the cities of New Bedford and Fall River, and the state of Massachusetts had the largest concentration of Portuguese, surpassing California (Taft 1923; Williams 1990). According to Silva (1976, 222–23) about half the Portuguese and Polish populations of Fall River were working in the mills by 1919. In other communities of Rhode Island, Portuguese men were working in unskilled mill jobs as combers, spinners, carders, and doffers, or in low-wage jobs in coal yards, produce houses, slaughter houses, small grocery, fruit, fish, or bakery shops, or as farm laborers (Lamphere 1987). The overwhelming majority of the Portuguese who arrived in this period were from the Azores. They were young, unmarried, largely illiterate, and unskilled.

Although the flow of Portuguese to the United States was by no means as large as those of Italians or eastern European and Russian Jews, it was also virtually halted by the 1924 National Origins Quota Act. The Portuguese quota was set at 503 persons per year (Baganha 1990). This was a dramatic limitation since, in the period between 1911 and 1920, almost 90,000 Portuguese had entered the United States. The 1930 census counted 109,453 Portuguese in the United States; 10 percent of all Portuguese-Americans lived in Rhode Island, 37.7 percent in Massachusetts.

In 1965 the National Origins Quota Act was replaced by the Immigration and Nationality Act. A new wave of immigration to the United States began, one that included the Portuguese.[1] The 1965 law was based on preferential categories, allowing first for the immigration of immediate relatives with no quota restrictions. In addition, 20,000 visas for each Eastern Hemisphere country were allowed (with a maximum cap of 170,000), with certain ranked preferences applied to those who had kinship connections to U.S. citizens or permanent residents. According to Immigration and Naturalization Service data, 76,065 individuals who listed their last place of residence as Portugal were admitted legally to the United States between 1961 and 1970, compared with 19,588 in the prior decade. Several of the Portuguese people whom I interviewed during the summer of 1971 were recent immigrants who had arrived in the United States under the preference or quota systems of the new legislation. Many found work in the textile mills and apparel factories of southeastern New England.

During the period between 1971 and 1980, 101,710 individuals who listed their country of last residence as Portugal were admitted legally to the United States, and the 1980 census listed 190,298 people of Portuguese ancestry in the country. Sixty-three percent of these were living in Portuguese-speaking homes. In 1980 Rhode Island had 61,756 people of Portuguese ancestry—about 10 percent of the Portuguese Americans in the United States (Williams 1990). After 1980 the number of individuals entering the United States as legal immigrants who declared Portugal as their last place of residence declined sharply, to 40,431 between 1981 and 1990 and to 22,916 between 1991 and 2000. Undoubtedly some of this decline was due to the political and economic changes occurring in Portugal, as the country moved toward full membership in the European Union. Many scholars of Portuguese history and society concur that Portugal has made rapid progress during the last two decades of the twentieth century.

It is important to note that between 1965 and the 1990s some Portuguese nationals, like immigrants from other places, entered the United States on tourist visas, overstayed their visas, and became illegal immigrants. At the beginning of this period they faced threats of arrest and deportation, as did immigrants of other nationalities, but many have been able to legalize their status. Today significant Portuguese communities thrive from Boston to Newark to Manassas, Virginia.[2] Indeed, it is the Portuguese, many of them initially illegal, who have helped to revive parts of downtown Newark where a couple of streets are lined with Portuguese bakeries and restaurants. In the mid-1990s the Portuguese made up 40 percent of the 40,000 residents living in the Ironbound area of Newark, a region bordered by the Passaic River on the north and railroad tracks on the west and east.

> In the compact 4.5 square miles of Ironbound, illegal immigrants own businesses, pay taxes and, in contrast to the raids of thirty years ago, walk the streets with little fear of arrest. "We are totally invisible," said Paul Quintela, 32, a bar manager who illegally came to the country in 1990. . . . Before coming to the United States, he had owned an ice cream parlor but saw little future for himself in Portugal. . . . He was startled to hear people speaking Portuguese everywhere on the street [in Ironbound]. . . . "I thought I was still in Portugal," said Mr. Quintela, who eventually became a legal resident of the United States through the sponsorship of his employer at the restaurant. (Dunn 1995, 2)

The invisibility that this man refers to is broadly characteristic of the Portuguese in America. They have rarely been written about in studies of either the third or the fourth wave immigration to the United States. Today, like other immigrants from Europe, they are overshadowed by immigrants from Asia and Latin America. And yet, in New Jersey, Rhode Island, and southeastern Massachusetts, their numbers are significant, and they are a fundamental part of the immigrant mosaic of the northeastern United States.

Since 1965 the Portuguese have migrated not only to the United States but also to Canada. During the summer of 1972 I spent two months in Toronto, living in the Portuguese community in the heart of that city. In 1953 there were somewhat fewer than 4,000 people of Portuguese origin in Canada. Some of them had arrived in response to advertisements in local Portuguese newspapers calling for agricultural workers for Canada (Anderson and Higgs 1976, 27). This was a period when Canada was extremely short of manual laborers and was encouraging immigration. According to Hawkins (1988), 900 Portuguese from the Azores and the mainland were recruited for farm, railway, and trade work in 1954 and

1955, and by 1957 2,000 farm laborers, 1,000 rail workers, and 50 trades workers had arrived. Once the beachhead was established, the Portuguese could take advantage of the 1952 Immigration Act, which allowed for the nomination and sponsoring of relatives as new entrants. Eventually the Portuguese community grew, and the population gravitated toward the cities, Toronto primarily and Montreal secondarily. They were attracted by a booming construction industry but also found work in hospitals as housekeeping staff, in factories, and in other cleaning jobs (Anderson and Higgs 1976; Alpalhão and da Rosa 1979; Noivo 1997).[3]

In 1960 there were 22,434 Portuguese immigrants in Canada; a decade later the number had risen to almost 85,000. By 1980 the official figure was over 150,000, although other estimates that included illegal immigrants put the figure at over 200,000 (Anderson 1974; Anderson and Higgs 1976; Giles 2002; Williams 1982). According to Statistics Canada there were close to 250,000 Canadians claiming Portuguese ancestry in 1991 (Statistics Canada 1991). While China, India, Pakistan, and the Philippines are the major sources for immigrants to Canada at the dawn of the twenty-first century, the Portuguese should not be overlooked, particularly in the province of Ontario, where 70 percent of them were residing in 1991, primarily in Toronto and its surrounding suburbs. Part III of this book discusses aspects of the early phase of this immigration and explores how an immigrant community is established in its earliest generation within a country and a city. It also addresses theoretical debates about ethnicity and the ethnic group, two key analytical concepts in the anthropology of migration.[4]

While 5.5 percent of Portuguese emigrants went to Canada in the period between 1950 and 1969 and 27.6 percent went to Brazil, 43.5 percent went to France (Antunes 1970). During the summer of 1972 I lived in a house with two Portuguese families, one from the Azores and the other from northern Portugal. The man from northern Portugal had spent five years in France before emigrating to Canada in 1965. He returned to Portugal in 1967 to marry his fiancée, and after eight months they came to Canada together. I listened carefully to his accounts of his illegal entry into France and of his life working in construction on a building near the Eiffel Tower. He told me that he had a brother and a sister still in France and four brothers in Germany; only his mother was left in Portugal.

I decided that summer that I would work on Portuguese emigration to France for my dissertation research. I was interested in whether or not the proximity between France and Portugal might result in more back-and-forth movement than was characteristic of the emigrations to the United States and Canada. This was also a flow dominated by people from continental Portugal rather than from the islands, and that too was of interest to me. Finally, my exposure to issues in the infant field of feminist anthropology through my Brown professor Louise Lamphere led me to focus on Portuguese migrant women, a subject that was virtually not discussed in the social science literature at that time, not even anthropology.

Europe became a receiving area for immigrants rather than a sending area in the post–World War II period. The first wave (1945–1960) included refugees returning from Eastern Europe and individuals coming from former colonies. The second wave, the one that brought the Portuguese along with Italians, Spaniards, and eventually Turks and Yugoslavs, occurred between 1960 and 1974 and has been labeled the "guest worker era" (Martin and Widgren 2002). However, the guests (who were mostly men) stayed, and eventually their families joined them. In fact, in France, unlike Germany, a concerted effort was made to reunify families.

While some Portuguese migrated to Germany (Bauer et al. 2002; Klimt 1992), Luxembourg, Switzerland, and the United Kingdom (Giles 1991, 1992), the largest number went to France. Indeed, during the 1960s and into the early 1970s, the Portuguese constituted the largest and most important immigrant population in France, and by the time of the 1975 census they numbered 758,000. The early period of Portuguese migration to France can be divided into roughly four phases: 1950–1961, when a fairly controlled number of immigrants entered per year (1,000–5,000), and clandestine immigration was low; 1961–1968, which saw a rapid increase in the annual rate of immigration (about 40,000 per year) and a surge in the number of clandestine immigrants; 1968–1971, when the rate of immigration accelerated and the Portuguese represented approximately 50 percent of all annual immigration to France (about 80,000 per year); and 1971–1974, which saw a decline in the annual rate, specifically because of an agreement signed by Portugal and France in 1971 that limited the annual number of Portuguese immigrants given entry to France to 65,000, and generally because of worldwide problems of inflation and unemployment.

This migration was male-dominated at its outset but gradually more women came, both as single women and as spouses. In 1962 women were 30 percent of the Portuguese population in France, and by 1975 they were 46 percent. While men found employment in the construction industry and in automobile plants, women found work in the domestic sector, as private maids for French bourgeois families or as members of cleaning staffs for office buildings and other institutions. Women's experience of migration and the impact of male emigration on women left behind are the focus of part IV of this book.

The number of Portuguese in France fell during the 1980s, but in 1990 they were still the largest immigrant population there, numbering

649,714, compared to 216,047 Spaniards (but 1,020,468 Spaniards who were French by acquisition), and 252,759 Italians (Ogden 1995, 293). Close to 50 percent of the Portuguese population live in Paris and the surrounding suburbs, where they have become part of the working class (Rocha-Trindade and Raveau 1998). The migration of Portuguese nationals to France is now regulated by the policies of free movement of labor in the European Community.

A third massive wave of immigration occurred in western Europe during the 1990s, and by the end of the decade close to 20 million foreigners were living there, 36 percent of them in Germany (Martin and Widgren 2002). This latest wave was composed of people from North Africa (primarily to France), Asia (primarily to Britain), Eastern Europe, and Turkey (primarily to Germany) (Massey et al. 1998). These were people who looked different and who practiced different religions from the resident populations. Immigration in France and in several other countries of northern Europe is as much about religion as it is about "foreignness," and it is certainly about racism (Wrench and Solomos 1993). In France today it is not the Christian, white, European Portuguese who are the objects of anti-immigrant sentiment. They have been fairly well integrated into northern European society and culture, and they move back and forth freely to their homeland. Their experiences are therefore germane to the issues of transnationalism that are hotly debated in current scholarship on immigration. These issues are discussed in part II of this book.

Luis Guarnizo and Michael Smith (1998; see also Guarnizo 2001) have distinguished between transnationalism from above (initiated by nation-states and the global economy) and transnationalism from below (the social networks that people forge across national boundaries). Chapters 3 and 4 offer discussions of these two dimensions of transnationalism as they have been created and sustained by the Portuguese state on the one hand and by Portuguese immigrants on the other. Not only have individual immigrants retained ties to their home villages, sent money back home, and built houses in their home communities, but the Portuguese state has constantly worked to sustain the loyalties of citizens abroad in order to support their own interests. Indeed the Portuguese case is interesting as an early example of precisely what Glick Schiller (1999, 95) describes, when she writes about "political leaders of emigrant sending states [who] . . . re-envision their states as transnational." This vision of Portugal is old, not new, although it has taken on a somewhat different character in the postcolonial world. The Portuguese case offers additional fuel to the debate about what is really new about transnationalism (Foner 1997; Gerstle and Mollenkopf 2001).

My research in France eventually took me to Portugal, where I began to work on the history of Portuguese emigration and look at its impact on village life over two and a half centuries (Brettell 1986). For much of the eighteenth, nineteenth, and early twentieth centuries, the major destination for Portuguese emigrants was Brazil. Despite the presence of Portuguese in the United States as early as the first decades of the nineteenth century, and the significant increase in immigration during the last decade of the nineteenth century and the first decade of the twentieth century, the flow to the United States was only 12 to 14 percent of the total migratory flow of Portuguese overseas (Baganha 1995, 91). Between 1891 and 1911 more than 90 percent of Portuguese emigrants went to Brazil (Nunes 2000, 27). It is perhaps for this reason that the Portuguese do not figure prominently in discussions of the third wave of immigration among scholars of U.S. immigration. And yet the Portuguese, unlike the Italians or Jews, were much more successful at spreading their language globally through both colonization and emigration. Portugal is a country of only 10 million inhabitants, but the Portuguese language is spoken in Brazil, a country with close to 175 million inhabitants, Mozambique, with a population of 19 million, Angola, with a population of 10 million, and beyond to Timor, Goa, and Macao. The Portuguese diaspora is extensive and significant and yet, ironically, it does not hold a central place in the historical and social scientific literature on global migrations and diasporic communities.[5] Thus one purpose of this book is to bring Portugal and Portuguese emigrants into such discussions. Certainly the Portuguese state has been and remains self-conscious not only about the Portuguese diaspora, but also about the contributions of both colonization and emigration to national history and national identity.[6] Furthermore, the Portuguese case reinforces the point of how deeply rooted migration is in human history.

As I have been suggesting, a second purpose of this volume is to draw on the Portuguese case for what it adds to the discussion within anthropology, as well as the social sciences more broadly, of key questions and concepts germane to our understanding of global migration at the dawn of the twenty-first century. I hope to suggest, through the introduction and elucidation of some aspects of this particular case, that there is a good deal of continuity over time in the experience of immigration. Indeed many of these essays offer not only a historical perspective on Portugal but also an analysis of what was going on in receiving societies other than the United States during the first decade after 1965—the earliest period of the massive late-twentieth-century migrations. Thus one of my primary aims is to suggest that our work in the anthropology of migration in the twenty-first century needs to be more broadly comparative across both time and space. The results of such comparisons are threefold: an avoidance of American exceptionalism, a sharper delineation of analytical concepts, and a broader theoretical formulation of structure, process, and agency in the study of migration.

Further, the book highlights what we can learn by varying our unit of analysis in the study of migration. One discussion looks at the instrumental role of the Portuguese state in shaping emigration, while others, by at least briefly delineating varying immigration policies and settlement patterns, focus attention on differences among receiving states. The family or the household is another unit of analysis that anthropologists have used in their studies of emigrants and immigrants, and it is certainly an important structural unit to examine in the Portuguese case. Community is yet another, be it the immigrant community in a major city or a village of origin. And finally, there is the agency of the individual migrant, a subject I address in chapter 2. While the political scientist focuses primarily on the state, the economist primarily on labor markets, and the sociologist on institutions, anthropologists generally acknowledge the significance of each of these units or levels of analysis and try to attend to all of them in their studies of migration. This comprehensive approach is, after all, the crux of anthropological holism.

One final observation is perhaps in order, because it holds out promise for future study. Portugal has become a country of immigration, much like Spain and Italy.[7] The earliest immigrants in Portugal were former emigrants repatriated from the African colonies after decolonization—the so-called *retornados* (Lubkemann 2003; Malheiros 2002; Ovalle-Bahamón 2003; Rocha-Trindade 1995).[8] These individuals were followed by skilled professionals from Brazil (Feldman-Bianco 2001) and unskilled workers from the Cape Verde Islands and other PALOP (Países Africanos de Lingua Oficial Portuguêsa) countries: Angola, Mozambique, Guinea-Bissau, São Tomé, and Principe (Solé 1995). According to Baganha et al. (2000, 11) "in 1997, of the 175 legally registered foreigners, 47 percent were from Africa, 28 percent from Europe, 14 percent from South America, and 6 percent from North America." The presence of large numbers of black Africans has been challenging for Portugal. There are now debates about racism in a country that has long prided itself on a multicultural tolerance rooted in centuries of colonialism. For the first time in recent history, Portugal is experiencing diversity in the homeland.[9]

More recently this diversity has extended to linguistic difference. According to Malheiros (2002, 5) "in a mere five years, Ukranians have become the third-largest group of foreigners [in Portugal], immediately after Cape Verdians and Brazilians." Although many of these workers initially entered Portugal illegally, in recent years the Portuguese state has given legal status to men from the Ukraine, Moldova, Russia, and Rumania who are working on construction projects throughout the country, men living in isolation and with no knowledge of the Portuguese language. In short, for several centuries the Portuguese have faced their own integration abroad, and now they are faced with integrating the foreign "other" at home. In May of 2002 Portugal moved to curb the number of non–European Union immigrants it was admitting, to control illegal immigration, and to promote special integration programs for second-generation immigrants. These are issues that have been debated for some time in northern Europe, in Canada, and in the United States, but they are new to a country like Portugal, which throughout much of its history was a country of emigration, not immigration.

Notes

1. Williams (1982, 103) notes the special Azorean Refugee Acts of 1958 and 1960 that facilitated the immigration of 4,811 Portuguese, largely from the island of Faial, which had suffered a volcanic eruption in 1957. These individuals established the foothold for the post-1965 wave of immigration.

2. Glader (2002, PW1) recently reported on Portuguese immigrants in the Washington, D.C., area. "Many of the nearly 2,000 Portuguese immigrants who live in the Prince William County area work with concrete and moved from New England states after home construction there slowed in the 1980s. . . . With 9,000 or so Portuguese immigrants in Northern Virginia, Manassas has been a cultural hub since 1993, when local Portuguese leaders built a large community center on Lee Avenue that includes a restaurant, dance halls, locker rooms for a soccer team, a library, and language classrooms for children. . . . At the Virginia Portuguese Community Center, there's Portuguese cuisine along with Sagres beer, Vinho Verde wine, and, on weekends, competitions with visiting soccer teams or celebrations with Portuguese bands."

3. Cole (1998) writes about Portuguese from the famous fishing town of Nazaré in central Portugal who settled and remained, together with immigrants from the Azores and Tras-os-Montes, in more rural communities in Canada on the shores of Lake Erie. They continued their work in fisheries.

4. For a more recent study of the Portuguese in Toronto see Giles 2002.

5. A special issue of the journal *Identities: Global Studies in Culture and Power* (8, no. 4 [2001]) begins to address this lacuna by focusing on empire and its aftermath in the Portuguese-speaking world.

6. Laguerre (1998, 8) argues that diaspora means both displacement and reattachment. "Diaspora denotes displacement in the sense that one lives outside one's primary land of attachment. . . . Diaspora also means reattachment and is a mechanism that expands the space of the nation beyond the borders of the state. . . . By diaspora, we refer to individual immigrants or communities who live outside

the legal or recognized boundaries of the state or the homeland, but inside the reterritorialized space of the dispersed nation." Portugal and the Portuguese abroad, from this perspective, indeed constitute a diaspora.

7. Massey and his colleagues (1998, 16) have recently written that "immigration into Southern Europe is so new that governments have not established reliable statistical systems for reporting the flows; and being closer to the Third World than other European nations, illegal migration has assumed larger proportions." Immigration was the key topic of discussion at a European Union summit that took place in Sevilla, Spain, during the summer of 2002.

8. See the excellent new book edited by Andrea Smith, *Europe's Invisible Migrants,* which focuses on the return migration to Europe of people from around the globe who were caught up in a decolonization process that began after World War II.

9. Malheiros (2002, 2) makes the astounding observation that in the first half of the sixteenth century 10 percent of the 100,000 inhabitants of Lisbon were Africans, the highest of any European capital. Lisbon also welcomed visitors from Spain, Italy, and Holland. By the middle of the seventeenth century, this "cosmopolitan profile" had eroded. Malheiros offers an excellent discussion of recent immigration trends in Portugal—people coming not only from the countries of Africa but also from Brazil, Pakistan, India, China, and the countries of Eastern Europe. For a discussion of Brazilian immigrants in Portugal, see Feldman-Bianco (2001). In the early 1990s a series of conflicts erupted over so-called "undesirable" Brazilians who had found their way to Portugal, and the restrictive Foreigners Law of 1992 limited the entry of immigrants arriving from former Portuguese colonies, including Brazil.

I

SITUATING THE ANTHROPOLOGICAL PERSPECTIVE
Macro, Meso, and Micro Approaches to the Study of Migration

Immigration is a subject studied by scholars from a range of disciplines (Brettell and Hollifield 2000), but no matter what the discipline, a shared set of questions relate to why people move, who moves, and what happens after they move. However, the emphasis in addressing these questions is variously placed. Political scientists and economists are largely interested in the flows that exist between two countries and how these flows are shaped by policy or by labor markets and trade agreements. Sociologists, who have generally focused on the receiving end, look at issues of integration. Anthropologists, by contrast, have tended to work at both ends of the migration process, beginning in the country of origin and asking what prompts individuals to leave particular communities and then what happens to them in their place of destination, including if and how they remain connected to their places of origin. Geographers, who have recently become active in migration studies (Gober 2000), focus on issues of space in the broadest sense of the term, looking, for example, at settlement patterns and residential segregation or at the cultural geography of immigrant communities.

The questions of why people move, who moves, and what happens after they move are also approached within these various disciplines from diverse theoretical perspectives and sometimes with distinctly different units and levels of analysis—the individual, the household, the state; the micro, the meso, the macro (Faist 1997; Gans 2000). The chapters in this section are about levels and units of analysis, about theoretical perspectives and how they influence the framing of questions, and about structure and agency in the study of migration.

Macro approaches to migration focus on broad population flows and the political and economic constraints and opportunities that influence these flows. Among the latter are the policies of a sending or receiving society that might either restrict emigration or foster immigration or that might control these in some way to support particular labor market needs, programs for development, or simply a balance of payments. For example, the need for the technological expertise of H-1B visa holders who hold temporary work permits in the United States influences the movement of significant numbers of workers from countries like China or India. Similarly, the Philippine government and private institutions play an important role in the organization, management, and regulation of "gendered patterns of labor migration as they pursue a labor-export policy that [not only] fits into a global economy" but also "offers solutions to homeland problems of unemployment and underemployment" (Tyner 1999, 685–86).

While anthropologists are obviously more comfortable working at a micro or meso level, they do engage the macro level, because they are interested in the structural and historical context within which individuals must and do act, including the choices they make in relation to migration. Anthropologists address the macro perspective through the lenses of world systems theory, dependency theory, or economy. According to world systems theory it is "the penetration of capitalist economic relations into peripheral, noncapitalist societies [that] creates a mobile population that is prone to migrate abroad" (Massey et. al. 1993, 444). Dependency theory, as a rather strong reaction to a modernization approach that suggested that migration would result in the development of sending societies through the ideas that supposedly progressive migrants brought home, suggests, by contrast, that migration spawns the development of underdevelopment (Frank 1967). And, within the political economy framework, anthropologists invoke dual labor market theory which argues that "international migration stems from the intrinsic labor demands of modern industrial societies" (Massey et al 1993, 440). In all these ways, anthropologists recognize, theoretically, how global capitalism has fostered the often exploitative relationships that exist between developing and labor-supplying countries and developed and labor-receiving countries. These unbalanced relationships often create the conditions that lead to emigration.

The first part of chapter 1 takes up some of these issues by discussing the historical and political-economic contexts, at home and internationally, that have fostered migration from Portugal, beginning in the colonial era, when a wealthy Portuguese nation penetrated Brazil in search of land and natural resources. It is equally important to understand that, by the time of post–World War II migration to France, Portugal found itself an underdeveloped nation in the southern periphery of Europe in relation to a developed northern Europe and hence a supplier of labor to a labor-hungry north. Only recently has this situation changed, as a more modern Portugal itself seeks labor from the developing margins of Eastern Europe. This is a perspective on emigration at the macro level and during what Fernand Braudel (1992) called the *longue durée* which outlines broad structural features of a changing global economy.

Of particular concern in chapter 1 is how population flows out of Portugal have been shaped by legislative policy that was, at times, rather ambivalent. How did the Portuguese state attempt to control flows, and how did individuals circumvent those controls? And how did the Portuguese state survive by turning its back on departures, such that it was unnecessary to tackle the problems of unemployment or underemployment in the northern countryside? With emigration as a "safety valve," aspirations for change are taken off the back of the state and focused on individual migrants who, by departing, can make some personal effort to improve their own lives or those of their families. At the same time, what migrants send back in the form of economic remittances sustains the state; it certainly did so in the case of Portugal during the 1960s, when the colonial wars in Africa were at their height and very costly. It should be evident that the questions that one can address at the macro and historical-structural level for Portugal are not only highly relevant to contemporary global migration flows more broadly but are also well understood in relation to ideas that emerge from world systems theory and a political-economy perspective.

But well understood does not mean fully understood. Thus the second part of chapter 1 takes up a different issue, one that I view as being closely allied to the more recent formulation of the concept of a "culture of migration." Massey and his colleagues attempt to review not only theories that explain how migration flows begin but also how they are perpetuated. "As migration grows in prevalence within a community," they argue, "it changes values and cultural perceptions in ways that increase the probability of future migration. . . . Migration becomes deeply ingrained into the repertoire of people's behaviors, and values associated with migration become part of the community's values. . . . For young men, and in many settings young women as well, migration becomes a rite of passage, and those who do not attempt to elevate their status through international movement are considered lazy, unenterprising, and undesirable" (Massey et al. 1993, 452-453).[1] Through such a process a "culture of migration" is created. In anthropological terms, cultures are rooted in symbols that manifest and express core values. In chapter 1 I argue that the emigrant has powerful symbolic meaning for the Portuguese people and the Portuguese nation. Until quite recently, to be

Portuguese was to emigrate or to have someone in one's family who was an emigrant. Emigration was, I have suggested elsewhere, an expected part of the life course, particularly for men growing up in the villages of the north (Brettell 2002b). Ultimately, then, my argument in the first chapter of this section is that Portuguese emigration is best understood if we examine it through multiple theoretical lenses, because a single lens offers only a partial truth.

But chapter 1 is itself partial and incomplete, because it ignores other levels and units of analysis that are, of course, well treated in later chapters in this book but perhaps more indirectly than directly. Thus chapter 2 attempts to approach the topic of migration from the micro and meso levels, returning to individuals, households, and social networks. From a micro-level perspective, it is the individual who decides to migrate, rationally weighing the costs against the benefits. This has been labeled neoclassical microeconomic theory.

> Potential migrants estimate the costs and benefits of moving to alternative international locations and migrate to where the expected discounted net returns are greatest over some time horizon. Net returns in each future period are estimated by taking the observed earnings corresponding to the individual's skills in the destination country and multiplying these by the probability of obtaining a job there (and for illegal migrants the likelihood of being able to avoid deportation) to obtain "expected destination earnings." These expected earnings are then subtracted from those expected in the community of origin (observed earnings there multiplied by the probability of employment) and the difference is summed over a time horizon from 0 to n, discounted by a factor that reflects the greater utility of money earned in the present than in the future. From this integrated difference the estimated costs are subtracted, to yield the expected net return to migration. (Massey et al. 1993, 434)

The strongest criticism of this microeconomic approach comes from anthropologists, who well know that individuals do not always leave for purely economic reasons and that the decision-making process is often more subtle and more far-reaching, shaped and reshaped by particular social and cultural contexts (Du Toit 1975, 1990). Indeed, very different factors than what is described above as the "pure" microeconomic approach may play into why women move in contrast with men and why they make the decisions that they do once abroad. The same could be said if we look at other aspects of social location—age, class, regional or ethnic background. We can, I suggest, get at some of these subtleties by listening to the voices of migrants themselves—how they tell their stories and what meanings they assign to their own actions. Chapter 2 introduces the notions of voice, agency, and life story into the debates about how we understand and theorize about migration.

By necessity storytelling must take the individual as the unit of analysis, so chapter 2 addresses the broader question of what we can learn about general processes by examining the experiences of particular individuals. This discussion also invokes problems that have long vexed anthropologists as they balance quantitative and qualitative methodologies in their research (Brettell 2002c). Patricia Pessar has recently written:

> In a formal research setting, such as one in which surveys or structured interviews are administered, an immigrant woman's decision to cloak her own and her family's experiences in a discourse of unity, female sacrifice, and the women's subordination to the patriarch represents a safe, respectful, and respectable 'text.' As I look back on my own research, this is the female voice that usually emerged from my own attempts at survey research. By contrast, my ethnographic collection of discourses that reveal family tensions and struggles emerged far more frequently out of encounters when my presence was incidental, that is, not the defining purpose for the ensuing dialogue, or after many months of participant observation had substantially reduced the initial formality and suspicion. (1999a, 586)

She goes on to suggest that "the chronicler of by far the best histories of divergent migration projects spent more than two years studying a limited number of immigrant families in both Mexico and Northern California and chose to feature in his writings only one family with whom he lived and socialized" (Pessar 1999a, 586–87).[2] What the ethnographer is balancing when she/he records the life history of one migrant or writes about one family is the detail, depth, and precise documentation of the ongoing process of making choices against a broader and undoubtedly more representative statistical sample that catches a group at a single moment in time. Is one better than the other or are they just alternative paths to understanding?

Individuals do not act in isolation. Indeed, a new economics of migration takes families or households as the unit of analysis and assumes that minimizing risk is as important as maximizing income. Households may send some family members out into foreign labor markets and keep others at home, thereby diversifying their risk. Further, "households send workers abroad not only to improve income in absolute terms but also to increase income *relative* to other households, and, hence to reduce their *relative* deprivation compared with some reference group" (Massey et al. 1993, 438). This approach is intriguing to anthropologists, because it situates individuals in relation to the social group, be it a nuclear family where men migrate while women tend to the fields, an extended family that sends some unmarried children into migration with or without a parent, or a village where families measure themselves against one another such that relative deprivation itself becomes a stimulus for departure.

This emphasis on groups of various kinds constitutes the meso level of analysis so well outlined by Thomas Faist (1997, 188). It encompasses the social relations between individuals in kinship groups, households, neighborhoods, friendship circles, and formal organizations. It is above all about social networks that not only facilitate departures but also help to keep emigrants connected with the homeland. Many individuals decide to move because they have a brother or a sister who is already abroad who can ease their entry, provide them with initial housing, and help them to find a first job. Social networks contribute significantly to the perpetuation of migration streams once they have started because "they lower the costs and risks of movement and increase the expected net returns to migration. Network connections constitute a form of social capital that people can draw upon" (Massey et al. 1993, 448).

Within anthropology the concept of a social network, as the web of social relations, can be dated to J. A. Barnes's (1954) research in a Norwegian fishing village. Rapport and Overing (2000, 291) observe rather intriguingly that the collective, depersonalizing, and distancing modeling that was characteristic of anthropological studies of social relations in other parts of the world seemed unsatisfactory in the study of the home environment. "Too much was known, and known experientially, to talk convincingly of 'Norwegian [à la Tallensi] descent systems' or 'Norwegian [à la Sherente] structures of marital exchange" (Rapport and Overing 2000, 291). The focus in network analysis is on individuals and their relationships, and the emphasis is on personal behavior and experience, on choice, action, and strategy.

Social networks received special attention in the work of British social anthropologists who began to study rural-urban migration among populations in sub-Saharan Africa in the late 1950s and 1960s. These anthropologists were looking for new ways to conceptualize how individuals related to groups in the more fluid social environments of cities. Building on this early work in Africa, anthropologists have continued to explore the role of social networks, largely based on ties of kinship and friendship, in the process of chain migration in a broad range of cross-cultural contexts (Butterworth 1962; Fjellman and Gladwin 1985; Graves and Graves 1974; Grieco 1995; Ho 1993). Wilson (1994, 275) has in fact argued that the network approach is preferable to the market theory approach, because it explains how people get to particular places not solely on the basis of a cost-benefit analysis of the most favorable destination but on the basis of whom they know and from whom they can seek help. Her argument is similar to that of Massey and his colleagues, who suggest that networks can become self-perpetuating to migration because "each act of migration itself creates the social structure needed to sustain it. Every new migrant reduces the costs of subsequent migration for a set of friends and relatives, and some of these people are thereby induced to migration, which further expands the set of people with ties abroad" (Massey et al. 1993, 449).

This is another way to approach the "culture" of migration—from a sociological rather than a symbolic perspective. It is an approach that I take up in chapter 2 by highlighting the networks of social relations among Portuguese immigrants in France. It is equally evident in chapters 7 and 8, and it is important to the transnational perspective that is raised in part II. Indeed, Nina Glick Schiller (1999, 99) argues that a transnational research paradigm necessitates adopting networks of social relationships that transgress national state boundaries rather than the individual as the unit of analysis such that "persons in the sending and receiving societies become participants in a single social unit." A further important insight is offered by Menjívar (2000, 36), who argues that the social networks of immigrants are "contingent and emergent." They are so because of the subtle interplay of structure and agency.

Marcus and Fischer (1986, 77) have argued that one of the challenges for anthropologists is "how to represent the embedding of richly described local cultural worlds in larger impersonal systems of political economy." How do we understand the former from the top down and the latter from the bottom up? Certainly this challenge exists in the study of migration, but it should be met. An anthropological approach to migration should emphasize both structure and agency; it should look at macro-level contextual issues, micro-level strategies and decision-making, and the meso-level relational structures within which individuals operate. It needs to articulate both people and process.[3]

Notes

1. Elsewhere I discuss how deeply ingrained migration has been in the everyday way of life of the European peasantry more broadly (Brettell 2002a).

2. She is referring here to the work of Roger Rouse (1989).

3. Glick Schiller (1997, 156) raises a similar challenge for transnational studies more generally. Such studies should attend to "the specification and location of agency; the relationship between transnational processes and states; and the historical simultaneity of and interaction between global, transnational, national, and local social fields." See also Kearney 1995.

1

The Emigrant, the Nation, and the State in Nineteenth- and Twentieth-Century Portugal

An Anthropological Approach

For a number of years, as both an anthropologist and a historian, I have been interested in the Portuguese emigrant (Brettell 1984, 1986, 1990b, 1995). Although I have sometimes considered the way in which state policies of emigration affect the individual emigrant, it has not been a problem central to my research. To rectify this oversight, in this chapter I will think more concertedly about the Portuguese emigrant in relationship to the Portuguese state from two distinct theoretical vantage points: political-economic and symbolic.[1]

From a political-economic perspective, the state is conceived of bureaucratically, much as Joyce Riegelhaupt (1967) conceived of it. It is a "legal and political organization with the power to require obedience and loyalty from its citizens" (Seton-Watson 1977, 1). Portuguese emigrants are also Portuguese citizens and, as such, they are subject to the laws that are promulgated to regulate the flow of people in and out of the country.

From a symbolic perspective, the state can be equated with nation and nationhood. A nation is "a community of people" with "supra-local identities and culture" (Seton-Watson 1977, 1; Grillo 1980, 6). In Portugal, the emigrant is a key symbol of national identity, or, to put it into Benedict Anderson's terms (1983), the emigrant is the vehicle for Portugal's "imagined community." If America is a nation of immigrants, Portugal is a nation of emigrants. This contrast is nowhere more apparent than in the prolific discourse about emigrants that exists in Portugal. It is this discourse that supplies me with the data, so to speak, for my discussion of the emigrant as a multivocal symbol for the Portuguese nation.

The Political Economy of Emigrant-State Relations

The political-economic perspective in anthropology is an attempt to locate anthropological subjects (the little people) within larger historical, political, and economic movements. In recent years this has led anthropologists to explore, for example, the way in which the slave trade and colonialism shaped the development of local communities, to trace the impact of the formation of postcolonial states on these local communities, and to assess the influence of boom-and-bust economic cycles and the spread of capitalism into various corners of the world system. Studies of emigration clearly fit neatly into this perspective.

Though many anthropologists have tended to view emigration from the point of view of the individuals or families—the actors—who are actually involved in making decisions to displace themselves from countryside to city or across international boundaries, such decisions are clearly not made in a vacuum. Nation states, whether as senders or receivers of migrants, shape both the structure and functioning of the international division of labor (Walton 1985). They do so as part of the larger process of state-building and empire-making (Roseberry 1988). In turn, emigrants themselves have an impact on local, regional, national, and international political economies.

More than a decade ago the historian Joel Serrão drew a distinction between the *colonizador* of the old regime and the *emigrante* of the modern period. The former, in Serrão's view was an individual who abandoned his native soil "under state initiative or as part of a national enterprise." The latter left "for exclusively personal reasons independent of official solicitations and sometimes in opposition to them" (Serrão 1974, 88). While this distinction is not incorrect, it tends to de-emphasize the role of the state in the process of emigration by contrast with its role in exploration and colonization.

As early as the seventeenth century the Portuguese state was conscious of the departure of its citizens for other than official business, and from that point on we can trace the development of an ambivalent policy that was rooted in the fact that emigration was considered to be both a problem and a solution. On the front stage, politicians, administrators, and leading thinkers of their day objected to massive and uncontrolled outflows. Underpopulation, *a falta de gente* in Manuel Severím de Faria's terms (Faria 1974), was a grave issue, and emigration was the culprit. From the seventeenth century until the twentieth century, in Portugal, as in other countries of the western world, it was believed that insufficient population made a state both militarily and economically weak (see Sampaio 1898; Carqueja 1916).

Faria and others writing in the seventeenth century recognized that emigration itself was caused by the lack of industry, the shortage of arable land, and the conquests. The state was called upon to address these issues. Two centuries later, Alexandre Herculano (1873) was pointing his finger at similar causes, which for centuries had made emigration a "constant structural reality of Portuguese society." Herculano, in fact, is responsible for one of the most perceptive and ringingly true statements about emigration, a statement that clearly challenges the sharp distinction formulated by Serrão. "Our best colony," he suggested, "is Brazil, after it was no longer a colony of ours."

Herculano had to shout loudly to drown out all the voices who condemned emigration because they thought that it was the primary if not sole cause of the increase in agricultural salaries (Carqueja 1916). Yet some of the same people who bemoaned, out of the right side of their mouths, the crisis caused by emigration, admitted with the left side that emigration constituted an effective strategy of survival for an economically fragile society that wanted to maintain the status quo.

Herein lies the contradiction of state intervention in the emigration process and in the lives of the individual emigrant, an intervention that operated largely through restrictions on access to passports. In the eighteenth century, passports to Brazil were limited to government functionaries and businessmen (Leite 1987). Though the formulators of the Carta Constitucional of 1826 recognized that individuals had a right to choose both their destination and the kind of work they would engage in once abroad, a fully liberal policy of emigration never developed.

By the middle of the nineteenth century, and well after Brazil had achieved independence from Portugal in 1822, state officials were primarily concerned about the number of minors who were being exploited on the one hand by the captains of ships and *engajadores* who, motivated by quantity rather than quality, arranged for their passage to Brazil, and on the other hand by the planters in Brazil who extracted their labor under onerous five-year contracts. For these people, emigration was a lucrative business. In 1858 a ship commander named Joaquim José de Sousa Breves and a businessman and supplier for the brig *Palpite* named João de Araujo Coutinho Vianna made a contract whereby Vianna provided Breves with workers (*colonos*) from Madeira under the following conditions: Breves would pay Vianna 50 *milréis* for each adult and 2000 *milréis* for all the children; Vianna would cede all his rights of engagement for work to Breves; Breves would transport these people to a coffee plantation in Brazil, where they would live and work. All the coffee was to be divided in two parts, one for Breves and the other for the settlers, who would not be allowed to leave until they paid Breves what they owed him (*Documentos* 1873).

According to several reports, those who went to the Brazilian *fazendas* (plantations) were badly fed, treated like slaves and punished like dogs (*Documentos* 1873, 170). One young boy of twelve or thirteen, originally from the island of Terceira, appeared before the authorities in the fall of 1859 in the company of a man who claimed to be his uncle. In tears, the boy laid bare the wounds on his legs that were made with a whip that his boss had administered because the boy could not do the work asked of him. This work, the tearful child testified, was above his abilities.

In the late 1850s, in an attempt to regulate the conditions of employment of Portuguese citizens who had emigrated to Brazil, the minister of foreign affairs in Lisbon specified that such contracts must include three meals a day, the noon meal to be followed by rest until two o'clock; laundry; and a limit of nine hours of work in open fields or ten in a covered area. Thus, rather than forbid contracts with minors altogether, this legislation allowed them to continue, partly in order to sustain the viability of Brazilian agriculture. In 1863 further legislation was enacted that required proof of a work contract and a prepaid voyage before a passport was issued. All this would help to eliminate the kinds of abuses mentioned earlier, whereby individuals were sold for the debt that they owed the sea captain who had ferried them across the Atlantic.

An explanation of why so many children emigrated was provided by the consul general of Portugal in Rio de Janeiro, in an 1864 letter addressed to the Portuguese minister. "The majority of emigrants," he wrote, "are minors of fourteen who, only to free themselves from military recruitment, are sent by their families to Brazil, without recommendation of any sort in the place of destination. The number of children who wander in this city without work is incalculable" (*Documentos* 1873, 169). Though it was quite apparent that the state, through its laws of military recruitment, was partially responsible for this emigration of minors, it was slow to change the regulations that made it possible to escape military service through emigration. Restrictions were eventually put in place; before obtaining a passport an applicant had to present proof of service or guarantee future service by means of a monetary deposit or a warrantor.

By the late nineteenth and early twentieth centuries, peasants were circumventing these and other restrictions by emigrating clandestinely. The Portuguese state, of course, was fully aware of the extent of clandestine emigration. In the 1870s letters passed between the consul general of Portugal in Rio de Janeiro and the minister of foreign affairs in Lisbon about the numbers of individuals arriving from Portugal without passports (*Documentos* 1873). Although severe penalties (including the possible confiscation of assets and the loss of citizenship) were put in place for those who were caught (Costa 1911), it is quite evident that the state never acted very rigorously on this issue of clandestine emigration. Indeed, a law of 1907 that raised the cost of a passport and emphasized it as a necessity only added further stimulation to illegal departure.

The same can be said for the emigration flow of the post-1960 period. Though the fear of apprehension remained real, stiff literacy requirements for securing passports led to ever-increasing rates of clandestine emigrants. In the Salazarist period, the peasants of Portugal engaged in a rare form of collective defiance of state law. It was a defiance tolerated by a government that less than half-heartedly took action against the numerous *passadores* who smuggled these peasants across Spain and into France.

Several scholars of Portuguese emigration (Leeds 1984; Baganha 1988, 1990; Pereira 1981) have suggested that the surface ambivalence and seemingly irrational stance of the Portuguese state vis-à-vis emigration—to encourage or discourage—masks a deeper rationality. The restrictive emigration laws were formulated to stimulate remittances. As the historian Maria Baganha (1990) has argued, by making it difficult for women to emigrate (legislation was sustained well into the twentieth century) and by averting its eyes from the clandestine emigration of men, the state fostered familial separation and thereby ensured the flow of money back to Portugal. Even the emigration of minors served this same purpose.

Although I use the word *masks*, one does not have to dig too deeply into the discourse about emigration to find rather blunt statements to this effect. Martins, for example, observed in 1885 that without the subsidies coming from Brazil through the Portuguese industry of "human cattle," it was indisputable that many in Portugal would have gone broke. "The exchange from Brazil," he claimed, "is the thermometer of our economic well-being and even of our constitutional stability" (Martins 1885, 251–252). *Engajadores* and *passadores* were ultimately tolerated precisely because they were capitalist middlemen for both legal and illegal emigration. Perhaps the most telling phrase in the wealth of materialist-oriented discourse about the Portuguese emigrant is that which refers to these men as the Portuguese state's most valuable capital. Yet they were capital not only for the remittances that they sent back to Portugal but also because of the market for trade that they stimulated with Brazil. Emigrants wanted Portuguese products (Manoco e Sousa, quoted in Serrão 1976, 166).

The effectiveness of this policy can be affirmed by the fact that it was maintained as a strategy well into the twentieth century. Elizabeth Leeds (1984) draws our attention to the fact that Salazar, in his Coimbra University dissertation, wrote of the need to have emigration to maintain remittances for foreign exchange. This policy, she argues, guided his approach to the African colonies, an approach whereby hegemony, economic advantage, and minimal social unrest were all part of a coherent political program. Colonial and emigration policies were intimately connected.

In addition to the question of exchange, the labor supply at home was never totally threatened, though some alarmists seemed to think so. Women who remained behind effectively worked the fields in the absence of men, providing the other half of a truly international division of labor. As one observer noted, "It falls to the women to carry out the heavy tasks of men. . . . There is a spot in the vicinity of Barcelos where there is a settlement where all is done exclusively by women—the hoeing, the pruning, the wine harvest, the treading in the presses, the carting. The men have all gone to Brazil" (Sampaio Bruno, quoted in Serrão 1976, 149).

By siphoning off excess population among the unemployed or underemployed, the Portuguese state relieved pressures that in other countries led to upheaval, if not revolution. It can also be argued that a policy that kept emigrants tied to Portugal and the Portuguese state served the interests of the receiving states, as well. A migrant worker population with its feet in both worlds does not develop the class consciousness and political action of a true proletariat. Nowhere was this more evident than in France in 1968. Portuguese workers did not join in the strikes launched by French workers. Some even chose to return to Portugal temporarily.

Afonso Costa best summed up all of this in his 1911 study of "the problem of emigration." "The interest of the state," he argued, "corresponds to that of the emigrant. If today, in his suffering and misery, the emigrant nevertheless contributes so effectively to the salvation of our finances, tomorrow, when emigration is carefully regulated and the emigrant, as an instrument of progress and wealth, is assisted and protected, how much more development would be achieved than what is achieved today in a spontaneous and disorderly fashion" (p. 183, loose translation). Costa went on to condemn the faults of a state administration that publicly disdained emigration and to laud the virtues of o povo who, in Costa's view, had saved the nation by giving it time to "find its own formula for a definitive political structure." "Emigration," he concluded, "is the touchstone of new governments in their work of rebuilding."

If I have emphasized the underlying logic behind state interest in emigration, what were the interests of the emigrant that Costa alluded to in 1911? At the outset, I think it is important to emphasize that the individual emigrant is best perceived as a mediator between the peasant household and the state. The household, as the basic unit of both production and consumption in peasant society, can adjust to a relatively inelastic and cash-poor labor market through migration or emigration (Tilly 1978). The peasants of northern Portugal survived by means of a rather efficient division of labor, whereby women, as producers of food and nurturers of offspring, reproduced a household to which male migrants contributed capital—capital that was necessary for the continuation of a local economic unit. To quote from the verse of Custódio José da Costa (1935, 127):

> *A vida não era cara* [Life was not costly]
> *Mas era caro o dinheiro* [But money was costly]
> *Por isso me retirei* [For this reason I went off]
> *Para o Rio de Janeiro* [To Rio de Janeiro]

A pattern that is emerging in much of the developing world today—the ever-increasing proportion of women who manage smallholder agriculture while husbands and sons seek waged employment elsewhere—has great historical depth in Portugal. It does because emigration is the vehicle of the delicate balance that exists between the strategies of sustenance of the peasant household and the political-economic aspirations of the state. Indeed, there is some evidence in the Portuguese case that emigrant sons provided the cash contributions to purchase a team of oxen or to bolster the marital bequests (*dotes*) of sisters (Brettell 1991). Where else, if not from emigration, was this cash to come, especially for peasant households that had already mortgaged (and I use this term loosely) their dwindling properties to the hilt to make improvements or to pay the always-increasing taxes imposed by the state? The options were limited. Sons were much more useful to the peasant household as emigrants than as soldiers. One can fully understand the peasant desire to avoid conscription, because this came at a time when the fruits of the labor of sons to the peasant household would be greatest.

To this point I have explored the political economy of emigrant-state relations in Portugal in the nineteenth and twentieth centuries. I now turn my attention to a consideration of the symbolic meanings of the individual emigrant and the implications that these meanings have for Portuguese nationhood—or the idea of Portugal.

The Emigrant as a Multivocal Symbol for the Portuguese Nation

In May of 1987, at a conference at the Woodrow Wilson Center in Washington, D.C., the then Portuguese foreign minister Pedro Pires de Miranda made a comment that has lingered with me since that time. He suggested that Portugal's heritage of discoveries, a heritage that made it a nation open to differences and a population adept in the field of cross-cultural understanding, could be its greatest asset and its most significant contribution to the European economic and political world of which it was increasingly becoming a part. If this heritage led Francisco Sá Carneiro to call Portugal a "nation of navigators," Portuguese emigrants are symbolic transformations of these navigators, for they have carried on the tradition of the Portuguese explorers—a tradition of reaching out beyond the shores of a small country situated at the margins of Europe.

Anthropologically speaking, it is through symbols that people represent the structure, norms, and ideals of the society that links them together. Symbols are vehicles for conception and thought. They are "objects, acts, concepts, or linguistic formations that stand ambiguously for a multiplicity of disparate meanings, evoke sentiments and emotions, and impel men to action" (Cohen 1974, ix). Victor Turner, a pioneer in the field of symbolic anthropology, was interested not only in this multiplicity or multivocality of symbols (Turner 1967) but also in certain core symbols that are central to the organization of specific cultural systems. Building on Turner's approach, Ortner (1973) has outlined several ways by which what she calls a "key symbol" can be identified: the "natives" say it is culturally important; they are positively or negatively aroused by it; it comes up in different contexts; it is the object of great cultural elaboration. Both Turner and Ortner argue that anthropologists must recognize and understand these core or key symbols as part of their efforts to understand the society that uses them.

I suggest here that in Portugal the emigrant is a core symbol. It is a symbol that is, in Levi-Straussian terms, "good to think" and one that is as highly charged for the Portuguese as the peasant is for the French (Brettell and Brettell 1983; Rogers 1987), the woman is for Italians (Giovannini 1981) and Greeks (Herzfeld 1986), the bandit is for Sicilians (Hobsbawn 1969), or George Washington is for Americans (Schwartz 1987). In the emigrant are vested certain ideas about Portuguese national identity.

But how do we get at these ideas? How do we engage in this search for symbolic meaning? We do so by turning to the representations of the emigrant that are contained in a wealth of texts. The volume of such texts is evidence in itself of how central to Portuguese thought the emigrant was and is. If the peasant was a dominant figure in the pictorial arts of France during the nineteenth century, a period when that country was developing its sense of nationhood, it is in Portuguese literary output that thinking about the emigrant prevails. In fact, I wonder if any other national literature has been as preoccupied with one social type as have the novels, poems, essays, commentaries, and orations of Portugal.

If we focus on one of the emigrant's alter egos—the *navegador*—this preoccupation can be traced back to Luis de Camões. But the real proliferation dates to the nineteenth century, a period during which new national or state identities were forged throughout Europe. In the Portuguese case, of course, it was the changing relationship with a former colony, Brazil, rather than the definitive establishment of nation state boundaries that was important, because Portugal's boundaries had been fixed six centuries earlier. This changing relationship led some of the greatest literary figures of the nineteenth century—Camilo Castelo Branco, Eça de Queiroz, Júlio Dinís, Gomes de Amorím, Ramalho Ortigão—to forge their fictional *brasileiros*—a term applied to a native-born Portuguese who emigrates to Brazil, makes it rich, and then returns to Portugal to display his wealth. The *brasileiro* was as much the subject of popular songs and rhymes of the nineteenth century as he was of printed literature, and, as Baganha (1990, 122–123) has recently pointed out, he was equally co-opted by political elites, who ridiculed him in their public speeches.

In the twentieth century, Ferreira de Castro, Aquilino Ribeiro, and Miguel Torga created their *brasileiros*, and most recently a new generation of writers have contributed stories, poetry, and songs to a burgeoning literature about the *francés*—the late-twentieth-century symbolic transformation. If the *brasileiro* of the nineteenth century was to some extent an antihero, mocked and ridiculed perhaps more than he was idealized, the *brasileiro* and *francés* of the twentieth century are more heroic, praised for the hardships they have endured. To quote from the poet Alberto Miranda, *glorificam a Terra na amargura da distancia* ("they glorify the homeland in the bitterness of distance," quoted in Pires-Cabral 1985, 363). Such contradictions and variations—positive and negative attributes—are, as Turner and Ortner have suggested, part of the multivocality of key symbols.

Since I have mentioned *a Terra*, let me take this up first as one of the voices or meanings of the Portuguese emigrant. The anthropologist Susan Rogers (1987) has pointed out that the French peasant symbolizes a central tension in French society—the tension between the centralized and modern state, on one hand, and a rural and traditional France that is anchored in the soil, on the other (see also Brettell and Brettell 1983). This association between the land, the past, and tradition no doubt motivated Salazar in his attempt to raise the peasant to the level of a core symbol in Portugal, through the contest that he promoted to find the most typical village (Brito 1982). This was Salazar's response to the forces of modernization that were proceeding all around him in the rest of Europe, a continent toward which his regime has been somewhat irresolute.

If Salazar's effort was not fully successful—though the contest proceeded and the village was chosen—it is because the rooted peasant is not as "good to think" in the Portuguese context as he is in France. Although the emigrant is generally a peasant, and therefore is in some sense associated with the land, it is his uprootedness that is good to think. And yet, uprooted from the land does not mean divorced from it, for one of the major attributes of the Portuguese emigrant is that he never fully abandons his homeland. His ambition is to return to his natal village (*a minha terra*, as an emigrant would say) but also to his nation.

But what does *nation* mean? One government official has bluntly stated that Portugal is more than a nation, it is *um povo peregrino* (wandering people) (Pereira 1983, 21). The emigrant is a pilgrim, a journeyer, and emigration is Portugal's national rite of passage. This rite of passage involves departure, the liminal status of being away, and the reintegration of return. As with all forms of identity, the emigrant feels his Portuguese identity once he is abroad and confronted by the other. But the emigrant also feels his marginality. When asked if he has *saudades* (nostalgia or yearning) for his country, the emigrant in Abel Botelho's *Amor Criollo* (1936) responds, "What country, sir? A person who comes here no longer has a country. They call us *galegos* [literally a Spanish Galician term but applied to the Portuguese in Brazil] here and if we return to Portugal we are *brasileiros*." And so it was with the Portuguese who went to France after 1960, who were *les étrangers* or *les portugais* in France, only to discover that they were *os franceses* at home. The ambivalence toward the emigrant that was manifested in political-economic policy is equally evident in the symbolic realm of thought and classification.

While the peasant represents the past to the French, it is the emigrant who serves this purpose for the Portuguese. This is the meaning that Sá Carneiro (1983, 26) attributed when he said "[the Portuguese] are a generous people without mental frontiers. . . . Emigration is for the Portuguese more than looking for the old in other lands—it is, in origin, the concretization of an interior will, of an impulse coming from the past— from the dreamers of the Sagres. . . . Wherever a Portuguese goes he carries the spirit of Camões and Vasco da Gama." Another official once referred to the culture that the Portuguese have transported abroad as the country's "inestimable patrimony" (Pereira 1983, 21).[2]

Earlier in this chapter I emphasized the role of the emigrant as economic capital for the Portuguese state, but here I stress his contribution as cultural capital. To the anthropologist, language and culture are fundamentally interconnected, and it is the emigrant who transported this language, and with it Portuguese culture, to almost all the continents of the world. Fundamental to this culture was an ecumenical and racially tolerant worldview. Anthropologists such as Leite de Vasconcellos (1958) and Pina-Cabral (1991), as well as myriad other scholars of Portuguese colonial history, have suggested that this racial tolerance is essential to Portugal's sense of itself, even if it is to some extent mythologized.

If the emigrant is a vehicle through which the Portuguese can think about their attachment to their homeland, their very nationality, if the emigrant is a vehicle through which the Portuguese can find their roots in their past, if the emigrant is a vehicle through which the Portuguese can represent their ecumenical and tolerant spirit, then the emigrant is also a vehicle for the expression of greatness—for the extension of thought beyond the boundaries of a small country wedged between Spain and the Atlantic Ocean at the very edge of Europe. The emigrant unbinds the Portuguese nation and Portuguese culture.

It is this desire for unboundedness, this desire to escape the ever-prevalent thought that Portugal is *um país pequeno* (a small country), that one can find an explanation for the symbolic transformation from *navegador* to *colono* to *emigrante*. Each was a symbol attuned to historical and political-economic circumstances: the *navegador* in the age of discovery, the *colono* in the age of settlement, the *emigrante* in the postcolonial period. The result of their journeys abroad is that Portugal is no longer a small country. It is this possibility for an international "Luso-American" nation that Nuno Simões (1934, 193ff) evoked when he called emigrants the spiritual force of Lusitanianism.

More recently it has been recognized by Freitas do Amaral (1983, 167). "Portugal," he has written, "is more than the simple and narrow European rectangle that is our territory of origin; Portugal is above all the Portuguese soul that we have irradiated throughout the world and that lives a little everywhere, a soul of sociability (*convívio*), of cross-fertilization (*cruzamento*), of the encounter of people and cultures." He goes on to suggest that the state should recognize this as the true nature of Portugal, and that any policy for emigrants and for Portuguese communities abroad was not merely a policy of social justice but an important national question. If I understand his comments well, and to put it in broader theoretical terms, it is an important national question, because all the Portuguese who have journeyed abroad, whether in the past or the present, are part of Portugal's imagined community. They do not exist without Portugal, and Portugal does not appear to exist without them. Herein, for Benedict Anderson (1983), lies the meaning of the nation as an imagined community.

And yet, to some, emigration and the emigrant also represented the death of a nation. "We are in the presence of an emigration that almost embarrasses us," wrote Afonso Costa in 1911 (1911, 73–75 and 170–171), "and that uncontestably bears witness to our profound physiological misery. The crises of the last few years have wrenched from us our life's

blood." Potential emigrants were warned that emigration meant death—
as in this popular verse:

> Brasil terra de enganos [Brazil land of deceptions]
> Quantos lá vão engandos [How many go there fooled]
> Tantos lá vão por três anos [So many go there for three years]
> E lá ficam sepultados [And are buried there] (Cortesão 1942)

Migration could mean either new life or certain death to the individual emigrant. If it represented both life and death for the nation as a
whole, it was because in the cycle of humanity itself life leads to death.
But, just as some die, others are born. The contradiction and the ambigu-
ity can be symbolically resolved, much like the contradictions in political-
economic policy that were explored earlier in this chapter can be
rationally resolved. Symbols function to synthesize complex and sometimes conflicting ideas.

If the emigrant represented positive features of hope and greatness
for the Portuguese nation, why was he so mercilessly ridiculed by late-
nineteenth-century Portuguese writers? What was ridiculed and satirized
most was the wanton display of wealth. Perhaps the best portrayal is that
of Júlio Dinís in A Morgadinha dos Canavais. His brasileiro Eusébio Seabra
returns home after forty years, a grave and rich man. He builds a house
with three floors and verandas, covered with tiles and appointed with
stone sculpture. The garden is filled with ceramic artworks, green and yellow flower pots, a parrot and a macaw. He builds a new church, sponsors
a festa, and circulates through the village in clothes that combine the various colors of a bird of America, accessorized with a profusion of gold. But
this is merely surface, and even Seabra comes to admit that deep down he
is a poor devil whom no one knows, an ignorant man lacking the basic
rudiments of knowledge and civilization. His wealth, Dinís is suggesting,
does not really mean anything.

Why were such aspersions cast? I think it is because the real-life
brasileiro represented a threat to the status quo and particularly to the self-
satisfied elites and the urban bourgeoisie who were faced with the competition of new enterprises established by immigrants returning from
abroad.[3] The idea that this new wealth, earned who knows how in a far-
off land, could buy social position had to be attacked as mere delusion. By
denigrating the brasileiro, these writers were representing the social order
as it should be, a social order based on ascription rather than achievement.

Like the peasant in France, the emigrant in Portugal has been given
both negative and positive value, partly because of particular historical
circumstances. The relationship with Brazil was much less clear to the
Portuguese state in the period immediately after independence than it

perhaps is today. Economically Portugal continued to depend on Brazil, but symbolically it served a purpose to downplay this dependence. A foppish *brasileiro* helped to resolve this ambivalent attitude toward the former colony. It provided the context for thinking about how to include Brazil and the rest of the colonial world as part of Portuguese national identity.

Conclusion

William Roseberry (1988, 33) has suggested that there is "a much richer interconnection between the concerns of political economy and those of symbolic anthropology than is recognized by those critics who repeat facile dismissals based on old-fashioned antinomies." I have tried to bring these two perspectives together in an analysis of the relationship between the Portuguese emigrant, Portuguese nationhood, and the Portuguese state. While I have barely skimmed the surface, it is evident that emigration was important both to the development of the colonial and postcolonial Portuguese state and to the production and the reproduction of the peasant household. The Portuguese state's sense of itself, both politically and economically, influenced migration streams. Yet the relationship between the individual emigrant and the Portuguese state is more than one of policy and lucre; it is, as I have suggested here, equally symbolic. Both conceptions, materialist and mentalist, contribute to an understanding about what it means to be Portuguese and what Portugal as both state and nation is all about.

Notes

This chapter was originally published in *Portuguese Studies Review* 2 (1993): 51–65. It is published here, with minor revisions, with permission.

1. The first version of this chapter was delivered as the Third Joyce F. Riegelhaupt Memorial Lecture in Durham, New Hampshire, September 21, 1989. I would like to thank the Gulbenkian Foundation for their generous support of this lecture. I also acknowledge the Wenner-Gren Foundation, the National Institutes of Health, the Social Science Research Council, and the Canada Council. All have supported my research on Portuguese emigration over the years.

2. For other examples of similar commentaries by politicians and government bureaucrats, see Rocha-Trindade (1984).

3. Baganha (1990, 124) shares this view. "Could the Portuguese elites subscribe to anything but a detrimental image of the emigrant? The most plausible answer is that unless it was stigmatized and restricted, emigration would have seriously interfered with the interests of the elites. Thus, the *brasileiro* must be seen as a device of social control and a coherent supplement to the legal restrictions."

2

Migration Stories
Agency and the Individual in the Study of Migration

In 1992, in an essay called "Migration and Culture," Tony Fielding drew attention to a central tension in the study of migration.

> There is something strange about the way we study migration. We know, often from personal experience, but also from family talk, that moving from one place to another is nearly always a major event. It is one of those events around which an individual's biography is built. The feelings associated with migration are usually complicated, the decision to migrate is typically difficult to make, and the outcome usually involves mixed emotions. . . . Migration is a statement of an individual's worldview, and is, therefore, an extremely cultural event. And yet, when we study migration scientifically, we seem to forget all this. Migration is customarily conceptualized as a product of the material forces at work in our society . . . [or] the migrant is seen either as a "rational economic man" choosing individual advancement by responding to the economic signals of the job and housing markets, or as a virtual prisoner of his or her class position, and thereby subject to powerful structural economic forces set in motion by the logic of capitalist accumulation (Fielding 1992, 201).

This chapter takes up this tension by asking what can we learn about migration as a general process by looking at the lives of particular individuals? More broadly it focuses on the stories of individuals and couples and on the personal decisions that are made in relation to migration projects. It is written in the same spirit that Lila Abu-Lughod (1991) writes "against culture." Abu-Lughod argues that focusing on the particular is not about privileging the micro over the macro. "A concern with

23

the particulars of individuals' lives [need not] imply disregard for forces and dynamics that are not locally based. On the contrary, the effects of extralocal and long-term processes are only manifested locally and specifically, produced in the actions of individuals living their particular lives, inscribed in their bodies and their words (Abu-Lughod 1991, 150).

Because the purpose of the chapter is to highlight individual stories, I begin with a brief discussion of the history of biographical narratives in anthropological research and move from there to an examination of immigrant narratives as a genre. I then turn to the stories of several Portuguese men and women who made their way to France in the 1960s. The particulars of their lives permit me to emphasize several aspects of the migration experience that are not always featured in the social science literature and to suggest that a handful of personal narratives can teach us a good deal about pattern, structure, culture, and the role of the individual in the migration process. They can also teach us something about what may have been distinctive about this particular population movement, but also about what is comparable to the experiences of other migrants in other places and at other times and hence can be generalized. I conclude the chapter by returning to a discussion of how the microanalytic perspective of the individual agent that emerges from biographical narratives can be integrated with the macroanalytic perspective of economic and political material structures.

Narratives and Life Histories in Ethnographic Research

When anthropologists conduct ethnographic research, no matter what the problem, they encounter people who engage in narrative and storytelling (Ginsburg 1987; Herzfeld 1985). "The telling of stories," Sarah Lamb (2001, 28) observes, "is one of the practices by which people reflect, exercise agency, contest interpretations of things, make meanings, feel sorrow and hope, and live their lives. Storytelling, the narrative presentation of self and culture . . . is a creative social practice. Viewed through such a lens, life stories can offer scholars of humanity a compelling mode of probing both the particular and the more generalized dimensions of the way people make, experience, and express their lives." Stories or narratives emerge in a range of ethnographic situations (during informal conversations, formal interviews, or in the interpretation of events that are at the heart of participant observation). They can be quite revealing and they are often autobiographical. Through narratives people weave their experiences into a coherent whole, documenting both their successes and their failures and drawing conclusions from these that help to explain the life choices they have made. Undoubtedly they also help the ethnographer to understand how people make sense of their world.

Sometimes, of course, anthropologists work with one or a small number of individuals to elicit, more formally, a life story or life history. The life history is an ethnographic genre that dates back to the 1920s.[1] The emphasis in the early work in this genre was on how the life of a single individual reflected a culture or a social group. The aim of some of these works was "not to obtain autobiographical details about some definite personage, but to have some representative middle-aged individual of moderate ability describe his life in relation to the social group in which he had grown up" (Radin 1926, 384). The genre was best defined in research on Native Americans, where it served as a form of salvage ethnography aided by individual memory (Dyk 1938; Simmons 1979; Underhill 1985). Theoretically, early proponents of the life history method were interested in the process of acculturation and how change was manifested in the life of a single individual over the life course and hence how the group to which he or she belonged also experienced change. However, another group who were more closely allied with the culture and personality school of the 1920s and 1930s were more interested in psychological theory, particularly that of Abraham Kardiner. Through the life history they wanted to test how personality was formed in relation to both primary (child-rearing practices) and secondary (art, myth, religion) institutions (see for example Du Bois 1944). Dollard (1949, 3), a proponent of this latter approach, thus defined the life history "as a deliberate attempt to define the growth of a person in a cultural milieu and to make theoretical sense of it."

Perhaps the culminating statement of this early phase of the use of biographical narratives or life histories in social research was the 1945 Social Science Research Council publication on the use of personal documents in history, anthropology, and sociology (Gottschalk, Kluckhohn, and Angell 1945). Assigned the task of discussing biographical and autobiographical materials in anthropology, Clyde Kluckhohn offered not only a comprehensive review of the work to date, both professional and "nonprofessional," but also an assessment of the strengths and weaknesses of the method. He was most critical of the absence of interpretation and analysis in most of the published works. But his final conclusion was that the "subjective factor in the lives of human groups is a problem of crucial importance" and if anthropologists do not develop methods to elicit it, it will remain the purview of literature rather than science (Kluckhohn 1945, 163). Frank (1996, 706) has argued more recently that Kluckhohn, and Langness (1965) after him, "tried to blend the demands of positivism (representative sampling, attention to truth telling, triangulation of sources) with an appreciation of the humanistic potential of the method."

But, despite Kluckhohn's belief in the possibility of bridging the positivistic and the humanistic branches of the anthropological endeavor through the life history, the method fell into relative disuse in the anthropology of the 1950s and 1960s, as a new scientific empiricism emerged. The one exception, of course, is to be found in the work of Oscar Lewis, whose collective family biographies that are at the heart of his books *The Children of Sanchez*, *Five Families*, and *La Vida*, allowed us to move inside the psyche of Mexican and Puerto Rican families. But Lewis was careful to set his overlapping autobiographical narratives into a broader demographic framework derived from an analysis of census records and survey data. And he certainly understood his role as an analyst, introducing the controversial concept of "culture of poverty" to help explain the worldview that his narratives appeared to evoke.[2]

A renewed interest in life histories developed with the growth of feminist anthropology, marked in the early 1980s by the publication of Marjorie Shostak's (1981) story of the !Kung woman Nisa, and followed by Hans and Judith-Maria Buechler's (1981) autobiography of Carmen, a peasant woman from Spanish Galicia, Margaret Blackman's (1982) record of the life of the Haida woman Florence Edenshaw Davidson, Laurel Kendall's (1988) account of a Korean woman shaman, Sharon Gmelch's (1991) life history of the Irish traveler Nan, Karen McCarthy Brown's (1991) "intimate spiritual biography" of the Vodou priestess Mama Lola, and Ruth Behar's (1993) life history of Esmerelda, a Mexican peasant. Although these works differ in the way in which they have given voice to the narrator and the extent to which they insert themselves collaboratively and analytically in the text, they all emphasize a story told from a subject's point of view. We learn much about the culture within which each of these women lived, as we learn about each woman herself, the challenges each faced, and the choices each made at different points in her life. In each of these life histories, the goal is not to present a typical or representative individual, nor to arrive at empirical truth or a "science of culture." Rather, it is to understand one person's life and its meaning to that person in the context of broader history and culture.

Migration Stories

It is in this spirit of trying to understand one person's life in the context of broader history and culture that some anthropologists, including myself (Brettell 1995), have drawn on life histories, or oral narratives, as a mechanism through which to comprehend the migration process. Gmelch (1992, 311) suggests that drawing on this genre helps to "get beneath the abstractions of migration theory and to understand migration from the insider's perspective."

Oral history data is quite unsuitable for determining frequencies, averages, and relationships between variables. But from narrative we learn the particular as opposed to the general, and we can understand what the abstract categorizations and generalizations about migration look like on the ground, from the individual's point of view. We get a sense of the degree to which migrants are free actors shaping their own destinies, as opposed to pawns merely responding to constraints imposed upon them by their society (Gmelch 1992, 324).

Gmelch also rightly notes that migration is not a readily observable event. Only once in Portugal did I actually hear the discussions leading up to and then witness an actual leave-taking, something I recorded at the end of my book *Men Who Migrate, Women Who Wait* (Brettell 1986). Generally ethnographers and others who study migrants and the migration process must rely on migrants' own detailed accounts of why they decided to leave, what the journey was like, what happened when they arrived in their place of destination, and, if relevant, why they returned home. These accounts emerge in the context of intensive and often repeated open-ended interviews, where an ethnographer asks a migrant to talk about his or her experiences. While the recounting of these events is obviously subject to lapses of or embellishments on memory, Gmelch (1992) stresses that migration is a paramount and disruptive event in anyone's life and is therefore likely to be recalled with more vivid detail than some other events. He suggests that people often omit the unpleasant, but when asked about it they are generally forthcoming.[3] This is certainly true of one of the life stories that I recorded in my book *We Have Already Cried Many Tears* (Brettell 1995), and it became crucial to understanding what motivated one of the woman whose narrative is included in the book to leave her village for France. I discuss this further shortly.

The use of the biographical method in the study of migration was, of course, pioneered by sociologists W. I. Thomas and Florian Znaniecki in their study of the Polish peasant in Poland and America. They argued that this method is "the only one that gives us a full and systematic acquaintance with all the complexity of social life" (1927, 77). But their use of this material was different from others who have tried to collect more comprehensive life histories of single individuals who have lived as immigrants.

An early but somewhat unusual example of the more comprehensive form can be found in *Between Two Cultures*, John Poggie's (1973) autobiography, as told to him, of Ramon Gonzales, a man who was born in Mexico in 1922 and brought to the United States by his parents when he was only six months old. Ramon grew up and lived in the United States until his early forties, and then he returned to Mexico. He remembers for Poggie his early years of helping his father pick oranges in San Bernardino, California, of going to school and for the first time being confronted with English, of his mother abandoning the family after his younger brother was born, and of his yearning for her to return. Ramon stayed in high school for two years but never finished. He recounts the ways that he earned extra money, selling newspapers and fruit to help his father, and of the petty thievery that got him into trouble.

Ramon's father bought him a car that he drove without a license. Indeed, cars and girls figure a good deal in his narrative, while little or no mention is made of either the Great Depression or World War II, both of which would have provided the larger economic and political context within which he passed from childhood to early adulthood. But Ramon does tell Poggie about his various jobs, what they paid, what he liked, how often he changed work and where he moved within the United States to find work, including as far north as Alaska.

Ramon never acquired U.S. citizenship, and during the war he was deported to Mexico for the first time. He was deported several more times, as he repeatedly jumped the border back into the United States because he was "not used to the kind of life that the people lead . . . in Mexico" (p. 3). His account is rich in the details of what it was like to interact with U.S. immigration authorities. But as his difficulties with the law increased, he decided to live in Mexico permanently, where he could be free from the fear of immigration authorities. His last deportation was in 1963. He lived in Mexico as an American Mexican, caught between two worlds and labeled *el pocho*, a pejorative term meaning someone one who is culturally prejudiced toward the United States or who has returned from there with little memory of the Mexican language and culture.

A second early example of a migrant life history is Marie Hall Ets's (1999) record of the life of Rosa Cavalleri, an Italian immigrant who came to the United States in 1884. Ets met Rosa shortly after World War I, when Ets was pursuing her social work degree at the University of Chicago and living at Chicago Commons, a settlement house in the city. Rosa was a natural storyteller who entertained the residents of the settlement houses, and indeed community groups at large, with tales she had heard while growing up in her native village in northern Italy. Gradually Ets took down Rosa's own life story and produced a document unique in the literature on the third wave of immigration to the United States. We learn about the culture and society of a Lombardian silk-making village, of Rosa's marriage at age fifteen to a man much older than she whom she did not love, of his departure for work in the iron mines of Missouri, and of her harrowing voyage across the Atlantic to join him. Then Rosa turns to her life in the United States, including her flight from her abusive husband, divorce and remarriage, life in the immigrant slums of Chicago, work as a cleaning lady, the challenges she met raising her large family, and the discrimination she faced. Rosa concludes by telling Ets what she has learned in America. "I could go anywhere—where millionaires go and high people. I would look the high people in the face and ask them what questions I'd like to know. I wouldn't be afraid now—not of anybody" (Ets 1999, 254). Rudolph Vecoli's assessment of the contribution of Rosa's life story is apt. "Beyond its value as an eyewitness account of certain historical events, Rosa stands as a personal document against which we can test certain ideas regarding the immigrant experience. While quantitative analysis may provide answers to certain questions, there are qualitative inquiries which numbers cannot satisfy. Subjective states of mind cannot be inferred with confidence from such 'objective data.' Unfortunately we have few autobiographical sources such as this which reveal in depth the effects of immigration upon particular human beings" (Vecoli 1999, x).[4]

Vecoli's assessment, written originally in 1970, held true for another decade until a few writers revived the life history method to explore the experiential aspects of late-twentieth-century migrations. This revival is perhaps best exemplified by the publication of *Through Harsh Winters*, Akemi Kikemura's (1981) life history of her Japanese immigrant mother, and more recently Dianne Walta Hart's (1997) *Undocumented in L.A.: An Immigrant's Story*, about a Nicaraguan woman named Yamileth Lopez who left her home country for Los Angeles.[5]

Kikemura tells us that she decided to use the life history approach "to investigate the continuity and change in the Japanese American culture by focusing on the life of an Issei woman—my mother" (p. 138). She adopted this method because it would capture the life experiences of an immigrant in more humanistic fashion and would address the relationship of the individual to her culture. Kikemura outlines the questions that she always had about her *issei* (first-generation) mother, Michiko Tanaka, who arrived in Liberty, California, in 1923. What was her life like before she came to America? Why did she leave her homeland? Was life in America anything like what she imagined? How did she survive extraordinary hardships, and why did she never return home?

Kikemura first sought answers by making a trip to Japan herself to learn about her mother's past. She went unaccompanied; her mother had no interest in returning to Japan after so long. And then Kikemura sat down to record her mother's story in her own words, beginning with her passage to America. "I was sick on that ship all the way to America. They fed us bread and butter. That was the first time I saw butter and just the sight of it made me sick. The ship was oppressively packed with people and the latrines were not like today's. We had to defecate into the ocean" (p. 27).

Michiko Tanaka tells her youngest daughter about her early life in the United States, about the birth of thirteen children and the death of two, about her husband's addiction to gambling and his imprisonment in San Quentin on the charge of bribing a federal agent. "In those days Issei were sent to prison easily. They didn't have a chance. But at least Papa didn't go to prison for stealing . . . he never did that. . . . Papa stayed in San Quentin for about a year. When he was there it was easy for me. The government gave me money for my children. I used to think that he should always stay there" (pp. 48–49). This is followed by accounts of surviving the war and the internment camps (which Michiko recalled as a carefree time because she did not have to worry about supporting her children), of celebrating the marriages of her children and mourning the death of her husband in 1953.

In 1956 Michiko moved from Liberty to Los Angeles. "When I was in Liberty I was dependent on everyone, but in Los Angeles I came to do things by myself. I was the pillar of the family. I had to bring home the money. . . . I found work right away. What kind of job do you think I got? A rotten job as a maid at Honda-san's hotel on Broadway" (p. 67). Michiko concludes with lessons in life, among them, show a happy face no matter what happens, have good manners, three times praise and one time scold when raising children, and rejoice in suffering, because it is then that you begin to understand life. At the end of the book Kikemura asks her mother why she chose to become an American citizen, which she did on May 15, 1980. "I have to protect myself. America will be facing hard times. They won't be helping foreigners. I've been here since 1923—fifty-seven years! I have eleven children . . . twenty-two grandchildren. All American citizens! I should be entitled to citizenship, but I'm still considered a foreigner" (p. 108).

Michiko's assessment of American attitudes toward foreigners and of her own attitude toward citizenship are honest and powerful and perhaps only emerged in the context of the repeated interviews that are part of the life history method. Dianne Walta Hart achieves a similar effect of brutal honesty in her record of the life of Yamileth Lopez, an undocumented Latina from Nicaragua who arrived in Los Angeles in January 1989. Perhaps of most interest in this story are the subtle reasons for Yamileth's departure from war-torn Nicaragua. On the surface Yamileth's migration was economically motivated—to make money and return to a better life in her own country—and shaped by the political context of her home country. But Yamileth also tells us that she left because she wanted to escape *el qué dirán* (what people would say about her sexual choices).

One of the women in my book *We Have Already Cried Many Tears* told a similar story. She migrated to the local provincial town to work as a domestic, but the consequence was that people in her village began to gossip about her, saying that she had lost her virginity. Although the gossip had no foundation, it was too much for her. She decided to leave for France.[6] Yamileth added one other reason for her departure. She was disappointed with the fact that the male leadership of the Sandinista revolution empowered women only in words and not in actions. All these are significant statements about the way in which gender ideology and patriarchal oppression figure into the decisions that women make with respect to migration. They emerge in narratives and are often omitted from broader theoretical discussions of the causes of migration. While economic motives may broadly explain why people migrate, these other motives might properly be considered precipitating factors to an actual departure.

Yamileth moved to the Pico-Union neighborhood of Los Angeles, and through her eyes we learn what it is like to survive in the urban ghetto. She too has a border-crossing story that culminates in northern Mexico. "The taxi stopped, and Mundo got out and went through an opening in the chain-link fence that divides Mexico from the United States. Beyond the fence is a riverbed, and beyond that, up a little higher, is a road where the Immigration vehicles go back and forth, making sure that no one gets across. We were tired of the cold. The entire trip had been horribly cold, but it was worse at the border, near the riverbed. . . . There must have been twenty to twenty-five people just where we were. . . . In the riverbed we saw . . . a dead man, or it could have been a woman. No one paid any attention to the body. It seemed to be a common occurrence" (pp. 22–23).

Yamileth tells Hart about the challenges she faced in trying to adapt to the United States as well as what struck her as so different from life back in Nicaragua. "The first day, I had to learn everything. I was afraid of using the dishwasher, so for two days I washed everything by hand. I didn't make much food because I didn't know what to cook" (p. 41). She recounts her life amidst the gangs of Los Angeles, her fears for her children, and her fears of *la migra* (the Immigration and Naturalization Service). "I get nervous when I go near MacArthur Park. I'm afraid the authorities will catch me and send me out of the country without my being able to say goodbye. . . . La migra spot the fear. They know if you have papers or not" (p. 56–57).

Yamileth and her son Miguel did return to Nicaragua during the time that Hart was working on the narrative, but they came back within a year. Yamileth was pregnant and in and out of work in the sweatshops of Los Angeles, earning little more than minimum wage. In 1996 she married a U.S.-born Latino. She was able to legalize her position, although she continued to worry about her son Miguel, who remained illegal. Other illegal family members stopped using public hospitals, clinics, and schools after the passage of Proposition 187. Yamileth continued to express concerns to Hart about her brother Omar, who had stayed in Nicaragua to fight with the Sandinistas and who was arrested in the early 1990s.[7]

These two volumes are each focused on a single life, but other volumes collect several life stories of the migration experience, devoting a chapter to each individual. This is the format that George Gmelch (1992) adopts in his book about Barbadian migrants and return migrants and that I use in my book *We Have Already Cried Many Tears*. An alternative format is to intersperse first-person testimonies that address particular issues related to the migration experience, as Nicole Constable (1997) does in her study of Filipina domestics in Hong Kong. But the effect is the same: to emphasize what generalizations about migration look like on the ground and to delineate how migrants make decisions, forge social relationships, and exercise agency in the face of various local, national, and international constraints. It is with this same purpose that I now turn to brief excerpts from some of the migration stories of Portuguese men and women who went to France in the 1960s.

Portuguese Migration Stories

Alcides F.

In October of 1974, Alcides F. and his wife Maria were living in a one-room concierge apartment in the eighteenth *arrondissement* of Paris. Their room was furnished with a small cot for their daughter Paula and a sofa bed for themselves. There was an armoire along one wall and a table in a corner surrounded by a few chairs. A few more storage cabinets, a television, and a sewing machine completed the furnishings. A small kitchen nook extended into the courtyard.

> *I left for France in 1965 soon after completing my military service. I was twenty-five years old. I discussed my plans with my parents. They were in favor of my emigration, saying that I should go to "arrange my life" (arranjar a minha vida). But I did not tell anyone else because they would be jealous and let it slip to the police. In Portugal at this time people were afraid of the secret police (the PIDE) and they kept their departure a secret. I crossed the border illegally with a neighbor who was a* passador. *This neighbor used to help men cross into Spain almost every day. It was November when I left, and it was raining, and we had to walk through the mountains. Once we were in Spain we joined up with other Portuguese men, and another* passador *took us through that country. There were about twenty men, and we went on foot for four days, always*

fearful that we would be caught. Finally we were put in two trucks to make the rest of the journey to the French border.

We crossed the Pyrenees on foot, and at night, with yet another passador. *While we were waiting on the French side for trucks to take us to Paris, we were caught by the police. Ten of the men fled, among them the man who was to become my brother-in-law and who was from another village near us. The rest of us stayed, and the police were very nice. We showed our identity papers, and the police gave us temporary passes for France.*

I went on by truck to Paris. I found a taxi and showed the taxi driver a slip of paper with the name and address of a friend who lived in a suburb. I spoke no French, but the taxi driver understood and took me there. My friend was expecting me, but he did not know precisely when. I spent twelve days looking for work, and then I found a job in construction with a crew composed entirely of Italians. I stayed at that work for a few months and then joined another crew, because I could work with other Portuguese. I found the second job through the friend of one of my cousins who was living in France. The work was easy to learn, and I was given housing in a shack with five or six other Portuguese men. I worked eight and a half hours every day for six days. On Sundays I did my shopping and washed my clothes. I sent money back to my parents in Portugal.

In 1967 I thought that I was old enough to marry, and I had managed to save a bit of money. So I returned to Portugal. There was no work for me in my village, and I wanted to return to France with Maria, who was now my wife. But my mother-in-law persuaded me to remain in Portugal and go to Lisbon, where some of Maria's relatives were working in a munitions factory. My mother-in-law said, "You will never be at home in France; they can kick you out whenever they want." The move to Lisbon was hard on Maria, because she had never done any work other than in her parents' fields, and now she had a job in a factory. She had to work, because otherwise we could not make ends meet. We also had to share part of a house with my brother-in-law. This was not good, two married couples living in one house together.

In 1969 we decided that we should go to France. We wanted our own house, but the salaries in Portugal just did not make it possible. It would take a lifetime to pay for a house. I left in November, and Maria joined me in February. When I arrived, I went to live with a cousin in the twentieth arrondissement *for fifteen days and then found a room in a hotel with two other men. The papers from my first trip had expired, and I had to spend three days securing a new working permit. My cousin had already found me a construction job, but I almost lost it because I could not show up to work without the proper papers. When Maria came I found work for her in a factory, and we moved into a room I had found in the eleventh* arrondissement. *I also worked in the factory for a time, but I found the work boring, making underwear for children. So I returned to construction work. When our daughter Paula was born, we moved to a larger place. But Maria was finding it difficult to work with the baby, so in 1971 she put an ad in the paper seeking a concierge position. The owner of this building called, and Maria took the job. Maria not only takes care of the building as a concierge, she also does private cleaning for some of the tenants to make extra money.*

I have some relatives in France. My younger brother came to France in 1966 and then returned to Portugal to complete his military service. After three years in the army, he returned to France in 1972. He also lives in the Paris area and comes every week to visit. He has a girlfriend in Portugal, whom he plans to marry and then bring to France. My sister and her husband live in Lille, so we do not see them very much. Another brother had emigrated to Africa but returned to Portugal after 1974, when Portugal got out of Africa. Most of Maria's family is in Portugal. They have more land than our family and can survive, but some members of her family are working in Lisbon. One of her cousins lives in Versailles, but that is far away so we do not see them very often.

At the time that I knew them, Alcides and Maria were planning to make their life in France. They did not discuss returning to Portugal, although the original reason for the returning to France was so that they could accumulate enough money to build a house for themselves back in their home community, a common goal among the Portuguese migrants during this period. Alcides first left Portugal with no passport and no immigration papers; in other words, he was a clandestine migrant, and his account of his border crossing is typical for Portuguese men of the period and tells us how individuals coped with state policies, which were simultaneously restrictive and liberal. Clandestine migration is one of the most characteristic features of the postwar movement of Portuguese people to France. Approximately two-thirds of all Portuguese immigrants to France between 1950 and 1970 arrived illegally. Clandestine migration developed, as one French scholar has observed, under conditions that were honorable neither to the country of origin nor to the country of destination (Tapinos 1975).

The high level of clandestine migration was due, in part, to the geographical proximity of France and to bureaucratic structures in that country which facilitated legalization after arrival. But it was also due to the rigid emigration laws in Portugal itself as well as the threat posed by the colonial wars in Africa that had escalated in the 1960s.[8] Although Alcides completed his military service prior to his departure for France, many other young Portuguese men at the time used clandestine migration as a way to escape *a tropa* (military service). By the mid-1960s Portugal had extended the period of military service to four years. Additionally, even those who had served had seen some of the rest of the world and found it difficult to return home and stay in their native villages.

Alcides's account of his voyage on foot through the Pyrenees is similar to those of many other men who left Portugal during the 1960s. They referred to it as *o salto* (the jump), and it is a defining and well-remembered feature of their migration stories. Most went with a *passador*, the Portuguese equivalent to the *coyote* who guides illegal Mexican immigrants into the United States. This intermediary figure in the migration process has deep roots in the history of Portuguese emigration. In the nineteenth century the popular term was *engajador,* a man who rounded up workers who were willing to go to foreign countries. The word *engajar* literally means "to hook," but its more conventional meaning is "to entice men for labor migration." One nineteenth-century observer remarked: "Before leaving, the *engajadores* read them the good word to prove to them that happiness awaits them; they point to the palaces, *quintas,* and belongings of their neighbors, whose fathers and grandfathers, like them, had nothing; they show them the sun that brilliantly breaks through the clouds, but hide from them the storm, whose destruction, from far away, they cannot see, nor even suspect" (Costa 1874, 274). Pereira (1981) describes various individuals from parish priests to the captains of ships who profited from the business of *engajamento.* Clearly, *engajadores,* like their twentieth-century counterparts, the *passadores,* were middlemen, serving the politics of migration in both sending and receiving areas. That these individuals figure in several migration narratives of the 1960s illustrates the continued significance of the "business" of migration. In fact, Douglas Massey and his colleagues (1993) have emphasized the important role that people like *coyotes* and *passadores* play in the perpetuation of migration streams as part of an underground market.

While Alcides does not discuss it graphically in his narrative, during the early years of Portuguese emigration to France, when rates of clandestine migration were so high, the Portuguese were sometimes subject to ruthless employers, who asked for long days of work at low pay. They often lived in crowded and unhealthy living conditions in shantytowns (so-called *bidonville*s) that were scattered around the periphery of Paris. It was difficult to return home, because the passage would be equally strenuous. These are conditions not unlike those faced by illegal immigrants in the United States in the late twentieth and early twenty-first centuries. One difference, however, and perhaps one reason that Alcides's narrative lacks a tone of fear and complaints of abuse, is that in France during this period it was quite easy for illegal immigrants to regularize their status and secure proper working papers. The French wanted and needed them, and their immigration policies reflected this need. This explains a lot about how the Portuguese fared in France, compared with undocumented Mexican workers in the United States.[9]

One of the most distinctive aspects of Portuguese immigrant women in France has been their high level of employment, domestic service being the predominant work. Maria's position as a concierge was characteristic of many Portuguese married women who migrated to France in the 1960s and 1970s. In pursuing this line of work, Portuguese immigrant women were making carefully considered choices among various labor market options. The position as concierge allowed them to balance their double responsibilities as mothers and wage earners. Alcides and Maria decided together to return to France, because they could not get ahead in Portugal. They went in search of better wages, and two earners are better than one. Yet other considerations come into play to shape the way that Maria, and Portuguese women like her, made their contributions to family income.

Gloria F.

In 1974, Gloria and Joaquim F. were living in one room on the third floor of a rather dark building in the first *arrondissement,* in a neighborhood occupied by many new immigrants from North Africa. They were paying 300 francs a month (about $50 at that time) for it. A cousin of Gloria's had a room on an upper floor of the same building. They shared a toilet in the hall. Their room was divided by a curtain, with the bed behind the curtain. In the other part of the room was a table with three chairs, a refrigerator, a large armoire, a smaller cupboard, a sink, and a stove. They had no television.

Joaquim, who was born in northwestern Portugal in 1938, first arrived in France in April of 1965 with a contract to work at an iron manufacturing company north of Paris. He left Gloria (who was born in 1941) behind in their village with their two children. There she could continue to tend to their small plots of land. He earned 350 francs per month and lived in company housing with three other Portuguese men. When he asked permission from the company to return home to Portugal in December to celebrate Christmas with his family, they said no. Joaquim had heard that there was work at Citroën, so he broke his contract, returned to Portugal for two months, and then returned to France to a job at Citroën. Joaquim once told me that through his job at Citroën he belonged to a union, and he remembered very well the strikes of 1968. "They tried to organize the immigrants. But I always vote for the boss. I did not come to France to make politics (*fazer política*)," he said, "I came here to work."

Joaquim returned to Portugal again in August of 1966 and in December of 1966 he brought Gloria back to France with him. She came on a tourist pass and then applied for legalization later.

I had had no intention of following Joaquim to France, especially without the children. But he persuaded me that if I joined him we could make more money together and more quickly. It would not be worth it to bring the children, because then I would not be able to earn anything. It was very hard for me to leave the children behind, even though they were in good hands with my mother, who was also taking care of my sister's children. They change while I am gone. They have become more used to their grandparents, who are not as strict with them as we would be.

When I first arrived in France, I stayed for two years; then I returned to Portugal for eighteen months before leaving for France again. We are thinking of going back at Christmas, and maybe next summer we will go back for good. We have bought a house in our village from a teacher who works in Porto, but we need to save money to buy new furniture, to paint it, to buy a car, and to put some money aside in the case of an accident. We are here to make money to make a better life for our children. That is impossible in Portugal. Life is hard in France, and we have to watch every penny. The French just earn and spend. They never put anything aside. That is not wise. We work all week, and then we have housework to do on weekends. On Sundays we go to mass, and then we have my brother over in the afternoon. There is a French priest who says the mass. But he is hard on us, always saying that the Portuguese are only interested in earning money. What he does not understand is the great pain that we suffer being away from our families. And the French do not really want us here with our families and to stay. Why do the Portuguese come here? Practically everyone has a bit of land, but people need money to build a house, and there is no other way but to emigrate. There is no great misery in Portugal; people grow things to eat and do not eat badly, but you cannot get ahead.

Joaquim used to work the night shift and on weekends at Citroën (he could make more money) until I came. Then he switched to the day shift and stopped his weekend work, except for one Saturday each month. He worked for eight hours each day, first the morning shift and then the afternoon shift from 3 p.m. to 11 p.m. When he worked during the afternoons, we did not see one another. Joaquim also has a job cleaning in a private home two days a week—washing floors and windows and making good money. He has been doing the extra work since 1970. He found the work through me.

When I came to France I first worked doing cleaning for private families, but then I found work with a service that cleans buildings. I work from 8 a.m. to 8 p.m. five days a week. But I like this better than cleaning in private homes, because the hours are regular. When you work in private cleaning they give you more than you can handle. I also like being with a group of other women. Most of them are also Portuguese. I am now the group leader. I receive my wages, money for transportation, and a month of paid holiday. So does Joaquim. I like cleaning more than working in the fields, because I can come home in clean clothes.

Joaquim's parents are very old, and they keep writing begging him to come home. Even though he is not the only son, he is close to his parents. We could go back for good, and if something unforeseen happened Joaquim could simply emigrate again by himself, to France or to Canada. It would not be hard. France still needs us. The French don't want to do the jobs we do. It would be easy for me to find work in a Portuguese factory, but it would be harder for Joaquim to find work in Portugal, because he does not have a trade.

> We both come from large families—we both had eight brothers and sisters, although one of my brothers died when he is very young. One of Joaquim's brothers has thirteen children, and he worked in Germany for a while. He also has a brother-in-law who worked in Canada. But his other brothers and sisters are in Portugal. Two of my older brothers have been in France, one with his wife. But they have both returned to Portugal, one in 1972 and the other this year (1974). I have a younger sister and a younger brother who are still here, and my brother lived with us for a while. The rest of my brothers and sisters are in Portugal, but one of my sisters has a husband who has worked in Germany, Africa, and France. He is now back in Portugal.

Gloria and Joaquim decided to leave their children behind in Portugal, and they were working long hours in France to amass savings so that they could return home. Gloria spoke about the priest's criticisms with a tone of resentment; they had not come to France to be like to the French but to meet their goals as Portuguese immigrants. The employment decisions that Gloria made were facilitated by the absence of childcare responsibilities. Indeed Gloria was a rather open and gregarious woman, and it was easy to see that she would opt for working with a group of women rather than for working alone in private domestic service.

Both Gloria and Joaquim admitted that they kept thinking that they would return to Portugal within a year, but the days and months passed and they remained in France. Indeed, during the year that I knew them, and every time I met with them, they would tell me their latest plan for returning—at Christmas, at Easter, during the summer. The date was always revised, with Gloria generally postponing permanent departure and Joaquim eager to set the date. Indeed, some time later Joaquim told me that he had once filled out forms in Paris to emigrate to Canada. He was told he needed a sponsor, so he let the whole thing drop. "But Canada is a good place to go because you can earn more money," he said.

This project of earning as much money as possible to realize certain ends which were constantly adjusted (buying a house, furnishing a house, saving more money for the future, and so forth) influenced an important decision for Gloria in December of 1974. Throughout the Fall of 1974 I attended Sunday masses at St. Eustache cathedral to meet with Portuguese families. In December I noticed that Gloria had missed a few Sundays. Joachim told me she was not feeling well. Then on December 22nd she came and asked to talk to me at the end of the mass. She wanted to know if I was interested in going to England with her after Christmas. I indicated surprise that she was making this trip, and then she told me that she was going to England to have an abortion. "I want you to come with me because you can speak English," she said. She then went on: "It is not the custom for Portuguese to abort their children, and if I could have the child I would not have this abortion. But I have not been feeling well, and I cannot work. The doctor has told me that if I have the child I will have to stay in bed for the rest of the pregnancy. And after it is born I would not be able to work. I am here in France to work, and anyway it is better these days to have a small family." She told me that the family-planning clinic had made the appointment in England for her, and it was all set for right after Christmas. I agreed to accompany her. Gloria then asked me not to tell any Portuguese about it. "We are always critical of one another," she said.

When I arrived on Friday the 27th of December at her house, Gloria was putting together a lunch to take with us on the train. She had gone to work in the morning and hoped to be back at work on Monday. Joaquim had bought one-way tickets for both of us, because he was not sure that she would be released from the hospital to return on Sunday. The cousin from upstairs arrived, and Gloria briefly mentioned that she was going to "take a little trip" (*vamos passear*). She whisked her bag into a corner. On the train I learned that she had told the cousin that she was being sent to England in connection with her work. No mention was made of my accompanying her; I had simply been invited to lunch. She had not even told her sister the real reason she was going to England. She told me that when her sister and brother-in-law heard that she was going to England, they had said that she would now "be standing above everyone else" (*as pernas acima de todos*).

Gloria told me that she and her husband had made the decision about the abortion together. "Joaquim was careful for nine years, and yet I got pregnant. The doctor suggested that I take the pill after this operation so as to avoid any more difficulties. But I am afraid it will make me fatter (*mais gorda*)." In England, when I was filling out the forms at the clinic for her, I learned that she had been pregnant five times: two of her babies were stillborn, two lived, and one died at the age of seven months.

I relate this event because it demonstrates quite powerfully the importance of a particular migration project and the extent to which migrants are social actors who make sometimes very difficult decisions in order to meet the goals that they have set out for themselves, albeit goals that can change, depending on both external and personal constraints. I found that married Portuguese women in France who had left their children behind were both extremely focused and deeply conflicted. The choices they had made aroused complex emotions. These emotions are rarely discussed in the literature of migration, but they frequently emerge in narratives and in the close-up context of participant observation.

Maria P.

In the fall of 1974, twenty-four-year-old Maria P. was working as a *bonne à toute faire* (full-time maid) for a French family. She was living in a maid's room on the eighth floor of an apartment building in the eighth *arrondissement* of Paris. The room was not very large and was sparsely furnished. In the center of the room, lit by a single window, was a small table, and along one wall was a couch that folded out into a bed. The room also had a dresser. Along another wall was a closet and a sink; the toilet was out in the hall. Other single people lived on the floor, including another woman from Portugal who was separated from her husband.

I come from a village in Tras-os-Montes, where many people, men and women, worked in tin mining in addition to farming. My father worked as a miner, but he died in the early 1960s. I was the fifth child, and I have one younger brother and two younger sisters. My oldest sister was born in 1941 and emigrated to Brazil in 1961, together with my older brother and another older sister. They went to join my uncle, my mother's brother, who had been in Brazil for a long time. My eldest sister met a Portuguese man from Minho in Brazil, married there, and had two children. Her husband set up his own business, as did my elder brother. My other sister found work as a stenographer and is not married.

Another older sister, who was born in 1943, married at age sixteen in 1959 and emigrated to France in 1964. Her husband had wanted to go to Brazil after his marriage, but because he had just turned eighteen the government insisted that he complete his military service. When that was finished, he decided to emigrate to France. At first he went alone, but eventually he called my sister to join him. She left all her children in Portugal, three of them with their paternal grandmother and four with my mother. Only recently she has taken her youngest child, who was born in France, back to Portugal.

I emigrated to France in 1966 at the age of sixteen. I came with the help of a passador, because I had no papers. My younger sister came in 1969 at the age of seventeen. My younger brother went to Brazil in 1968 to live with my older brother; that way he could avoid the tropa [military service]. My youngest sister, who was born in 1960, is still living with my mother in Portugal. I also have an aunt living in France who arrived in 1972 to join her husband, who emigrated in 1964 to work in construction. Finally, I have some other cousins in France. They are the children of one of my mother's brothers. On my father's side most of the family has passed away, but we have some relatives in Brazil.

Children in Portugal work from an early age, in the fields or in the mines, and they give their earnings to their parents. I only attended school for four years, and then I stopped to help my mother in the fields and taking care of my younger brother and sisters in the house. I decided to come to France, because life in Portugal is so poor. There are rich people in my village who have a lot of land or a business, and with their presence the poor want to be rich, too, and gain their level of living. The only solution is to emigrate. No one is left behind in the villages of northern Portugal but older people and young children.

My father was already dead and my mother was not well, and so when I came to France it was to earn money for the family. I paid a passador 6,000 escudos to help me to cross the border. One other woman from my village came with me.

The passador *left us at St. Jean de Luz in southern France, and we had to buy train tickets for Paris, where the aunt of my traveling companion lived. We couldn't speak any French, and we were lucky, because a taxi driver in Paris took us to her aunt's house for nothing.*

I found this position as a maid through my brother-in-law. This was the only kind of work that someone like me could get, but it is a good position because it comes with a free room. My boss helped me to get my working papers. During the week I begin my work at 8 in the morning, and I work until 8 o'clock at night. I also work between 8 in the morning and 2 p.m. on Saturdays, but I have Sundays off, and I spend Sundays with my sister and with other Portuguese friends. I like the family I work for; they treat me very well. This is different from Portugal, where maids are treated badly; here in France you are like one of the family.

For three years I did not return to Portugal; it would have been hard to get a passport to reenter France. I was very lonely during those years, and until my younger sister arrived. Now it is better, because my sister is here and I have made some friends at church. But we came to France to work. We do not go out much, and we economize.

My younger sister and I send money back to our mother, because she needs it to live; what she does not use she sets aside for us. I want to return to Portugal one day, but not to my village. I will go to the city, perhaps Bragança, and get an apartment and a job, and maybe I will study at night, like my brother is doing in Brazil. My mother can come to live with me.

Maria P.'s story demonstrates the extent to which her family, across generations and across a genealogy, was involved in migration. Her family is no different from many more in northern Portugal who witnessed the departure of young people in the prime of life to make their living elsewhere. Indeed, Maria's account of her diasporic family offers a concrete example of how Portuguese emigration fits the model of a self-propelling cycle of departures outlined by Massey et al. (1993) to describe the process by which migration streams are perpetuated more generally.

Marcelo Borges (2000) has found this life-cycle expectation to migrate to be equally true for the Algarve region in the south of Portugal. Like the north, the Algarve is also a region characterized by extreme division of property and limited resources. Borges views seasonal migrations, migrations across close frontiers (to Gibraltar for example), and trans-Atlantic migrations as part of a single system. "Emigration constituted one of the regular strategies used by Algarvian farmers and rural workers to complement the production on their own or rented lands, to acquire cash income, and to buy land. . . . Algarvian peasant-workers incorporated seasonal migration in the regular activities of the agricultural year" (p. 176).[10] In both northern Portugal and in the Algarve in the south, internal and international migration (especially when it was not trans-Atlantic) were part of a strategy for household reproduction. Older children left progressively, leaving younger children to care for elderly parents and to tend to the family lands. Once France began to admit immigrants, more and more young working-age adults left, such that the villages, as Maria observes, were made up only of old people and children.

Historically, the normative expectation for migration was more characteristic of men, whether single or married, than of women. If single women did migrate, it was primarily within a regional context or as far as Lisbon to work in domestic service. It is from such experiences that Maria and others draw comparisons between the treatment of maids in Portugal and in France. The fact that they do so suggests that dignity of work may have been as important to the decision to emigrate as economic opportunity. Maria's story helps us to understand the role of unmarried women in the post–World War II Portuguese migration stream to France. Certainly word filtered back to villages about the opportunities for women who were willing to work as hourly house cleaners and private maids for bourgeois and upper-class families in the cities of France, particularly Paris. The latter position was particularly attractive to single women, because it came with free and safe housing. However, what is also important in Maria's story is how her own migration fit into a household strategy. She went to France in order to help support her mother and her younger siblings, and she was routinely sending money back to Portugal. Maria was left in this position because all her older siblings had emigrated to Brazil and made lives for themselves there; the sister who proceeded her to France was already married and had her own family to take care of. It is not apparent in Maria's narrative how much her mother was involved in the decision, but clearly Maria was not just looking out for herself.

Maria's migration was facilitated by the fact that her sister was already in France, and Maria in turn facilitated the arrival of her younger sister. Kinship networks are important to the majority of Portuguese immigrants in France and are also fundamental to recent theorizing about why people migrate. People get to particular places because of these networks, not solely on the basis of a cost-benefit analysis of the most favorable destination but on the basis of whom they know and from whom they can seek help (Wilson 1994). This is an accurate if partial explanation of why some of Maria's siblings went to Brazil and why she and others went to France.[11] The only exception, perhaps, is Maria's brother-in-law, who established the family "beachhead" in France, choosing this destination because by the time he got out of the military it had become the most popular destination for the Portuguese.

Another important observation made by Maria is that relative deprivation spurs emigration. Those without land want to be like those with land, and the only way to achieve this is to earn cash in the larger national or global economy. These baseline economic differences within localized systems of social and economic stratification are important to a determination of who leaves first and then who follows. Often it is neither the extremely poor (who have no money for the passage and no social networks abroad) nor the richest who pioneer a migration stream, but those with some but not great resources. But as cash becomes increasingly important in a localized economy, those from families who may have been rich in land but not in cash follow. This is yet another way to approach and understand how a culture of migration emerges.

Conclusion

The methods of anthropology are well suited to the task of eliciting data from individuals, including the collection of individual stories of life experiences. In research on migration, anthropologists have a unique contribution to make by elucidating how the process looks from the inside out and from the ground up. What they learn often confirms economic and sociological theories about why people migrate—to improve their standard of living by going to places where wages are higher or jobs more plentiful. But ethnographic data often suggest other dimensions that ultimately lend important support to a more comprehensive approach that combines levels and units of analysis. As Massey et al. argue, "sorting out which of the explanations are useful is an empirical and not only a logical task" (1993, 455).

The small number of brief narratives included in this essay reinforce this point. They show us how state policies of one sort or another structure a particular migration stream and how individual migrants respond to these structures. They illustrate the context (familial, local, national, international) in which decisions are made and actions are taken and perhaps most importantly how these are affected by social locations of age, gender, region, class, and so forth. They reveal the importance of kinship networks and intermediaries not only in facilitating but also in generating migration. They demonstrate how gender ideologies and gender roles can shape migration decisions, both before and after departure. And, to return to the observations of Tony Fielding with which I opened this chapter, they sometimes demonstrate the complex feelings associated with leaving one's homeland and becoming an immigrant. Through individual stories we learn how the migration process is patterned and subjectively experienced. We also learn about how migration is part not only of an individual but also of a collective biography—something extremely important in the Portuguese case. Anthropologists, no matter what they study, must be mindful of both the general and the particular. As Sarah Lamb (2001, 22) writes, "even if our aim is to better understand and represent particular people's lives, we cannot do so adequately without scrutinizing the very kinds of generalized, broader forces and categories through which people make these lives."

Notes

1. For comprehensive discussions of anthropological approaches to life history, see Angrosino (1976, 1989), Crapanzano (1984), Frank (1996), Langness and Frank (1985), and Watson and Watson-Franke (1985). The life history has been described as "an extensive record of a person's life told to and recorded by another, who then edits and writes the life as though it were autobiography" (Langness 1965, 4–5).

2. Two other works from this intermediary period are also worth mentioning— Sidney Mintz's *Worker in the Cane* (1960) and David G. Mandelbaum's "life history" of Gandhi (1973). Mintz strongly asserts that the Puerto Rican sugarcane worker Don Taso was anything but typical, but he also argued that he was "representative of his time, his place, and his people. . . . What happened to him happened in the broadest terms to his society as well" (Mintz 1989, 792).

3. The Italian immigrant woman Rosa, who is the narrator of the life recorded by Marie Hall Ets (discussed later in this chapter), says that she is deliberately going to omit her husband Santino from her story. "But I have to leave that man out of this story. The things he did to me are too bad to tell! I leave him out, that's all!" (1999, 174).

4. Another early example is Monica Sone's (1953) autobiographical account of her childhood, adolescence, and young adulthood as part of a Japanese immigrant family in Seattle.

5. Another recent example worth mentioning is Tung Pok Chin's (with Winifred Chin) (2000) autobiographical account of his life in Boston and New York from the 1930s to the mid-1970s. Through Chin's eyes we come to understand the real impact of the Chinese exclusion laws on an individual life, including the strategy of becoming a "paper son" who entered the United States with fake documents that claimed that the bearer was an American citizen or the son or grandson of an American citizen. Chin's book is a good example of how immigrants themselves have appropriated the narrative format, whether in the form of autobiographies, diaries, or even fiction. See Parati (1997) for further discussion.

6. See Brettell (1995) for further discussion of this case. As I was taking down this story, this woman gave me a set of dates that indicated that in France she had become pregnant prior to her marriage. When I finally asked about this, much more information came out on the reason for her departure, including the fact that her fiancé *(namorado)*, who was a cousin, had heard the stories and wanted to be sure of her virginity before he married her. She told this story with tears in her eyes, evidence of the emotional pain that it caused her.

7. It is interesting that both of these accounts are about women immigrants and that often it is women ethnographers who help to launch these projects. Some time ago Isabelle Bertaux-Wiame (1982, 192–193), writing about migrant narratives, noted important differences between how men and women tell stories:

> Men seldom talk spontaneously about their family life—as if it was not really part of their life. *Their* life: men consider the life they have as *their own*; . . . Men present their life as a series of self-conscious acts, a rational pursuit of well-defined goals—be it success, or simple . . . quietness and security. Their whole story revolves around the sequence of occupations they have had, as if they insisted on jobs because work is the area where they are active. They present themselves as the subjects of their own lives— as the actors. Women do not insist on this. Self-conscious acts are not their main interest. Instead, they will talk at length about their *relationship* to such and such a person. Their own life stories will include parts of the life stories of others. In contrast with men's accounts, women will not insist on what they have done; but rather on what relationships existed between themselves and persons close to them.

Although it is not my goal to explore this point further, it is certainly an interesting observation and one worthy of further consideration by those interested in migrant narratives as a genre.

8. The Portuguese constitution that was put into effect in 1933 under Salazar's Estado Novo (New State) gave the state the right to control emigration, and an additional law of 1944 forbade issuing passports to workers of any industry or rural workers. It was a crime to leave the country without a passport until 1974, when the Portuguese revolution ushered in a new system. Political scientists are interested in how the state controls population flows across borders. Alcides's narrative shows how the state may not always be successful at controlling flows, but it can certainly shape their nature—often illegal or clandestine.

9. It should be noted that French immigration policy at the close of the twentieth century was much less tolerant of clandestine immigration than it was in the 1960s, when Portuguese immigration was at its height. This is a reflection not only of changed economic circumstances but also of changes in the source of the flows—primarily from North Africa, and primarily Muslims.

10. Borges notes the similarities between the system in the Algarve and that described by Douglas Holmes (1989) for the north of Italy.

11. I say "partial" because state policy shaped destinations for Portuguese emigrants prior to 1960. The Junta de Emigração, established in 1947 to regulate emigration, sent the majority of legal emigrants to Brazil.

II

RETURN MIGRATION, TRANSMIGRANTS, AND TRANSNATIONALISM

In 1977 Robert Rhoades proposed a session for the annual meeting of the American Anthropological Association that would focus on the phenomenon of return migration. Rhoades observed that, despite Donald Bogue's observation that "for every migration stream there is a corresponding counterstream flowing in the opposite direction" (Bogue 1969, 765), little social scientific attention was paid to understanding the phenomenon of return migration. Rhoades's argument was clearly not persuasive enough to the program chair serving that year; the session was rejected. Rhoades suggested to those of us slated to participate that we nevertheless write a paper for *Papers in Anthropology*, a series from the University of Oklahoma. This became the first collection that wrestled in print with the phenomenon of return migration. A few years later return migration had clearly "arrived" in the discipline, marked by an essay in the *Annual Review of Anthropology* by George Gmelch (1980), one of the authors in the *Papers in Anthropology* volume.

Gmelch began his review essay by noting that, in a migration bibliography published in the early 1970s, only 10 of the 2,051 titles listed were studies of return, this despite the fact that an estimated 25 percent of the 16 million Europeans who came to the United States early in the twentieth century returned (Gmelch 1980, 135; see also Cinel 1991; Foner 1997; Morawska 2001; Wyman 1993). Gmelch defined return migration as "the movement of emigrants back to their homelands to resettle" and addressed questions of why people return, how they adjust once they are at home, what return means to them, what changes they bring to their home communities, and why some choose to reemigrate. While Gmelch eventually published a book that had as its central subject matter the definitive

47

return of Barbadians from London to Barbados (Gmelch 1992), it is safe to say that during the 1980s and the early 1990s there was little interest coming from other directions on the subject of return migration, except among those studying intra-European migrations (Hoffman-Nowotny 1978; Hudson and Lewis 1985).[1]

Those who did write about some aspect of return talked about "sojourners" (Chavez 1988; Margolis 1994) or simply back and forth movement (Grasmuck and Pessar 1991). As recently as 1997 Luis Guarnizo, in an article titled "The Emergence of a Transnational Social Formation and the Mirage of Return Migration among Dominican Transmigrants," offered an explanation for this lack of interest by noting the important conceptual distinction between individuals who were classified as settled (that is, immigrant) and those classified as temporary (that is, migrant). "In effect," he argues, "being cataloged as either settled or temporary greatly influences whether a given group receives more or less attention as a subject worth studying with returnees receiving much less attention than so-called definitive immigrants" (1997a, 284; see also Guarnizo 1997b).

Guarnizo was of course trying to deal with the relationship between transnationalism and return migration (as mirage or reality), for by 1997 the former concept had exploded on the scene of migration studies, if not in anthropology more generally. Transnationalism was defined as a social process whereby migrants operate in social fields that transgress geographic, political, and cultural borders (Glick Schiller, Basch, and Szanton Blanc 1992b, ix; see also Basch, Glick Schiller, and Szanton Blanc 1994). The concept emerged from the realization that immigrants abroad, rather than being uprooted, maintain ties to their countries of origin, making "home and host society a single arena of social action" (Margolis 1994, 29). Transnationalism was, as Glick Schiller, Basch, and Szanton Blanc (1995, 49) argue, formulated as "part of an effort to reconfigure anthropological thinking so that it will reflect current transformations in the way in which time and space [are] experienced and represented."

As her own thinking about transnationalism became more refined, and in part in response to how the concept was being appropriated by other disciplines, Nina Glick Schiller (1997, 155) formulated careful distinctions among (1) transnational cultural studies that focus on "the growth of global communications, media, consumerism, and public cultures that transcend borders to create a global ecumene"; (2) globalization studies that call attention to "the recent reconfigurations of space and polity and the growth of global cities; and (3) transnational migration studies where scholars are "concerned with the actual social interactions that migrants maintain and construct across borders." She has come to speak and write more firmly about transmigrants rather than transnationalism and to emphasize this concept as a way to rethink older categories of circulatory, permanent, and return migration. "Transmigrants are people who claim and are claimed by two or more nation-states into which they are incorporated as social actors, one of which is widely acknowledged to be their state of origin" (Glick Schiller 1999, 96).

Glick Schiller illustrates the concept of the transmigrant with the story of a Haitian woman named Yvette, who was living in New York and yet pays for the weddings and funerals of her nieces and nephews in Haiti. These are heavy responsibilities, but as Glick Schiller points out they also have rewards. "In the United States, [Yvette's] earnings would make no social mark, even if she were to hoard them or expend them on consumer goods. To her network in Haiti, Yvette is a person of influence. . . . Yvette's continuing home ties, her experience of being identified as Haitian while living and working in the United States . . . all contribute to her understanding that her life is connected to Haiti, even as she and her family strive to become further incorporated into the United States" (1999, 94).

In another essay Glick Schiller takes on the nostalgia for home, arguing that it is not useful "to equate transnational migration with the longings that immigrants may feel for home, if these sentiments are not translated into systematic participation in networks that cross borders" (1999, 96). Certainly in both anthropology and literary studies, the question of how "home" is thought about and/or imagined has become of increasing interest in recent years (Constable 1999; Klimt 2000a; Rapport and Dawson 1998; Robertson et al. 1994; Stack 1996). Zetter (1999), for example, addresses how the protracted exile of a Greek Cypriot refugee population influences their perceptions of home and return.

While this literature does indeed focus more on meaning or ideas than on action, the two aspects of return need not be mutually exclusive and were not conceived as such in my essay "*Emigrar para Voltar*" (literally to emigrate to return), chapter 3 of this volume. When I wrote about an "ideology of return" it was meant to capture the longing for home felt by Portuguese nationals living in France in the mid-1970s. But it equally demonstrates how people are actively involved in their home society through economic remittances, the building of houses, and participation in the social and religious life of their native villages. The essay is not, in short, only about intentionality or a "myth" of return. Although I never use the term *transmigrants*, preferring instead to write about return migration, because, as the title of the chapter suggests, the Portuguese themselves conceptualize it this way, I am in fact describing transmigrants. The *brasileiros* and *franceses* about whom I write are perhaps comparable to the "dominicanyorks" described by Guarnizo (1997a, 1997b); and the idea of *emigrar para voltar* is not that different from Eugenia Georges' (1990, 223) portrayal of transnational Dominicans who have their feet in two worlds, one here and one there (*un pie qui, el otro alla*). Finally, when Peggy Levitt (2001a, 11) writes about migrants who "still use their sending community as the reference group against which they gauge their status," she is describing something similar to what I observed when I suggested that the Portuguese are *travailleur* in France, to be *petit bourgeois* in Portugal. For all these reasons, the chapter *"Emigrar para Voltar"* still has theoretical and empirical resonance in the early twenty-first century. It offers an earlier example, in a European arena, of what has been so elaborately described for Dominicans, Haitians, and others in the U.S. immigration arena of the 1980s and 1990s (Laguerre 1998).

In my view it is extremely important to bring the Portuguese case into the discussion of transnationalism and transmigrants. Maintaining links with the homeland and sustaining the idea of return for as long as one is abroad is, as my essay argues, deeply rooted in Portuguese history and culture (Brettell 1990b; see also Meintel 2002). The Portuguese state for several centuries has fostered continuing ties with its population abroad (Rocha-Trindade 1990). In the post–World War II period, the Portuguese state, and Portuguese institutions such as banks and the Catholic Church, took an active interest in supporting ties to the homeland among those who had emigrated to France, to Canada, to Venezuela, and to the United States.[2] The remittances of emigrants during the late 1960s and early 1970s helped the balance of payments and sustained Portugal's colonial wars in Africa. In 1960, according to the annual report of the Bank of Portugal, the total remittances amounted to a little more than 1.5 million *escudos*, and the balance of payments was –3.0 million *escudos*. By 1975 remittances were at 25.5 million *escudos*, and the balance of payments was 9.3 million *escudos*. In 2000 remittances still accounted for roughly 3 percent of the gross domestic product.

After the loss of the African colonies in 1974, the Portuguese state became more aggressive in reaching out to Portuguese immigrants dispersed throughout the globe, as part of a new concept of nation based on population rather than place (Feldman-Bianco 1992). In the 1980s Portuguese laws were changed so that emigrants and their descendants could retain their Portuguese nationality while they were simultaneously citizens of another country. The Ministry of Foreign Affairs has registered and maintains contacts with close to 4.3 million Portuguese people and their descendents who are living abroad (Malheiros 2002). Furthermore, the government has begun to offer financial support to the more than 2,000 Portuguese associations that have emerged in Portuguese immigrant communities around the world, in the hope that this will help to sustain the knowledge of Portuguese language and culture among young people who are growing up in other societies (Stalker 2000).

What I describe in chapter 3 is certainly not unique to Portuguese emigrants in France, nor is it simply a function of the early period of post–World War II intra-European migration patterns. Meintel (2002) describes transnational lifestyles that characterized nineteenth-century Cape Verdean migration. Chapin (1989) describes Azorean fishermen in Provincetown who, while not recent immigrants to the United States, nevertheless maintained ties with their homeland. And Andrea Klimt (2000a, 262) writes that none of the Portuguese migrants she interviewed in Hamburg, Germany, in the mid 1980s "had any intention of settling permanently in Germany or acquiring German citizenship, despite their increasing entanglement with German society. . . . Their sense of self was firmly linked to an anticipated return, and their resources and ambitions were all aimed at creating the perfect 'home' in Portugal." When she returned to Hamburg in the late 1990s she found that the rhetoric of return was still present among Portuguese immigrants, who wanted to keep all their options open and live across national spaces. "Even those who have lived their entire lives in Germany and know Portugal only through stories and vacation visits . . . [hold a] sense of self . . . firmly linked to 'being Portuguese'. Most express that commitment through investing in a future in Portugal" (Klimt 2000b, 517).

What is perhaps of most interest theoretically is that even in the arena where the concepts of transnationalism and transmigrants has been most pervasive in analyzing immigrant behavior and the immigrant experience in the late twentieth century—that is, the United States—there are those who were equally writing about return migration. Two particular examples in anthropology are Patricia Pessar's edited volume *Caribbean Circuits* (1997) and Peggy Levitt's book *The Transnational Villagers* (2001a), but I should also draw attention to the work of geographers (Bryon 1999, 2000; Bryon and Condon 1996; Condon and Ogden 1996), for whom return migration is perhaps a natural outcome of their disciplinary focus on questions of space.

In the Pessar volume, Guarnizo (1997b) focuses on actual return migrants who planned to stay in the Dominican Republic for good. These people were middle-aged, slightly better educated than the general Dominican population, and married. Guarnizo found that most individuals returned not primarily for economic reasons but because they had family obligations or because they preferred life on the island. His results are similar to those of others who have studied actual return flows (Gmelch 1983), but what he adds is the assertion that even those who have returned "for good" remain part of a transnational social field, and one-third of his sample wanted to reemigrate. He also describes a growing hostility toward returnees who have settled in the better neighborhoods of Santo Domingo.

In her essay in that volume, Lourdes Bueno (1997) addresses the particular experience of women who return. What she discovers about the significant losses in social gains acquired in the United States has been documented by those who have studied the role of gender in this process in other countries (Gmelch and Gmelch 1995). But the losses are weighed against what women perceive to be the real advantages of return—a better education for their children. Finally, Chevannes and Ricketts (1997) look at the role of return migrants in small business development in Jamaica, thereby addressing a much older question first raised by anthropologists in the intra-European arena (Rhoades 1978). Contrary to what others have argued, they found a positive impact on some forms of development (see also King et al. 1985).

These chapters in the Pessar volume deal with actual return, something that I do not address in my essay "*Emigrar para Voltar*," because at that stage of the migration of Portuguese nationals to France, the mid-1970s, the return flow was negligible. However, by the early 1980s scholars were beginning to write about these return flows (Comissão de Coordenação da Região Centro 1984; Poinard 1983a, 1983b; Silva et al. 1984; Sousa Ferreira and Clausse 1986), many of them occurring with assistance from the French and German governments.[3] By the end of the decade the numbers of returnees had declined, and in the 1990s attention has been redirected to the study of Portugal as a country of immigration as well as emigration (Baganha 1997).

Levitt's characterization of Dominican immigrants in the Boston area is perhaps closer to what I am describing in chapter 3. Almost everyone who leaves the community of Miraflores in the Dominican Republic, she observes "does so with the intention to return" (2001a, 92), but few actually do return. Nevertheless, Levitt describes three groups of actual returnees: those who leave poor and with minimal education who return with negligible English, few skills, and, with the possible exception of a new home, little advancement from where they were when they left; those who return with jewelry, cars, and other attributes of wealth that everyone assumes is linked to the drug trade and who engage in circular migration rather than permanent return; and a smaller and more successful group who left with more education and resources and who return with English, significant skills, and a changed social and economic status. Levitt refers, as I do, to an altered system of social stratification; a two-class society has become one with many rungs on the ladder. This is a direct result of the impact of returnees, be they temporary or more permanent.

Perhaps of more significance in Levitt's book, for my purposes here and particularly for introducing chapter 4 of this volume, is the chapter on the role of religion and the church. Not only does she describe the Spanish-language masses that Dominicans supported in the Boston area but also the influence that migrants had in moving the celebration of religion in the sending community "away from popular religious practices toward more officially sanctioned, church-based rituals" (Levitt 2001a, 176). She describes the choice of migrants as baptismal godparents because they were thought to be more able to assume the financial obligations. And she describes migrants who could afford to make pilgrimages to holy places and supported the local church when they organized such tours.

Chapter 4, "Emigration, the Church, and the Religious Festival in Northern Portugal," addresses the religious ties that Portuguese emigrants have maintained with their communities of origin. When I wrote this essay, and still to a large extent today, more attention was paid to the role of religion in communities of immigration than on the impact of emigration on the church and religious practices in sending societies. Most recently, this is exemplified by several of the essays in two recent volumes, one edited by Stephen Warner and Judith Wittner (1998) and the other by Robert Orsi (1999).

The Warner and Wittner volume is the result of the New Ethnic and Immigrant Congregations Project. The focus of the project was how immigrant identity is shaped in relation to religious communities but also beyond them and how such organizations help new immigrant groups to take a seat at the multicultural table. The book includes an essay on how Mayan immigrants in Los Angeles find a place in Catholic churches that cater to Hispanics and Latinos but at the same time reject this place because they are also Indians. It also contains essays on various Protestant Asian communities. The Orsi volume also addresses how immigrant communities, through various religious institutions, create their own social space and negotiate the differences between America and the home culture and society. It includes essays on a church that serves as a gathering place for Cubans in Miami and a Hindu temple that serves a group of Asian Indian immigrants in the Baltimore area. But the book also includes an essay by Karen McCarthy Brown that addresses the links that Haitians maintain with their homeland through the practice of voodoo. Brown writes about "the parallel Vodou ceremonies . . . performed, following the same ritual calendar, in both Haiti and New York, [and] the more interesting circumstances that make Vodou a key player in the exchange of people, goods, and money between Haiti and the continental United States (Brown 1999, 97). Brown is writing about the transnational links that sustain religious activity in sending societies.

These are the same issues that I address in chapter 4. My argument is that in one village in northern Portugal—and I have no doubt that this was occurring elsewhere in this region[4]—the annual celebration of an important religious festival was revived through the economic support and participation of emigrants, who timed their return to the community to coincide with this event. While they are at home emigrants also baptize children born in France and celebrate weddings, their own or someone else's in their extended family. When in France they remain tied to the life-course events of villagers through their subscription to the parish newspaper. The motives for their extensive support of the *festa* are similar to those described by Levitt for Dominican immigrants to the United States. They can convert economic capital into social capital within a social system that remains meaningful to them. They operate as transmigrants within this social system.

By way of conclusion, it is probably useful to address the difference between return migrants and transmigrants. The first concept should be reserved for those individuals who do go back to live in their sending communities. Sarah Mahler (1999) has identified Salvadorans who fall into this category: They have no desire to return to the United States. Certainly some former Portuguese emigrants also fall into this category. Of course, one should at least acknowledge that some returnees may eventually reemigrate. "Transmigrant" then remains a concept used to refer to individuals who maintain ties with their homelands and become involved in the economic, social, religious, and political spheres of their sending communities as well as the host society. They move back and forth and are, as Glick Schiller has argued, simultaneously incorporated within more than one nation-state (1999, 98). The Portuguese I studied fall into this category, guided by an "ideology of return" that helped them to justify their behavior. Certainly this has become even more complex and interesting since Portugal became a member of the European Union. Movement across national borders within Europe is free, and the Portuguese can identify themselves as Portuguese, as French, and/or as European.

It is worth emphasizing another important insight offered by Glick Schiller (1999, 114): that many nation-states do not want their emigrants to return permanently. They could not absorb them. But they do want them to make investments in home and hence remain "permanent long-distance nationalists." Portugal had a hard enough time absorbing the more than a million *retornados* from the former African colonies in 1975 (Lubkemann 2003; Ovalle-Bahemón 2003). They could not possibly take back the more than one million Portuguese nationals who now reside in northern Europe. Finally, I cannot overestimate the significant theoretical contribution that anthropologists, among them those whose work I have cited in this introduction, have made to a new understanding of the migration process, of how immigrants are incorporated in their host societies, and of the impact that they continue to have on their sending communities. Chapters 3 and 4 indicate that these patterns have been around for some time and are inevitably discovered by anthropologists, who generally have field experience at both ends of a migration stream.[5]

Notes

1. The focus on return among scholars of European migration streams was unavoidable, given that implicit in the immigration policy of some receiving societies, Germany in particular, was the idea of a guest worker who remained for a short period of time and was expected to go home. Of course, the reality is that these individuals did not go home, that families of workers began to arrive, and that new policies about immigrants and citizenship had to be formulated (see King 1978; Rhoades 1978). The one area on the American side of the Atlantic where scholars addressed the issue of return, and Gmelch's work is one example, was in the Caribbean (see also Pessar 1997; Thomas-Hope 1985, 1986).

2. Those writing more recently about other transmigrants have equally noted the important role of the state in maintaining ties to the homeland (Guarnizo and Diaz 1999; Mahler 1998; Smith 1998).

3. At the same time, Portuguese scholars were also beginning to examine the impact of the population of so-called *retornados* from the former African colonies (Pires et al. 1987).

4. Frances Chapin claims that the largest influx of visiting emigrants to São Miguel in the Azores occurred at the time of the *festa* honoring Santo Cristo in Ponte Delgada. "In 1978, the newspapers estimated that twenty-five to thirty thousand tourists of Azorean descent attended this *festa*. Charter flights for the occasion brought visitors from both coasts of the U.S. and from Canada. . . . Many emigrants send money to pay off a promise to Senhor Santo Cristo dos Milagres, the bejeweled statue of Christ that has been on the island since the sixteenth century and reputedly performs curing miracles." (Chapin 1989, 136).

5. From somewhat different perspectives, Foner (1997) and Mintz (1998) have cautioned us about the newness of transnationalism.

3

Emigrar para Voltar
A Portuguese Ideology of Return Migration

Between the mid-1950s and the mid-1970s, over 10 million people emigrated from the underdeveloped countries of southern Europe and North Africa to the more developed and industrialized nations of northern Europe, tying north and south together into what one writer has referred to as a "symbiotic relationship based upon the transference of labor" (Kramer 1976, 47). This intra-European population movement was born in the economic advantages (primarily to the countries of northern Europe) of a foreign labor force that could satisfy demands for cheap labor, increased production, and the desire for expanding profits without further augmentation of salaries or alterations in working conditions. Inherent in the immigration policies of most northern European countries in the postwar era was the temporary or semipermanent status of these workers in the countries to which they had migrated. After a period of residence and work abroad, they were expected to return to their homeland. By the mid-1970s the problems of reintegrating these returned migrants assumed major proportions in several countries of southern Europe, and return migration itself emerged as a field for systematic study and analysis.

In early research on intra-European return migration, the problem was analyzed primarily at the macrostructural level (Organization for Economic Cooperation and Development 1967). The emphasis was largely upon demographic studies of the actual number of returnees (Lianos 1976), upon an examination of the sectors of the economy into which migrants return (Pascual 1970), upon their impact in changing the social and cultural attitudes of those who left behind (Baucic 1972), or upon the actual temporary nature of return itself (Gregory 1976; Paine

Table 3.1. Portuguese Legal Immigration to France, 1946–1975

Year	Permanent Workers[a]	Seasonal Laborers[b]	Familial Immigration[c]
1946			
1947			
1948			
1949			86
1950	72		242
1951	260		158
1952	472		178
1953	438		252
1954	459		288
1955	949		387
1956	1,432		419
1957	4,160		480
1958	5,054		1,210
1959	3,339	126	1,499
1960	4,007	937	2,427
1961	6,716	1,328	3,776
1962	12,916	1,368	3,882
1963	24,781	2,269	5,062
1964	43,751	3,729	7,917
1965	47,330	4,190	12,937
1966	44,916	3,035	18,695
1967	34,764	3,131	24,833
1968	30,868	3,110	27,873
1969	80,829	3,063	29,785
1970	88,634	3,004	47,033
1971	64,328	2,821	47,492
1972	30,475	2,837	38,217
1973	32,082	2,674	31,861
1974	14,329	2,094	23,398
1975	4,946	2,138	18,490
Total	582,307	41,854	347,877

Source: Office National d' Immigration, *Statistiques de l'Immigration,* 1975.

a. Permanent workers includes those issued work and residence permits.
b. Seasonal workers are those issued temporary permits, normally for nine months.
c. Familial immigration includes women and children who enter France under the title of familial immigration rather than that of permanent worker.

1974). Although these studies all examine important aspects of the problem, none of them, except insofar as they deal with emigrant remittances, give attention to return migration as an important element in the decision-making process of the migrant or migrant family prior to migration and as an important factor affecting their behavior once abroad—that is, an important facet of the migrant's self image and of the individual or familial "plan" of migration. It is this latter issue that is addressed here.

This chapter examines a particular case of intra-European migration and "return migration," Portuguese migration to France (see table 3.1).[1] More specifically, it focuses upon a particular paradox that seems to characterize the Portuguese case, a paradox perhaps best resolved by Bovenkerk's (1974) typological distinction between temporary and permanent migration along the axis of intention to return. I argue that an analytical distinction should be maintained between the goal of return and actual return. Whereas the latter is a variable affected by such factors as the immigration policies of the receiving society, the emigration policies of the sending society, the possibilities for employment in the sending society upon return, and other socioeconomic or demographic conditions, the second is more dependent upon a series of social, cultural, and historical traditions or attitudes toward migration. In short, return migration is affected not only by the way the host society receives and accepts migrants but also by the way the migrant views both his or her own society and the host society.

The distinction between the goal of return and actual return will first be illustrated through a discussion of what I am calling here the Portuguese cultural ideology of return migration. In employing the concept of "ideology," I am borrowing from Philpott's (1973) usage in his discussion of West Indian migrants in Britain, a usage that conforms to Geertz's (1966) "ethically neutral sense." "Every migrant," according to Philpott, "carries ideas as to the nature and goals of his migration, a cognitive model . . . an ideology" (p. 188). Philpott allows for a continuum on the basis of migrant ideology in order to distinguish those migrants who are totally committed to the host society from those who remain totally committed to the sending society. For the most part, first-generation West Indian migrants in Great Britain, like the Portuguese in France, fall at the latter end, because they perceive migration as a temporary state and expect to return one day to their homeland. This expectation to return is not unique, however, to the Portuguese or the Montserratians. Lee (1960), Loewen (1971), and Watson (1975) have described a similar attitude among Chinese emigrants in Great Britain and the United States, as has Dahya (1974) for Pakistanis in the United Kingdom and Kenny (1976) for Spanish expatriates in Latin America. Kenny has labeled this goal or desire to return "institutionalized nostalgia." To a certain extent this return orientation is "nostalgic," and here I explore this element of the cultural ideology of return migration in Portuguese society. However, there are other factors that contribute equally to the goal or intention to return, which will also be considered in the body of this chapter.

0 Brasileiro: Origins of the Ideology of Return

Emigration in Portugal is a tradition that dates back to the age of discovery and the colonization of the island of Madeira in 1425 (Serrão 1974). Since that time, it has never ceased to be an important aspect of the demographic, economic, political, and social history of this small seaboard nation. However, while the history of emigration spans several centuries,[2] it was really only during the latter half of the nineteenth century that significant numbers of rural peasants became involved in emigration. At that time the *brasileiro de torna viagem* (the returned Brazilian) emerged as a kind of national archetype of the Portuguese emigrant.

Brasileiro is a term that, since the nineteenth century, has been used to refer not only to a native-born Brazilian but also, and often more frequently, to a native-born Portuguese who emigrates to Brazil, makes it rich, and then returns to Portugal to display his wealth.[3] Substantial evidence for the vitality of this archetype can be found in writings on Portugal—historical, philosophical, and literary. Every peasant family was thought to produce at least one *brasileiro*:

> The race of the peasant is prolific. In youth he has ordinarily more brothers on the fig tree than sparrows above him chirping away. As a result, since the figs cannot feed them all, it is necessary to send each one out according to the vocation and talents which God has bestowed upon him. The stupidest becomes a teacher; the most disorganized a chief magistrate; the laziest a priest; and the cleverest goes to Brazil. The teacher dies of hunger; the priest turns fat and procreates; the magistrate mistreats everyone; and the Brazilian either establishes himself there and no one talks of him anymore or he comes back to establish himself in his own village and becomes a viscount. (Ortigão 1944, 24)

Some essayists refer to these returned emigrants as "deceived compatriots who see in Brazil a new promised land" (Percheiro 1878, dedication). The emphasis on "deceived" is important, as it suggests that the disadvantageous expenditures (both monetary and emotional), which are necessary in order to get to Brazil, outweigh all the advantages. But "the Portuguese who emigrates does not see it this way. He only thinks that at the end of several years he must return from Brazil" (p. 18). It is this desire to return that gives *brasileiro* its true meaning. The first idea, perhaps, that this word suggests is of an individual whose principal and almost exclusive characteristics are to live with more or less largesse and not to have been born in Brazil; he is a man who left Portugal in his boyhood or youth, more or less poor, and who, many years later, returns more or less rich (Herculano 1873, 111–12).

Not only do they return rich, they return displaying their wealth. The most common way to display this wealth is to build a house, a tiled extravaganza with "columns painted in green and walls with yellow bases and scarlet vertexes" (Castello Branco 1966, 24). These so-called *casas brasileiras* appeared throughout northern Portugal in the latter half of the nineteenth century as symbols of the financial success and newfound prestige of the returned emigrants from Brazil. They represented, in the words of the novelist Luiz de Magalhães, "the necessity to shout, to publicize through unusual forms and bright and ridiculous colors, a vital energy which explains the fiat of the emigratory movement" (Magalhães 1886, 76). Cesar (1969) notes that in the twentieth century the image changed.[4] The *brasileiro* was treated with more humanity and sympathy by writers like Manuel Torga, José Maria Ferreira de Castro, and Joaquim Paço d'Arcos, who had experienced emigration themselves. In the works of the latter two, in particular, emigration is represented as an illusion, a dream mysteriously impelling people outward in search of a fortune.

> In all the villages there was the same anxiety to emigrate, to go in search of riches and far continents. It was a dense dream, a profound ambition which dug deep into the souls of young and old alike. The gold of Brazil was part of the tradition and had the prestige of a legend among simple souls. They saw in the fluorescence of churches, in the palaces, schools, bridges, and new roads that the rich men on the other side of the Atlantic ordered to be built, the magic of emigration. . . . The idea of emigration resided in the breasts of each man and was an implacable arrogance which even reached the sentiments of the poorest. It came from their great grandfathers . . . or further still—an inheritance which hung as a heavy weight. All generations are born already with that aspiration which incommodates when it remains unrealized (Ferreira de Castro 1928, 32–33).

One cannot leave this discussion of the *brasileiro* without some reference to the concept of *saudade* that, as many writers argue, has its roots in the tradition of emigration in Portugal. *Saudade*, which only roughly translates as "nostalgia" or "yearning," was what brought the *brasileiro* home again, and their magnificent buildings were the "realized dreams of a long-lasting nostalgia (*saudade*) which made the emigrants feel more

Portuguese each day" (Casanovas 1937, 8).[5] Although associated with the literary movement *saudodismo,* founded by Jaime Cortesão, *saudade* is not merely a concept of the literati. It pervades popular song and poetry as well, generating verses such as:

> *O triste segunda feira* [Oh sad Monday]
> *Da semana que há de vir* [Of the week which has to come]
> *O meu amore diz que embarca* [My love says he is embarking]
> *Quem o há de ver partir* [Who has to watch him go]
> *Tenho o peito fechado* [My heart is closed]
> *A chave está em Brazil* [The key is in Brazil]
> *O meu peito não se abre* [My heart will not open]
> *Sem a chave de la vir* [Until the key comes from there]

The *brasileiro* as an archetype is fundamental to the image of Portugal as an emigrating society. It embodies both hope and nostalgia, emigration to return, *emigrar para voltar.* Furthermore, it represents a set of goals for the potential migrant prior to departure as well as a set of expectations for his behavior upon return. The *brasileiro* is the kingpin of the Portuguese ideology of migration and return migration, an ideology that has survived to the present.

From *Brasileiro* to *Francés*

The Portuguese migrant who traveled to France in the 1960s and 1970s carried a "cognitive model" of migration (Philpott 1973). This model underlies not only how one should think but how one should feel and behave as a migrant. It also justifies or reconciles any differences that might arise between the ideal "oughts" and the realities of the migration experience. The *brasileiro* archetype has served as a guide, however conscious or unconscious, for the behavior of twentieth-century Portuguese migrants. It orders various elements of the migration process within Portuguese society: emigration as an illusion or dream, emigration as a way to make a quick fortune, return as an implicit part of the process, return to display one's success or to quell one's feelings of nostalgia.

One of the most common words used by Portuguese migrants to describe France is the word *illusion:* "France is a great illusion." *Illusion* has two different but related meanings in this context. The first meaning refers to a precise or unchanging image of France as an El Dorado where fortunes can be gained quickly and easily. However, the illusion in this meaning only becomes clear to the migrant post facto, when the images or expectations he or she had before leaving are confronted with the reality encountered upon arriving in France. El Dorado is a deceptive image and the migrant sees himself or herself and others swept away in the pursuit of money. As one informant commented, "It is the illusion of money which brings us here. We can live in Portugal. We have enough money to eat, but not to buy a car or a house. At the end of a year there is never anything to put aside. People know it is all an illusion, a dream, but they still live with it and by it. There are always rich people around. We see what we do not have but might have."

On occasion, migrants comment upon individuals who are already *rico* and who had no need to emigrate but who were, nevertheless, equally caught up by the glitter and gold of France; that is, by the same "illusion." They fear being "left behind." They become "jealous of the people who were once poor but who return better off. They feel they have to emigrate too."

The second meaning of *illusion* refers to illusory or deceptive behavior. Emigrants who have prospered, but especially those who, at least so far, have not, depict their supposed successes glowingly and deliberately to friends and family remaining in the village. The visit of one such emigrant to the homeland to display his wealth (or illusory wealth) is enough in itself to sow the seeds of restlessness among fellow villagers.[6] The hardships of life abroad are rarely represented completely or honestly to those who stay behind and who may become next year's emigrants. One informant summarized this spiraling process quite well:

> There are Portuguese who arrive in Portugal during the summer holidays and who make themselves more important than they really are. They say they do this or that in France, that they are *senhor* of this or that. And the truth is that they clean office buildings and toilets. Sometimes they do work which is worse than what service people do in Portugal. There are Portuguese here who leave factory jobs, good jobs, in Portugal to work in France as domestics. All with the same illusion and all who return to perpetuate the same illusion.

Upon return, if only for a summer visit, the emphasis is on display. Weddings are evaluated by the number of guests and the number of cars. Information on how much one has paid for a new house or a new car is readily volunteered. Lavish meals are planned, and on every occasion bottles of port wine are opened. Throughout the north of Portugal, the annual summer festivals in honor of village patron saints or other important local saints have become festivals essentially supported and enjoyed by returning emigrants, who plan their summer vacations to coincide with these occasions. If they cannot return for the holidays, they send money back to their villages to cover the expenses of events that become more and more elaborate with each passing year. In addition to festivals, emigrants make annual contributions to the renovations of the church or to the parochial newspaper, which brings them news of the village throughout the year when they are in France. As a result of all these activities they gain prestige and importance within the village. They are clearly recognized as *os franceses*, a new social class in late-twentieth-century rural Portugal. One young and well-educated male migrant from the city of Pombal in central Portugal living in Paris expressed this behavior as follows:

> Emigration happens like this. First one person goes. He lives very badly in France in order to save a lot of money, and then he goes back in splendor for vacations. He throws his money around, and everyone is jealous. He shows off that he is richer now than when he was born. He wants to prove that he can be successful, but only by going away can he do so. He could improve himself if he lived there as he lives in France, but he is too proud to do so. The Portuguese have been oppressed for so long. The emigrant is like a handicapped person who all of a sudden loses his infirmity. He finds he can run, so he runs and runs to keep ahead of others.

The house, for these twentieth-century emigrants, like their nineteenth-century "Brazilian" predecessors, becomes a symbol of their success abroad. Almost all of my informants in Paris showed pictures or plans for their new houses. They readily rattled off the price they had paid for the land and/or the house. The *casa francesa* or *casa*-type *maison* has usurped the place of the *casa brasileira*. It is more modest but also more widespread, because emigration itself has become more widespread. Furthermore, the proximity to France makes it possible to return more easily to supervise the building of a house or to enjoy it once it is finished during summer vacations. These new houses, sheathed in bright-colored stuccoes, fancifully tiled and "visibly modeled upon those which Portuguese bricklayers are building throughout the year around French urban centers" (Kayser 1972, 49), have burgeoned throughout the northern countryside of Portugal, particularly in the districts of Braga, Porto, and Viana do Castelo. They bestow upon this countryside some aspects of a modern suburb, a suburb of the city of Paris.[7]

It is in the building of the *casa francesa* (or the saving to build it) and in the cluster of behavior patterns demonstrating success abroad that are associated with it that one finds some explanation of return-oriented migration as a goal or expectation for Portuguese migrants in France. In emigrating, Portuguese migrants are looking outside their own social system for a way to gain prestige and social mobility within that system.

Emigrar para Voltar: Emigration and Social Mobility

Until the collapse of the Salazar regime, Portugal was a country dominated by a rigid social structure that denied educational or occupational mobility to the lower classes of Portuguese society.[8] In this context, emigration has been the only possible channel of upward mobility for the peasantry of rural Portugal.

For many centuries Portugal was characterized by a strong division between the poor, illiterate classes and the wealthy, educated aristocrats and bureaucrats of the upper classes. This sharp class division was reinforced by a division between the center and the periphery, based on the concentration of economic resources, human capital, and political power on the narrow Portuguese seaboard and in the hands of a few. Furthermore, the sharp class division based on economic and geographical differences was sustained during forty-three years of Salazarism by the attitudes that the Salazar regime held with regard to the poorer and rural classes of Portuguese society. Sjoberg (1964) quite appropriately applied Barrington Moore's concept of "catonism" to Portugal under the Salazar regime. The concept refers to a repressive social order that supports those in positions of power, prevents new developments that would favorably affect the peasantry, and opposes ameliorative social changes (Moore 1961, 491). Catonism assumes a romantic view of the past to further its purposes, stressing the "organic" and "whole" nature of peasant culture and of the peasant's attachment to the soil. Moore further adds that this alleged attachment to the soil becomes the "subject of much praise but little action."

Moore's analysis seems well substantiated by the pastoral ideology that Salazar insisted on during the decade of the 1950s (Figueiredo 1975, 164–165). He organized, for example, a competition to select the most typical village in the country.[9] The attention bestowed upon the countryside during the competition was an excuse to do little else to improve social conditions for most of the Portuguese people. "Backwardness" was a virtue. The pastoral ideology was designed to suppress any feelings of class antagonism or animosity, aiming instead to promote a sense of admiration and respect for the rich and an implicit acceptance of class differences. These were attitudes with deep roots within Portugal.[10] Emigration, under these circumstances, is not only a result of a rigid and stable system of stratification, it is also a cause of its perpetuation. As Martins (1971) perceptively noted, it eliminates possible tensions by channeling out the frustrated. A person improves his social position by emigrating, not by rebelling against working conditions in the countryside and social inequality.

Portugal had a small upper class, an "overeducated familistic oligopoly with aristocratic pretensions and ostentatious display patterns" (Martins 1971, 69). This upper class consisted of leading industrialists and other businessmen, the upper echelons of the officer corps, the civil service, the Catholic episcopate, the top ranks of the liberal professions, who traditionally held important political offices (Schmitters 1976), and finally the latifundists, large-scale, often absentee landowners of the rural south.

The Portuguese middle class, especially in the countryside, was historically weak, a factor not uncharacteristic of other Mediterranean societies (Giner 1971). The implications of this weak middle class are significant, for it means not only an economic gulf between rich and poor but also a social one between those who work with their hands and those who do not. This social gulf was further enhanced by a system of education that was for the advantage of a few at the expense of the many. In Portugal, as in most of southern Europe, the historical weakness of the middle class meant that the universities never lost the monopoly of training for the higher professions and were able to maintain their aristocratic ethos, their scholastic pedagogy, and their archaic cultural mentality. They acted as agents of cultural immobility rather than of social mobility (Martins 1971, 81).

Cultural immobility provided a definite mark of separation. It allowed for a special kind of familiarity or intimacy in Portugal, similar to that which Barrett (1972) described for Spain. Titles, forms of address, and social facades rigidify social separateness and legitimize paternalism. A formal title (*Exa Senhor, Senhora Doutora*) is combined with an informal first name. One informant mentioned an experience she had while serving for a wealthy family in Lisbon when she was a teenager. She was severely scolded for improperly addressing the five-year-old child of her employer. Another informant commented, "Here in France everyone is madame. My mistress calls me madame. But in Portugal, I was always just Julia. And I had to call my employers Senhora Doutora and Senhora Dona."

A third informant told of a visit that she made back to her former employer (a well-to-do woman who lived in Lisbon and for whom she had served as a maid for several years prior to her emigration) to tell of her financial success abroad. The employer responded that it was "all very nice, but to me you will always be Maria!" This statement itself confirms the inflexibility of the social system. Wealth did not necessarily buy social position or social mobility in the national social hierarchy. Indeed, social facade itself, through the use of titles and through other forms of behavior, was important among "noble" and bourgeois families in order to *manter o brilho* (maintain the glitter) (Chantal 1962, 104).[11] Women of bourgeois families who were obliged to do the shopping themselves were considered to be "victims of difficult circumstances," and the maids of wealthy or supposedly well-to-do families had to emerge from the house with "just the right kind of shopping basket so as not to be confused with poor women who are buying for their own families" (Fryer and McGowan 1963, 56). This attitude, as Fryer and McGowan have noted, also affected university students, whose parents of modest means found it difficult to pay for their children's education. Unlike their American counterparts, Portuguese students did not work to fund their studies because such work, mostly manual labor, was considered demeaning and dishonorable.[12] These characteristics of middle- and upper-class behavior, particularly the emphasis upon the symbols (manners, dress, speech) of prestige and wealth, are important to the present discussion, because they define a matrix of behavior to which those of the lower classes could aspire or according to which they could organize or justify their own actions.

The distinction between manual and nonmanual labor is itself an important motive for emigration, expressed most frequently in the disdain that migrants have for peasant life and for work which is *sujo* (dirty). It is further expressed in the desire of many emigrants to one day own a store or another small business and work *por minha propia conta* (for myself). Manual labor in France, although less *sujo* than agricultural labor in Portugal, is therefore a means to an end: The prestige accorded to an emigrant who is able to move out of the agricultural sector and up the social ladder.

The desire for prestige exists in all societies, but the value placed on it and the means by which it is procured vary. In Portugal it is clearly associated with the concepts of *vaidade* and *inveja*, concepts that are prevalent among the lower classes as well as the upper classes. *Vaidade* (vanity) involves the presentation of self in public, particularly the way one dresses. Among peasant women it came to be associated with the gold jewelry that is part of the traditional costume worn by women of rural Minho on feast days to show off the worth of their family. Not to wear some gold was to admit misery. Lamas (1948) has attributed such *vaidade* particularly to the wives of emigrants, "peasant mothers who stop being a peasant not because of a change in their condition of life or their intellectual development, but only because of a sudden increase in money which they can spend freely" (p. 103). In the peasant context, where titles are absent, money and the things that money can buy serve to mark differences.

In more contemporary times, *vaidade* is manifested in modern dress but more so in the new cars and the new houses purchased or built by emigrants. Each tries to outdo his neighbor, and with every passing year these houses become more elaborate. Everyone shows off newfound wealth, but such behavior also draws criticism and envy.

Envy is a concept that several writers have referred to in their discussions of peasant society (Foster 1967, Banfield 1958, Bailey 1971b). Foster (1972) and Simmel (1955) distinguish between envy and jealousy: Envy expresses a desire to acquire that which someone else has; jealousy, on the other hand, expresses a fear of losing that which you already have. Foster further differentiates two axes of envy, one prompted by fear and the other by competition. In the case of emigration, the competitive aspect seems more important. The prosperity that accompanies emigration leads to a liberal display of one's successes. "To induce envy in another through conspicuous consumption or other means is to raise or further secure one's status vis-a-vis the competitor" (Foster 1972, 166).

Competition and envy thrive not to create equality but to create inequality through symbolic evidence of status differences. Envy, however, does emerge from an egalitarian ethos, where one individual feels himself no more inferior than the next. If Fernandes can emigrate, earn money, and build a fine house, then Pereira can, too!

Envy is related to gossip or, as the Portuguese refer to it, *as críticas*. As one informant noted, "*Críticas* exist in Portugal because we are all after the same thing (*Procuramos todos o mesmo*)." In the Portuguese village, everyone makes it his business to know about everyone else. Thus Daniel, the young hero of Júlio Dinis's novel, *As Pupilas do Senhor Reitor* (1963), complains bitterly of the wagging tongues. "This life of the village. This life of slander and gossip. The misfortune of small places where there are few serious things to think about. Look what these people occupy themselves with. In knowing what I do, how I live, where I go, with whom I speak; this is what entertains them" (Dinis 1963, 236).

It is precisely because everyone knows about everyone else, especially their social background, that it is difficult to create envy and therefore gain social prestige. Instead people are criticized for their pretensions to grandeur, and gossip serves as a means of social control and the maintenance of social equality. Only through emigration can one really make successful use of the symbols of social prestige. Individuals, by emigrating, escape the mechanisms of village social control. They can earn money in whatever way they like, and those who remain in the village can only admire the returned emigrant for the successes he or she readily displays on return visits. Those who remain become envious, and thus the desire to leave is born in them, as well. The important factor, however, is that the village remains the jury of an emigrant's success and prestige. This newfound wealth does not buy social prestige and social mobility in the Portuguese world outside the village, where social position is ascribed or achieved through a system of education closed to the Portuguese peasant. Nor is it possible to achieve rapid social mobility in the country of immigration, where the Portuguese migrant, as a foreign worker, enters at the bottom of the social ladder.

Emigration therefore brings a curious type of social mobility, one based upon the geographical (and social) distance between France and Portugal. The Portuguese migrant is a *travailleur* (working class) in France in order to be "petty bourgeois" in Portugal. He or she works with his or her hands in France so as not to have to work with his or her hands in Portugal. Return to Portugal or at least an intention to return is fundamental to the entire process. By retaining an association with the village in Portugal, the migrant can aim at achieving the prestige of being a property owner or perhaps a small entrepreneur.[13] Until the migrant has actually achieved this goal, as a summer returnee he or she can at least give the impression of having achieved it.

Unlike Loewen's Mississippi Chinese (1971) or Cohen's Hausa Traders (1969) who found themselves special niches within the foreign or urban "receiving society," the Portuguese in France are *les Portugais*, but this is only a way of saying that they are *les Étrangers*. In Portugal, on the other hand, they are *os franceses*, a new rural social class. They have left Portugal to escape the low prestige accorded peasants. But higher prestige is not conferred on them in France, where they become part of a mass society, part of the French working class, doing the jobs that the socially mobile French do not want to do. As these migrants see it, only by eventually returning to the village or entertaining that possibility and thereby justifying their living conditions in France can they achieve this goal. As one informant commented: "We do not lead a normal life here, but it is in order to lead a normal life there. We do not come here to make a life. This is not our country, and we are always foreigners."

The problem is therefore one of changing the goal or expectation into reality, of realizing the hope or dream of return. We come full cycle to the problem or paradox with which we began this chapter. Why, if Portuguese migrants are oriented to eventual return, have so few of them actually returned?

Obviously the answer to this question is multifaceted. However, one important factor is the shift that occurred in French immigration policy after 1968, marking a return to the "natalist" propaganda of the immediate postwar period and emphasizing the reunification of the migrant family abroad.[14] As Minces (1973, 33) has noted,

> Among migrants, there are proportionally more adults of working age than among the French. It is precisely because their demographic dynamism is high that the French government aims at settling them more permanently in France, facilitating procedures for naturalization and

the introduction of families . . . A strong State is a peopled State. Immigration represented one-third of the total demographic growth between 1969 and 1971, and approximately 12 percent of the annual births are of foreign parents.

This shift in policy had its greatest impact in bringing more and more Portuguese women to France, reducing the proportion of male migrants from approximately 80 percent of the total migrant population at the beginning of the 1960s to roughly 47 percent by the end of the decade. This can be contrasted with Spain, where the proportion of male migrants remained constant at about 79 percent of the total between 1962 and 1968 (Livi Bacci 1972). The fact that fewer women were remaining in the villages necessarily altered the context of migration, making permanent emigration a viable alternative.

However, there are also concrete reasons for a low rate of actual return within Portugal itself. The lack of jobs is one important factor. Little or no investment was made in rural industry and other forms of rural employment, and salaries remained low throughout the 1960s and into the 1970s. The massive remittances sent back by emigrants were not invested in agricultural development. Moreover, the countryside itself, as a result of the suburbanization process of the construction of *casas franceses,* began to lose its agricultural viability. Emigrants, as has been noted, have little desire to return to agricultural work as full-time farmers, and the villages can absorb only a limited number of small entrepreneurs. The industrial sector, concentrated around the cities of Porto, Lisbon, and Setubal, was not expanding like the industrial sectors of Spain and Italy, and the jobless rate was aggravated by the return of several hundred thousand Portuguese nationals from the former African colonies—a group officially labeled as *retornados* (returnees). As short-term migration plans become more long-term, those who had been working for many years in France in order to send their children to school in Portugal were confronted with the realization that the only solution for the security of their educated offspring in the near future might be the solution they themselves had chosen: emigration.

But perhaps the greatest impetus to remain in France for "just a while longer" is *vaidade* itself. Social aspirations continue to rise. New needs have been created, and these in turn create still further needs. The Portuguese best express this phenomenon by the phrase *quando maís tem, maís querem* (the more you have, the more you want). One young Portuguese mother living in Paris put it as follows:

France made many leave the life they had there—the illusion of coming to make money, nothing more. There were many who came here with the idea of staying only a short time and then returning. It was difficult at the beginning, but then they began to like it and did not want to go back quite so soon. The time arrives when you have enough money already to build a nice house. And then you tell yourself that you are going to stay a bit longer to buy some furniture, a car, a small business, or just to put money aside. And with all this, time passes. Counting on being here three or four years, you are here six or even more. The more you have, the more you want. The more you see in the bank, the more you want to put there. So you never stop working; you never leave France.

Yet, despite this "staying power," many Portuguese immigrants in France continue to view themselves as "transients rather than permanent settlers" (Dahya 1973). Few adult Portuguese migrants in France have taken French citizenship, and most young parents of newborns are careful to register their offspring in a Portuguese consular office abroad.[15] While some families in France have managed to secure apartments in public housing, many still live in cramped living quarters. They continue to send remittances back to Portugal and to spend their savings on new homes in the village. Thus, while proportionately fewer Portuguese migrants to France in the 1960s and early 1970s actually returned to their homeland by comparison, for example, with Spaniards from West Germany (Pascual 1970; Rhoades 1978) or Yugoslavs from West Germany and Scandinavia (Baucic 1972), they nevertheless maintained the same goal of return and have certainly produced similar changes in the rural countryside of Portugal as if they had returned.

In one sense, this maintenance of an intention to return alongside the postponement of actual return is a way of dealing with the insecure environment abroad, where the position of the migrant is very much at the mercy of fluctuations in the international economic system. Many informants commented that "the French do not really want us here, at any point we may have to leave." Indeed, during the fall of 1977, France altered its immigration laws to discourage further familial immigration and to encourage return to the homeland: No more work permits were issued; no families of migrants residing abroad received authorization to join those abroad; aid was to be extended to all those migrant workers residing in France for more than five years who wanted to return home.

In short, the Portuguese ideology of migration, the notion of *emigrar para voltar* (to emigrate to return), as it has emerged within the historical tradition of emigration in Portugal, was well adapted to the short-term political and economic changes associated with post-1960 intra-European migration. It allowed the migrant to keep his options open, to live in or straddle both worlds.

Conclusion

For six centuries, the Portuguese have been an emigrating people, leaving their homeland in search of fortune, in search of El Dorado. While many of them left for good to settle in a new land, others have consistently viewed their departure as temporary and, even after twenty years abroad, have still maintained a hope of eventual return, a hope rooted in nostalgia for the homeland. Indeed, the centrality of the concept of *saudade* in both literary and conversational contexts underscores the force of a return orientation and its relation to the tradition of emigration. However, this return orientation was not, and is not, merely nostalgic. It is associated with a very specific goal—to leave poor but to return rich and display one's wealth to those one has left behind, to prove that one has become a *fidalgo* (from *filho de algo*, "son of someone"). In the words of the great Portuguese novelist Eça de Queiroz, the Portuguese emigrant leaves "in the hold of a galley ship with a pair of clogs, a pine box, and a mattock" and returns "on the deck of a royal ship with new varnished boots and grayed hair, and with ideas of inviting the abbot to dinner" (Eça de Queiroz 1886, vii).

The goal of eventual return is at the very heart of the Portuguese ideology of migration, an ideology which, as this chapter has shown, has survived well into the twentieth century to motivate the wave of Portuguese emigrants who crossed the frontiers of Spain and France rather than the waters of the Atlantic in search of their El Dorado. Instead of leaving on a galley ship, they left on foot or crowded secretly together in a refrigerated truck with little else but the clothes on their back, and they return for their vacations in a shiny new black Citroën, wearing the latest Paris fashions.[16]

This ideology has influenced many of the decisions that individuals make prior to migration, leading some couples, for example, to emigrate without their children, hoping to earn more money in a shorter time and thereby hasten the date of definitive return. It has influenced many of the decisions they make once abroad about housing, spending and saving, or the education of their children. It is profoundly rooted in the Portuguese migrant's (or Portuguese peasant's) view of his or her own society and the few opportunities that that society provides for social mobility. Concomitantly, it has affected the way migrants view the host society as a detoured route to social mobility and social prestige within their own society. Finally, it explains, at least partially, the rapid success of the postwar intra-European movement. The aims of migrants converge closely with those of host society policy makers, who see immigration on a temporary basis as the best means to bring about rapid economic growth.

Notes

This chapter was originally published in *Papers in Anthropology* 20 (1979): 1–20. It is published here, with minor revisions, with permission from the University of Oklahoma.

1. The research on which this chapter is based was conducted between July 1974 and January 1975 in both Paris and northern Portugal and was graciously funded by the Canada Council and the Social Science Research Council.

2. Serrão (1974) distinguishes between pre- and post-eighteenth-century Portuguese emigration. In his view it was only after 1700 that the Portuguese emigrant *strictu sensu* came into being. Unlike the *colono* of the earlier centuries, the eighteenth-century Portuguese emigrant to Brazil left his homeland on his own initiative rather than through state initiative.

3. Cesar (1969) traces the etymology of the word *brasileiro*, contrasting it with the earlier noun *brasiliense*. The former, he claims, developed during the nineteenth century to refer to inhabitants of Brazil but also more generally to refer to Portuguese emigrants who had returned from Brazil. The definition in the *Pequena Diccionário Brasileira da Lingua Portuguesa* (1964) is as follows: "the nickname given by the Portuguese to their compatriots who return as rich men from Brazil."

4. I owe much of this discussion to Cesar's fine study (1969).

5. More recently, Bela Feldman-Bianco (1992) has written about *saudade*.

6. There are migrants who rent cars in France in order to return to Portugal in style. They are frugal for eleven months of the year in order to be able to spend their money freely when they are back home. Nonmigrants frequently complain of rising prices during the month of August, when *os franceses* have returned on vacation.

7. An article that appeared in the *New York Times* titled "American Dream Is Ghana Home" (Berger 2002) suggests that this interest in building homes is widespread and still current among diverse immigrant groups. The article refers to a company, Ghana Homes Inc., in the Bronx, whose "principal enterprise is helping Ghanaian immigrants, some of them living pinched lives as taxi drivers and nursing home aides, to buy houses in Ghana, even if the buyers may never actually return to Ghana to live (p. A17). The Ghanaian quoted at the close of the story reflects sentiments similar to those expressed by the Portuguese thirty years earlier. "For a lot of people it's a status symbol of getting out of the position you were in. Someone who's not highly educated and works at a low-income job comes up with the down payment on $30,000 and achieves that type of house in a very nice area. You can be someone coming from a village but you return in a totally different class because of the power of what you've been able to earn here."

8. I discuss the social structure of Portugal essentially in prerevolution of April 25, 1974, terms, because the majority of Portuguese migrants in France left their country prior to this revolution and the changes it has brought. They were raised under the Salazar regime.

9. The village selected was Monsanto in Beira Baixa, close to the frontier with Spain, deep in interior Portugal. I met a man from there who was very proud to

tell me that he came from *a aldeia mais típico do Portugal* (the most typical village of Portugal). A monograph on Monsanto was published in 1961 (Buescu 1961). A plaque commemorating this award is on exhibit in the lobby of the Ethnographic Museum in Lisbon.

10. The priest in Júlio Dinis's nineteenth-century novel *Os Fidalgos da Casa Mourisca* lectures on the justness of the distinction between rich and poor: "Nobility is nobility. It is evil to forget one's duties and to mix with those of the upper classes. Society needs these distinctions. If not, there would be no order, no government" (Dinis 1962, 385).

11. Officially, titles of nobility were eliminated in 1910, when the Portuguese monarchy fell. However, informally they were still in use throughout much of the twentieth century. The descendent of an old enobled family in one village in northern Portugal is still referred to as Senhor Conde.

12. Beals (1953) noted similar behavior in mid-twentieth-century Latin America. "The middle-class family with two cars and no servants, the banker who washing windows in preparation for his wife's tea party, the professor with overalls wielding a shovel in his garden all are incomprehensible in Latin America" (p. 339).

13. The fact that this goal must be realized in Portugal is further imperative, because it was illegal for non-French citizens to operate such enterprises in France. Thus in the 1970s you could not find ethnic stores in Paris like you could in some of the "immigrant cities" of North America, except for those owned and operated by Algerians.

14. France has been relatively underpopulated for over a century and at various times has followed a "natalist" population policy in order to expand the rate of demographic growth. This policy was particularly characteristic of the post–World War II era, after the population losses of the war.

15. The Minister of Labor for France provided the following figures for naturalization of Portuguese citizens in France for the decade 1964–1973: 1964, 309; 1965, 747; 1966, 535; 1967, 1,231; 1968, 976; 1969, 1,365; 1970, 1,947; 1971, 2,780; 1972, 3,233; 1973, 3,800. In comparison with the total number of Portuguese nationals in France (table 3.1) these figures are, of course, extremely low.

16. One of the most important characteristics of post–World War II Portuguese migration to France is clandestine migration. The word *secretly* refers to this characteristic. The predominance of illegal or clandestine migration, especially during the 1960s, was due largely to lengthy military service for the wars in Africa which were, of course, at their height during that decade. Many young Portuguese men chose to migrate to France instead of fulfilling their military service. Only in France was their position legalized, and until the 1974 revolution many could not return to Portugal without fear of being caught and imprisoned.

4

Emigration, the Church, and the Religious *Festa* in Northern Portugal

The relationship between the Portuguese Catholic Church and Portuguese emigration has deep roots, dating back to Age of Discovery. Blanshard (1962, 198) cites an old English saying: "Where the English settle, they first build a punch house, the Dutch a fort, and the Portuguese a church." For three centuries, the church served as the state's accomplice in Portuguese overseas expansion, and state wealth was matched by church wealth. In the twentieth century, this association was renewed with the virtual hegemony granted to the Portuguese church in the African colonies. While one of the major responsibilities of the Portuguese Catholic Church abroad has been to "christianize the natives," it has also served the needs of Portuguese nationals living abroad. In this sense, the Portuguese Catholic Church differs little from other ethnic churches that, particularly in North America, performed a vital role in the integration process of foreign immigrants (Dolan 1975; Krickus 1976; Miller and Marzik 1977). Indeed, the international Catholic Church has always been interested in the moral and religious aspects of migration.[1]

Although social scientists have written extensively on the role of the church and religion in communities of immigration, to date there has been little discussion of the importance of the church in communities of emigration. More precisely, how has emigration affected the position of the church at the local level? In addressing this latter question, one is necessarily raising the more general question of whether emigration brings social change or preserves social continuity in local sending communities. Those who have studied the impact of emigration in regions and communities where it is a tradition of great historical depth generally describe it as a conservative force. Emigration preserves the traditional social

75

structure and serves as an escape valve for demographic pressure (Davis 1963; Dunn and Dunn 1967; González 1969). Some scholars who have studied regions where emigration is a relatively new phenomenon have also documented an absence of change. For example, Levine (1966) and Plotnicov (1970) both argue that, in the context of an industrializing Africa, labor migration brought an "accentuation of traditional patterns" (Levine 1966, 188; see also Sweet 1967).

On the other hand, some scholars identify the important modifications in village life that result from emigration. Both Goldey (1981), in a study of a village in northern Portugal, and Watson (1975) in a study of the Man Chinese in London and at home, describe changes in the way the godparents of marriage are chosen which are the direct result of new ideas accompanying emigration. Watson also describes other changes in the local economy, including a shift from production to consumption. "Household income in the village now depends more on the number of emigrants in the family than on the amount of land owned. Emigration may not have turned San Tin into an egalitarian community, but the restaurant jobs [in London] have given a large number of talented, achievement-oriented men the opportunity to excel and find economic success abroad" (p. 158).

The "sterling houses" built by the Man Chinese emigrants that Watson describes are similar to the *pakka* houses of Indian emigrants described by Dahya (1974) and the *casa francesas* referred to by various observers of northern Portuguese rural society. In effect, the shift from production to consumption is one explored in many studies that focus on the impact of post-1960 intra-European labor migration on the sending communities of southern Europe. Rhoades (1978, 1979), for example, describes a process of economic change in Spain that was initially quite superficial, modernization rather than development (Schneider, Schneider, and Hansen 1971). The remittances of emigrants have been concentrated in construction, small enterprise, and the trappings of consumption more than in agricultural or other forms of development.

The social and economic changes studied by Rhoades and others have been occurring in the north of Portugal as a result of emigration to France in the post–World War II period. Yet, beyond the impact on the economy and on local family structure, emigration has also had an impact on religious activities. It is this impact in particular that I explore in this chapter. Based on an analysis of data collected in northern Portugal in the village of Lanheses (district of Viana do Castelo) and in the province of Minho, I argue that, during a period of extensive out-migration and significant social and economic change, certain religious activities and institutions that one might expect to disappear as a result of a general process of "modernization" have displayed a definite survival, if not reinvigoration, largely through the interest and support of Portuguese emigrants.[2]

Emigration and the Village of Lanheses

An analysis of population censuses and parish registers demonstrates that a significant number of individuals have emigrated from Lanheses over more than a century (table 4.1). From the late nineteenth century until the 1950s, the major destination for Lanhesan emigrants was Brazil, although many also emigrated to Spain on a more or less temporary basis, particularly during the decade of the 1920s (Brettell 1986). There are numerous tales of success—the migrant who returned from Brazil to set up the first café, the woman whose social and economic status changed when she inherited from a celibate uncle who had made his fortune abroad. But there are also tales of hardship—women who have not seen their husbands since the day they departed for Brazil, years of sacrifice, ill-health, eventual death. However, it was really only the emigration to northern Europe, particularly to France after 1960, that brought significant changes to the village. Emigrants to France can remain in contact with their villages to a greater extent than trans-Atlantic emigrants and can therefore sustain a dream of eventual return, which is nourished every year when they return home on vacation.

The northern European phase of Portuguese emigration evolved through the interaction of two needs: the need of the developed countries

Table 4.1.   Rates of Migration and Sex Ratios in Lanheses, 1864–1869

Years	Rate of Migration	Year	Sex Ratio (No. of Men per 100 Women)	
			Single Men	Married Men
1864–1878	15.9	1864	85.9	102.4
1878–1890	9	1878	67.4	90.2
1890–1900	4.3	1890	53.4	78.1
1900–1911	5.1	1900	64.2	87.4
1911–1920	3.7	1911	63.9	72.5
1920–1930	0.9	1920	66.5	80.3
1930–1940	5.7	1930	82.1	86.9
1940–1950	2.7	1940	81.3	87.8
1950–1960	13.3	1950	77.2	91
1960–1970	14	1960	84.6	91.1

Sources: National Population Census, 1864–1970; Parish Registers, Lanheses

for workers to fill the posts that their own countrymen would no longer fill, and the need of the underdeveloped countries to export their surplus population. "The postwar immigration of labor (within Europe) . . . has bound the north and the south into an intricate symbiosis. The new migrants are the labor by which northern industry survives and dominates, and they are equally the source of the foreign exchange capital with which their countries manage to survive that domination and the unemployment that the domination has produced" (Kramer 1976, 47).

The capitalist enterprises of northern Europe came to rely on a reserve army of foreign workers who would help satisfy the demands for cheap labor and increased production and the desire for expanding profits, without further augmentation of salaries or alterations in working conditions. Immigrant workers would accept lower salaries, longer and irregular working hours, dangerous jobs, and unsatisfactory living conditions. The less-developed countries of southern Europe saw this new intra-European movement, especially if it was carried out on a temporary or semipermanent basis, as a means of bringing new wealth into their countries (through emigrant remittances) and of obtaining free vocational training for their semiskilled labor force.

Although there are Portuguese nationals in most of the receiving countries of northern Europe, the majority emigrated to France. In 1976 the total number of Portuguese immigrants in France was estimated at 853,929.[3] These emigrants were primarily from northern Portugal (table 4.2). In the village of Lanheses the effects of emigration to France are apparent in census figures, which indicate that the variation in population between 1960 and 1970 was –4 percent. Records kept by the village priest show that, in 1975, 173 families or individuals from Lanheses resided in France, among them complete families, married men who left their families in the village, single men, single women, and married couples who left their children behind (table 4.3). This represented about one-quarter of the total population of the village and would, of course, be higher if emigrants to the United States, South America, Canada, Australia, South Africa, and Germany were also included.[4] While the general level of definitive return migration to Portugal from France during the 1970s remained relatively low, particularly in comparison with Spanish migrants returning to Spain (Rhoades 1978), the visible effects of emigration are quite apparent. In Lanheses many new commercial enterprises were opened by returned emigrants (os franceses, as they are called), including two carpentry workshops, two small inns, and a couple of cafés. However, the most important visible result of the post-1960 emigration from Lanheses and from the province of Minho in general has been the construction of new houses.

Table 4.2. Portuguese Emigration by District of Origin, 1950–1974

	1950–1959		1960–1969		1970–1974	
District	Total Emigration	Annual Average	Total Emigration	Annual Average	Total Emigration	Annual Average
Northern						
Braga	20,715	2,071	60,215	6,021	20,848	4,170
Braganca	21,673	2,167	24,451	2,445	6,146	1,229
Guarda	23,186	2,319	37,538	3,754	6,436	1,287
Porto	35,909	3,591	55,295	5,529	25,074	5,015
Viana	15,910	1,591	36,432	3,643	8,887	1,777
Vila Real	18,990	1,899	25,122	2,512	11,735	2,347
Viseu	36,300	3,630	30,607	3,061	17,878	3,576
Total	172,683		269,660		97,004	
Central						
Aveiro	36,830	3,683	42,821	4,282	21,592	4,318
C. Branco	4,895	489	33,447	3,345	6,297	1,259
Coimbra	16,449	1,645	18,343	1,834	12,117	2,423
Leiria	13,633	1,363	49,555	4,955	22,526	4,505
Lisbon	7,439	744	52,400	5,240	31,457	6,291
Santarem	6,668	667	24,517	2,452	10,829	2,166
Setubal	1,114	111	11,305	1,130	8,253	1,651
Total	87,028		232,388		113,071	
Southern						
Beja	619	62	7,015	701	7,398	1,480
Evora	329	33	2,427	243	2,534	507
Faro	7,720	772	23,886	2,387	7,882	1,576
Portalegre	529	53	2,384	238	1,017	203
Total	9,197		35,712		18,831	

Source: Annual Bulletin, Secretary of State for Emigration, Lisbon, 1975.

Table 4.3. Residents of Lanheses Living in France, 1975

Complete families	97
Married men	45
Single men (without families)	8
Single women (without families)	22
Married couples without their children	1
Total families and Individuals	173

These houses, plastered in brightly colored stuccoes and fancifully tiled are "visibly modeled upon those which Portuguese bricklayers are building throughout the year around French urban centers" (Kayser 1972, 49), or based on models of the provincial Portuguese bourgeoisie. They have burgeoned throughout the northern Portuguese countryside, bestowing on it the air of an urban suburb—a suburb of the city of Paris. In the period between 1970 and the early 1980s, approximately fifty new houses were built in Lanheses by emigrants, most of them with two stories, at least two bathrooms, a modern kitchen, a garage, and a television.[5] To build a house is the first goal of virtually all Portuguese emigrants, because it represents for them a symbol of their success abroad.[6] Although many of those houses are only occupied for one month out of the year, when the emigrant family returns for summer vacation, the hope of the emigrant family is that one day they will be able to return for good.[7]

Emigration and the Church in Lanheses

Approximately 95 percent of the Portuguese are Catholic, although only about one-eighth to one-third of nominal Portuguese Catholics attend church regularly. Both church attendance and the distribution of the clergy vary regionally. Northern Portugal has demonstrated, throughout Portuguese history, stronger religious devotion than southern Portugal.[8] In the twentieth century, the anticlericalism of the First Portuguese Republic did little to diminish the power of the church in the rural north, the area that subsequently offered the least opposition to forty-eight years of Salazarism.[9] After the revolution of 1974, some leftist groups began to predict the demise of the Portuguese church in the post-Salazar era, but this has not happened. Indeed, behind the eventual weakening of the Portuguese Communist Party were popular mass demonstrations during the summer of 1975 which expressed support for the church and for the right-wing Partido Popular Democrático (PPD).[10]

In Lanheses the church and the priest are still focal points of village life. While there is some criticism of the village priest, church attendance remains high, and participation in the major religious events is strong and active, despite the fact that older people do complain on occasion that there is less faith today, especially among the younger people. Masses that are, for the most part, in honor of Lanhesans who have passed away, are held every morning at seven o'clock. Although these weekday masses are usually attended by no more than a dozen people, the two masses on Sunday are both well attended.[11] On Sundays between a third and half of the participants take communion. Virtually everyone in the parish takes communion on important holy days like Christmas and Easter. At Sunday masses, the priest, in a semiofficial capacity, often takes the time to make announcements of relevance to the secular life of villagers. On one occasion, for example, he read a government directive about the vaccination of farm animals; on another, he read a list of property for sale. He frequently devotes his homily to a discussion of problems in the village school, of which he is the director. The priest leads the community in praying with the rosary on Sunday afternoons, and throughout the year there are various religious activities, in accordance with the annual religious calendar.

The cult for the dead continues to flourish in Lanheses. On Saturday evenings it is common to see young girls going to the cemetery with flowers to place on the graves of their ancestors, and every year on All Saints Day solemn ceremonies are held. Almost all villagers (including emigrants and young children) belong to one or more of the five local *confrarias* (brotherhoods), some of which date back well into the eighteenth century. Membership in these *confrarias* involves paying annual dues and, for some individuals, serving on the board (*mesa*) of the *confraria*.[12] Membership ensures villagers that a certain number of masses will be said for them after their death. One informant commented that there is a degree of pressure to belong to at least one *confraria*, because if there are no *confraria* banners at one's funeral then people will gossip and criticize, saying that the person was "not very Catholic."

If the role of the priest is important in the strictly religious life of the community (funerary rites), his role in support of local economic institutions is equally significant (at least historically) and perhaps explains the existence of so many *confrarias* in this community. The extant registers demonstrate that many residents borrowed various sums of money from the *confrarias*, generally with an interest rate of 5 percent. Borrowers designated certain properties as a guarantee against the loan, and sometimes individuals stood as guarantors on the loan. For example, an entry in the register of the Confraria das Almas dated February 1876 recorded a loan of 20$000 to José Machado da Rocha of Lanheses at an interest rate of 5 percent. This transaction was also registered with a notary named Barreto of Viana do Castelo. As a guaranty Sr. Rocha offered an arable field, with vines and olive trees adjacent to his house, and as a guarantor he named his son José. In 1975 another inhabitant of Lanheses acquired land and other buildings in the central square from a widow of the community who had remodeled it into a café. The domicile and property had been mortgaged to the Confraria of Rosário in February 1889 for 60$900 (i.e., almost 70 *escudos*, although at the time the currency was *reís* and *mil reís*) at an interest rate of 6 percent. When the widow paid the debt, almost a century later, the sum owed was 7,000$00 (7 *contos*, or almost 100 times as much). Frequently these debts were passed on from one generation to the next, and this perhaps explains the continued association of particular families with particular *confrarias*. At the very least these transactions indicate the significant role of the church not only in the religious life but also in the economic life of rural Portuguese families.

Lanheses also contains several small chapels in addition to the parish church, each of them dedicated to a particular saint and several of them the focal points of religious activities at specific times of the year. One, for example, is dedicated to Santo Antão, protector of cattle, for whom a small *festa* is celebrated in May on the Thursday of the Ascension. Others are dedicated to S. Frutuouso, a religious monk and the archbishop of Braga who founded several monasteries in Portugal in the seventh century, and to Nossa Senhora de Esperança.[13]

Although the position of the church in the village generally remains strong, emigrants have contributed in significant ways to its continued importance. In the late 1960s the village priest initiated a campaign to collect funds for the restoration of the church, and in 1973 the new church was inaugurated. A major portion of the money for the restoration came from emigrant donations. In addition, special gifts were made. For example, two young men working in Australia donated the entire sound system for the new church. A second way in which emigrants have supported the village church, although perhaps more indirectly, is by celebrating many important life-cycle events in the village, even if it means postponing a baptism, first communion, or wedding for several months. Table 4.4,

Table 4.4.   Baptisms in Lanheses for Children Born in France to Native Lanhesan Parents, 1967–1977

Year	%	Total Baptisms
1967	13.2	38
1968	26.8	41
1969	12.2	41
1970	30	30
1971	42	50
1972	37.5	32
1973	50	32
1974	27.3	44
1975	37	46
1976	33	39
1977	39	41

Source: Parish Registers, Lanheses.

for example, gives the percentage of baptisms between 1967 and 1977 performed in Lanheses for children born in France to native Lanhesans. Most of them took place at Christmas time or during the months of July and August, when emigrants return to the village. On weekends during the summer months the church bells ring two and three times a day to indicate a wedding or a baptism. All of this puts money into the village church coffers and into the pockets of the village priest, but it also reinforces the role that the church plays at crucial points of transition in the lives of individual villagers.

A third way in which Lanhesan emigrants have continued to sustain the village church is through their monetary support of the parish newspaper, which brings them monthly news of the village. For many Lanhesans abroad, as for many villagers, it is the only newspaper they read. In every issue, the newspaper publishes a list of those who have contributed money to its continuation, and the largest donations come from emigrants. Indeed, the priest maintains that the newspaper is published essentially for emigrants, because nonemigrants "know what is going on anyway." In addition, through this mechanism the priest can communicate with his parishioners abroad and provide them with moral guidance and even, on occasion, political guidance. No doubt the priest himself, through the publication of the parish newspaper, has become a vehicle through which Lanhesans living abroad can maintain contact with their home village.[14]

All the examples mentioned illustrate mechanisms through which emigrants in France can support and maintain their connections with religious life in Lanheses. However, one of the most important ways in which emigrants have supported the local village church is through their support of the annual *festa* of Senhor dos Necessidades, celebrated every year on the fourth Sunday in July. This is the time when many emigrants make a trip to Portugal for their summer holidays. The relationship of emigrants to this *festa* is so important that it merits detailed discussion.

Emigration and the *Festa* of Senhor dos Necessidades in Lanheses

The *festa* of Senhor dos Necessidades in Lanheses is dedicated to an image of Christ which is housed throughout the year in the chapel of Senhor de Cruzeiro e dos Necessidades, a chapel of significant architectural importance and for which there is good documentary information specifying a mid-eighteenth-century date of construction. Records in the District Archives in Braga reveal that in 1756 Padre Manuel da Silva, the mayor, and other officials of Lanheses, in a petition to the archbishop of Braga, claimed that they had "a large cross, with the image of a crucified Christ in the churchyard; that the image had made and makes miracles; and that with donations they hoped to cover the image with a sculptured arch and a closed niche."[15] As a result of this petition, a chapel was built. In 1767 the *confraria* of Senhor do Cruzerio was founded with the following statutes: (1) There will be in this brotherhood a *juíz* (chairman), secretary, treasurer, and two *mordomos* elected by the officials of the previous year (the *mesa* of the *confraria*). (2) The officials will be obligated, through their revenues, to celebrate a solemn *festa* each year in the said chapel on the day of the invention of the cross (May 3).[16]

After its creation, the *confraria* had a period of prosperity, augmenting the benefits to the brothers and establishing a new festivity to be realized on the fourth Sunday in July in honor of Senhor dos Necessidades. In the last years of the eighteenth century, the *confraria* reached its heights but subsequently suffered during the nineteenth century, as a result of general anticlericalism and the new civil laws which required the alienation of church goods and which prohibited any further increase in capital.

Much of the rest of the pre-twentieth-century history of the *festa* is uncertain, although there is good documentation on the chapel itself.[17] One story relates how at one time in the past (I could never ascertain exactly when) people from as far away as the fishing town of Esposende (at a distance of approximately twenty-four miles) belonged to the *confraria*. These sailors used to come to Lanheses every year to carry the *andor* (float or litter) of Senhor dos Necessidades in the procession. Other stories recount that in the past, in years of prolonged drought, the image of Senhor dos Necessidades was carried in procession to the marshlands down by the river. And the rains came.[18]

In the twentieth century a second period of decline occurred under the First Republic, and by 1933 the *confraria* was totally inactive, although villagers claim that the *festa* has always been celebrated, if less elaborately in recent years. According to several informants, the village priest who officiated from 1927 to 1967 was "not too interested in *festas*," and it was only when his successor took over full responsibility for the village in 1967 that the *festa* and the *confraria* were revived.[19] In fact, the most important stimulus for the revival of the *festa* came from two emigrants who returned from Brazil during the summer and in little more than a week had hired two bands and organized a *festa*. No one I interviewed was sure whether they did it to fulfill a religious vow (*promessa*) or not, but it did mark the beginning of the important input of emigrants in this annual *festa*. This also occurred at a time when the village priest began his campaign to raise money for the restoration of the church and the chapel of Senhor dos Necessidades. During the 1970s, largely through the prosperity brought to Lanheses by emigration to France and through the direct contributions of emigrants themselves, the *festa* became more elaborate and increasingly lucrative.

According to the priest and villagers, the *festa* of Senhor dos Necessidades is a "strictly religious" *festa* and can be distinguished from other *festas* and *romarias* (regional pilgrimages) which are "more profane" or which have "profane" elements.[20] While the program each year includes a band and fireworks, villagers comment that these events *não prestam* (are not worthwhile).[21] They claim that the priest, because he wants to keep much of the profits from the *festa* for the church (*não quer que o dinheiro saia de Lanheses*; he does not want the money to leave Lanheses) hires only one band and there is, therefore, no musical competition (which is, according to villagers, what makes the music good). Although the band remains playing in the square outside the church on Sunday after the procession, the focal point of the *festa* is the procession. This takes place on Sunday afternoon and involves a walk of about two kilometers from the church to the central village square (*feira*) and back again. Although traditionally the *festa* involves a single weekend, the priest extended it to include a week of nightly masses, with special sermons given by an invited preacher. This week begins on the Sunday preceding the *festa* with a high mass, a sermon, and a small procession to a nearby chapel. In this procession the Holy Sacrament is carried by the priest under the pallium.

The priest and the officials of the *confraria* of Senhor dos Necessidades are responsible for the organization of the *festa* each year. They start early hiring the band, confirming the date with the *armador* (church decorator), who comes to decorate the *andores* (floats), and arranging for the arches, lighting, and fireworks.[22] A month before, letters are sent to emigrants in France and elsewhere asking for donations. Villagers, for the most part, make their donations in person during the week of preaching prior to the *festa*. The raising of funds for the *festa* is perhaps the major way in which emigrants have contributed both to its survival and elaboration. While villagers (nonemigrants) on average give donations of 100 *escudos* each, emigrants give 500 *escudos* or more.[23] If we compare the expenses and receipts for *festas* in the early 1960s, when emigration to France was just beginning, with those of the early 1970s. when emigration was at its height, the monetary input of emigrants is quite clear (table 4.5).

Several weeks before the festa, the *juizes* of the *festa* and the *mordomos* and *mordomas* are chosen. The *juizes* are the honorary officials who march with the priest around the pallium during the procession. They are chosen from the important men of the village (the president of the *Junta*, the *Conde*,[24] important merchants). The *mordomos* and *mordomas* are unmarried boys and girls (usually sixteen and older) who are chosen each year

Table 4.5.   Receipts and Expenses for Special *Festas* in Lanheses, 1964–1978

Year	Receipts[a]	Expenses	Net
1964	1,301$40	1,000$00	301$40
1965	1,443$40	550$00	893$40
1975	145,389$20	77,717$10	67,672$20
1978	187,467$00	133,328$90	53,638$20

a. All amounts in *escudos*.

by those of the previous year. It is an honor to be nominated as a *mordomo* or *mordoma*, and supposedly only those young people of "good moral conduct" are chosen.[25] The major responsibilities of the *mordomos* is to carry the various floats (*andores*) during the procession. Each image (there are five, now although in the past there were only two) has from eight to twelve nominated *mordomos*. The *mordomas* for each image walk behind with an offering. This offering provides another focal point for emigrant interest in the *festa* of Senhor dos Necessidades.

Fifty years ago it was customary for the *mordoma* to carry, as an offering, an ornamented candle.[26] After that it became customary to bring a small round of bread called a *redonda*. Today, however, the *mordomas* bring *tabuleiros*—elaborately decorated tray structures that they carry on their heads, filled with food: cooked chickens, sausages, cheese, ham, fruit, bread, cakes, bottles of wine, port wine, and *champanha*. The cost of putting one of these *tabuleiros* together frequently runs close to 1,000 *escudos* ($22). Each *mordoma* tries to make a *tabuleiro* that is more spectacular than the next. According to one informant, "When the *tabuleiros* started, everyone wanted to do it so as not to appear poorer than the others." Another commented, "It is better not to go at all than to have the shame of only giving a little."

The *tabuleiros* are auctioned off at the end of the procession, and the proceeds go to the church. It is customary for the *mordoma* to keep her *tabuleiro* (or to try to), and it is therefore the responsibility of her father (who has already spent money to prepare the *tabuleiro*) or her boyfriend to buy it back for her. On occasion there is bidding competition, especially between young men vying for the favors of the same girl. The important point is that these *tabuleiros* are auctioned off today for anywhere from 1 *conto* (1,000 escudos) on up. During the summer of 1978, one *tabuleiro* sold for five *contos* ($110) to the uncle of a *mordoma*. He was an emigrant, a *francés*. Indeed it is only the emigrants who can afford these inflated bidding prices, and emigrant daughters are therefore frequently sought after to serve as *mordomas*. In 1975, out of a total of fifty-one *mordomas* nominated, thirty-six were the daughters of emigrants. In 1978, of the eighteen *mordomas* who appeared in the procession, fourteen were the daughters of emigrants and one was an emigrant herself.

A third way in which emigrants provide funds for the *festa* is through the vows they make. Here we have an important change in the *festa*. These *promessas*, fundamental to the *romaria* and *festa* tradition in northern Portugal, are made to a particular saint (in the present case to Senhor dos Necessidades, whose name itself implies that he fulfills the needs of the people) imploring his or her help and promising to perform a particular service or sacrifice in gratitude for the help given. The major portion of promises are made in connection with some problem of health,[27] but since 1960, throughout northern Portugal, many vows have been made by, or on behalf of, both military men[28] and emigrants who have sought the protection of a particular image of devotion as they embarked to foreign lands. Traditionally these *promessas* involved specific sacrifices on the day of the *festa* or *romaria*. Araujo for example, describes a series of *promessas* associated with the annual *romaria* to the chapel of S. João de Arga (August 29) in the Serra de Arga near Lanheses, a *romaria* that is apparently very popular with emigrants from the region:[29] "To do the pilgrimage (crossing seven hills) with only bread and water to eat or without talking, to carry *ex-votos*, to go wearing a shroud, to carry an offering of a sack of salt, to walk barefoot, or on one's knees once one comes in sight of the chapel" (Araujo 1957, 94).

Such vows persist in the *festa* of Senhor dos Necessidades. For example, during the summer of 1978, several people, mostly women and among them the wife of an emigrant, walked the length of the procession barefoot, enshrouded, and carrying offerings of candles, which they left under the image of Senhor dos Necessidades when the procession was over.

However, increasingly and largely through the influence of emigrants, the more sacrificial *promessas* are giving way to monetary *promessas*.[30] For example, in 1976 a young emigrant made a vow to Senhor dos Necessidades because he had to undergo a serious heart operation. In the event of a successful operation, he promised to pay for the decoration of all the floats and for the major sermon on the day of the *festa* (this involved approximately 5000 *escudos*). The following year he repeated the promise but also promised to carry the float of Senhor dos Necessidades in the procession. Another emigrant gave 10,000 *escudos* ($220) as part of a promise. Finally, a few years ago there was a man, an emigrant as well, who had an accident in France and fell into a coma. His wife vowed in France to pay for the *festa* sermon if her husband was cured.

Indeed, during the week of preaching prior to the *festa*, virtually all the sermons are paid for by such *promessas*.

The priest has been fundamental to the revitalization of the *festa* of Senhor dos Necessidades in Lanheses, and from year to year he has assumed increasing responsibility for its organization and administration. His behavior can be contrasted with that of priests who have a more "modern" outlook (Pina-Cabral 1981b, Riegelhaupt 1973). These modern priests tend to discourage the celebration of similar religious festivals in other communities. Pina-Cabral describes these "modern priests" as clerics who avoid the use of religious habits on a daily basis, who live in new houses, drive cars, and teach as a second profession. The priest of Lanheses, despite being a bit older than the majority of modern priests (he was in his fifties at the time of my research) is in all these senses modern. And yet he encourages the celebration of the *festa* each year. Why?

On the one hand his behavior can be explained if we focus on the fact that he has been responsible for a renewed emphasis on the sacred elements of the *festa*. In fact, this separation of the sphere of the sacred from the sphere of the profane in popular *festas* has been a constant preoccupation of the Portuguese Church. In 1943 a Pastoral Sobre as Festas called for "restoring to *festas* their religious aspect which has been lost little by little, to the destruction of faith and the detriment of souls . . . because it is not appropriate to mix sacred things with profane things. . . . Religious festivals should not include profane distractions, above all nighttime dances that frequently become affronts to God and the ruin of good habits" (Sousa 1943, 5–7).

The Pastoral went on to emphasize that the objective of *festas* should be to "honor God and the Saints, to express adoration for Jesus Christ, to achieve pardon and mercy for the sins of humanity." The priest of Lanheses adhered to the principles of this Pastoral, and the result was a division within the community, which I return to shortly.

But it is important to note that even the elaborate revitalization of what was essential to a religious festival cannot be understood outside the context of emigration and the economic advantages that it has brought to the church in Lanheses. The *festa* may have become more religious (sacred), but it also has become more monetarized. The priest of Lanheses is in one sense an opportunist who maintains links with parishioners abroad through the mechanism of the *festa* in order to maintain the demographic and economic foundation for his church. His actions are parallel to those of the Portuguese state, which has encouraged remittances from Portuguese emigrants in France in order to sustain the national economy.

It remains to be asked, however, why emigrants continue to support so generously the village church and its activities. One could argue that this support is partly sustained, at least with regard to the *festa*, through their continued personal faith in the image of Senhor dos Necessidades, particularly given some of the insecurities they experience as emigrants abroad. One could also argue that the traditional diversionary role of the *festa* (one of the most important times of leisure and celebration within the agricultural year) remains important for Lanhesan emigrants in France, who have little opportunity for festive activities while abroad.

However, the most convincing arguments for this sustained interest on the part of Lanhesans for the village church, and for the *festa* of Senhor dos Necessidades in particular, are those related to the social aspects of religiosity and to the display component of religious ritual mentioned by Freeman (1978). The church and its various activities and campaigns provide a context whereby Lanhesan emigrants can convert economic success abroad into social prestige. In addition, the village church and the *festa* are centripetal forces which provide a symbolic focal point for the reintegration of emigrants into village life each year when they return home on vacation (and, for that matter, even if they do not return but nevertheless make a donation).

The desire for social prestige exists in all societies, but the value placed on it and the means by which it is procured varies. The newfound wealth of the Portuguese emigrant did not buy social prestige in the Portuguese world outside the village where social position is ascribed or achieved through a system of education which, until recently, was essentially closed to the Portuguese peasant.[31] Nor is it possible to achieve rapid social mobility and social prestige in the country of immigration, where the Portuguese immigrant, as a foreign worker, enters at the bottom of the social ladder. It is in the village back home, where everyone knows from whence the emigrant came, that the degree of social mobility can be truly valued and the appropriate social prestige accorded. Villagers are the jury that measures the success of the emigrant abroad. The various public activities of the church become an important mechanism for asserting or affirming this success, because they provide the emigrant with an opportunity to display his wealth overtly.[32] Thus, behind the economic motives for emigration are social motives. It is not a matter of survival, but of improving life (*melhorar a vida*),[33] of social mobility.

In some ways, the emigrant has simply "modernized" some of the traditional functions of specific church activities. For example, the gold jewelry that is an essential part of the traditional costume worn by *mordomas* on annual feast days is meant to show off the wealth or solvency of the family.[34] However, not only does this opportunity for display enhance the social prestige of the emigrant, it also sets him firmly into a new socioeconomic class within the village. These social differences are fundamental to the organization of the procession. As mentioned earlier, the *juizes* are always nominated from among men of distinction in the village and, increasingly, emigrants have been chosen. The *pessoas de massa* (people with money) who can pay for *tabuleiros* and make large contributions to the church are the emigrants, the *franceses*. As one villager (a nonemigrant) commented "the poor cannot afford luxury."

Thus, contrary to evidence elsewhere in the world where fiesta complexes supposedly act as equilibrating mechanisms (Suttles 1960, Cancian 1965, Chinas 1973), in northern Portugal such rituals affirm hierarchy. Foster (1967), in what is now considered a classic debate in anthropology, associates the Latin American fiesta complex with his idea of limited good. He argues that:

> [peasants] see their social, economic, and natural universes—their total environment—as one in which almost all desired things in life such as land, other forms of wealth, health, friendship, love, manliness, honor, respect, power, influence, security, and safety exist in absolute quantities insufficient to fill even minimal needs of villagers. Not only do 'good things' exist in strictly limited quantities, but in addition there is no way directly within [their] power to increase the available supplies. (Foster 1967, 123–124)

Foster based his argument on his analysis of behavior in the Mexican village of Tzintzuntzan, using Wolf's (1957) concept of a closed corporate community (see also Freeman 1970) to characterize the village—a community that is relatively self-sufficient, closed in on itself, and with few connections to the outside world.

With respect to the data on Lanheses, in the context of the questions addressed by Foster, Wolf, and others, it is important to recognize that the wealth of emigrants comes from the world outside the village. Thus it can be converted into prestige but without necessarily eliminating all the social and economic differences. The concept of "limited good" does not adequately explain a peasant village like Lanheses, where the opportunities to obtain wealth outside the village have a long tradition.

A second way in which the *festa* marks identity is to reassert that emigrants are Lanhesans. Since they were baptized in the village, they will be married there and baptize their own children there. This provides continuity and rootedness to the otherwise discontinuous and uprooted life of an emigrant. The tradition of the *festa* provides another point of continuity to counter the detachment resulting from emigration. By returning for the *festa* or at least supporting it, Lanhesan emigrants reaffirm their goal of eventual return and their sense of belonging to the Lanhesan community. The community is, as Durkheim and his followers have argued, defined through religious ritual.

The reinvigoration of the church, and particularly the *festa* tradition, in northern Portugal is directly related to the return orientation of Portuguese migrants to northern Europe. This point becomes clearer when contrasted with Portuguese migrants to North America, for whom return is much less likely.[35] In North American communities, it can be argued, the continuation of these public religious festivals in the community of immigration, as well as the general orientation of an immigrant community around the church, is a means by which that community can establish or assert its ethnic identity within a society that places a great deal of value on the social and political benefits of ethnicity. In France, on the other hand, the overall immigration policy has been one that emphasizes acculturation, and ethnic differences do not carry the same power of political persuasion. As a result, neither the ethnic church nor religious *festas* have evolved in immigrant communities in France. Instead, local *festas* and village churches in Portugal continue to provide Portuguese emigrants with their community (Brettell 1981). A further comparison can be made, for example, with Brandes's (1975) study of a Spanish town, where he notes the disappearance of religious processions largely as a result of rural out-migration; there is, in this case, a real abandonment, both physical and mental.

Emigration and the National Portuguese Church

Before drawing some final conclusions, two further points can be made about the relationship between the church and emigration. So far, I have focused on the effects of emigration on the church at the local level. However, since the church is perhaps the most important national institution within local communities, the discussion of institutional decay or institutional change is not complete without some mention of the relationship between the Portuguese church and emigration at the regional and national levels.

The reinvigoration of church activities in Lanheses is not unique but rather is characteristic of much of northern Portugal, particularly in the province of Minho, where *festas* and *romarias* have received new life since 1970. Indeed Lanhesans, both emigrants and nonemigrants, spend most of their summer weekends going to other villages to attend a variety of *festa* activities, more as spectators than as participants. While one cannot deny that the spectacle aspect of these ceremonies has always been present, this aspect has been enhanced by the Portuguese Department of Tourism, which began in the 1970s to provide subsidies, particularly for those *festas* that included folkloric elements, such as dancing groups (*ranchos*). The rituals become part of the local color, and the public and ceremonial aspects frequently overshadow the devotional bases of the *festas*. Of course, the connection between tourism and these religious *festas* and *romarias* is not altogether unusual, if we recall that in western Europe early touring was often associated with religious pilgrimages.[36] Furthermore the emigrants themselves, in their rather ambiguous position as dual residents, now constitute the bulk of summer "tourists" to Portugal.[37]

On a national scale, the Portuguese church has found a new range of activities in dealing both with emigrants and returned emigrants. One of the most important activities, and one that is also based on the relationship between tourism, emigration, and religion, is the annual pilgrimage to Fátima and coincidental celebration of the Semana Nacional de Emigrantes (National Emigrants Week) in mid-August. This pilgrimage is organized by the Secretariado do Arquidiocesano de Emigração, an organ of the Portuguese church founded by decree in 1965 to help emigrants in the best investment of capital, give moral and educational support to families in the absence of heads of household, and foment campaigns of evangelization and catechism abroad.[38]

Since its inception, the pilgrimage and the National Week for Emigrants has focused, each year, on a theme or a set of problems of relevance to Portuguese emigrants. In 1978 the major concern was the provision of Portuguese language education for the children of emigrants living abroad. In 1977 the theme was "the emigrant in the renovation of the Church." In his introductory remarks to the program issued that year, Padre Pereira dos Santos noted the contributions that emigrants had made to the revitalization of the Catholic community in the countries of immigration and emigration: "Equally one should consider and profit from the richness of spiritual and Christian experiences which the emigrant brings back with him. If it is true that many emigrants lose certain Christian habits and flee from religious practice, others come to live in a more conscious faith. Their reintegration into their place of origin will certainly be a factor in transformation and renovation."

This statement fundamentally questions the old idea that emigration necessarily leads to the abandonment of religion. This idea, which has been often refuted in studies of ethnic churches in America, is also rejected by the Catholic ministry in France, who attribute a revitalization of Catholicism in France to the presence of Portuguese nationals. However, the important point about the pilgrimages to Fátima is that they are essentially massive rallies that reinforce the importance of the Portuguese church in the life of Portuguese nationals at home and abroad and in the life of the Portuguese nation in general.

Conclusion

Based on research in a village located in the district of Viana do Castelo in northern Portugal, this chapter has suggested that, owing in large part to the fruits of emigration, the local religious *festa* has been reinvigorated, or at least continues to be celebrated, in the context of an increasingly secular world. But this reinvigoration is not simply about the preservation of a tradition, because the way in which the *festa* is celebrated has also changed. It has become both more elaborate and more religious and also more monetarized. The same process of consumerism that has influenced social and economic life, in northern Portugal as well as in other regions of southern Europe that have experienced emigration after 1960, has also influenced religious life. But while emigrants can support this process of monetarization, what of those who do not emigrate? Residents of Lanheses complain bitterly about the sums of money that the priest asks for to officiate over a baptism, marriage, or burial. The tradition of offering eggs to the priest at Easter (*o folar*) has been replaced by the distribution of envelopes in which residents are expected to place money. This brings me to a final point worth emphasizing.

Earlier in this chapter I made reference to the issue of anticlericalism in Portugal. In Lanheses there is a degree of what one could call popular anticlericalism (Riegelhaupt 1973; Brettell 1990a). It involves a negative attitude against the priest as an individual, not against the church as an institution or against religion as a body of beliefs (see Pina-Cabral 1981b). Villagers frequently have nothing good to say about the priest. They call him hypocritical and criticize him for many of the same things for which European Catholics have been criticizing their local religious leaders for years.[39] The oldest inhabitants compare the present priest to all previous priests they remember: the priest who served the community between 1890 and 1911, who was a peasant like them and who only worried about having his devout women (*beatas*) on Sundays; the "saintly and pious" cleric who ran the community between 1911 and 1927 and who, everyone said, slept on a bed of nails; the severe disciplinarian who dominated the life of the village throughout most of the Salazarist period (1927–1967); and the present priest, who is "only interested in money." One hears other criticisms, mentioned also by Pina-Cabral (1981b), and, particularly after the revolution of 1974, there has been a growing understanding that priests are just like everyone else. They are "employees of the village," not superiors as they were under Salazar and before educational opportunities became more widespread. Among some inhabitants the animosity against the person of the priest has become quite strong, manifesting as a subtle struggle for power in the context of the village. This conflict between the forces of the sacred and the secular has emerged most dramatically in debates about the celebration of the *festa*.

In 1973, while the renovations on the church were being completed, the musical component of the *festa* of Senhor dos Necessidades that traditionally took place in the open plaza in front of the church (the sacred center) was transferred to the village square (the secular center). During the evening there was a dance and other popular entertainment. The priest was offended, as were some residents, and there was a quarrel. This quarrel clearly has its precedent in previous objections that priests have raised against secular festivities (as in the Pastoral previously cited; see also Sanchis 1976) [40] In the following years, the priest completely abandoned the musical entertainment in order to avoid any possibility of "scandalous" behavior. But some residents, supported by the majority of youth in the community, considered the music at night to be an important part of the *festa*. Furthermore they thought the priest had too much control of the *festa*. In the late 1970s this group organized a *festa* of their own for the first Sunday in August. It was a strictly secular event, unassociated with any saint, and a local band was contracted to play so that people could dance. The organizers were even able to secure support from the Department of Tourism, and their *festa* was listed in the cycle of "typical *festas*" in the region of the Lima valley during the summer months. In the following years the recently organized dance troupe (*rancho folclórico*) in Lanheses performed, and there was also a show of farm animals with a jury from the nearby provincial town to judge them.

Celebrated for a few years, this *festa* began to absorb the economic resources of the community. Families, both those of emigrants and of nonemigrants, were making two contributions. During the summer of 1980 the secular *festa* was not organized, while the *festa* of Senhor dos Necessidades continued to be observed in all its splendor. Some of the organizers of the second *festa* stopped attending church in Lanheses. Their rupture with the priest was permanent. The point I wish to make here, with regard to emigration, is that emigrants are, by virtue of their absence, essentially left out of these conflicts and factions and the changes in the position of the priest in the village. Whereas many villagers, especially the young people, are adopting new ideas toward the priest, the church, and the *festa*, emigrants, who essentially perceive the goings-on of the village through the priest and his newspaper, are not. As a result of their absence, they remain conservative in their attitude toward the village priest and the importance of the church in their own lives and the life of the village.

Notes

This chapter was originally published in Portuguese in *Estudos Contemporâneos* 5 (1983):175–204. It is reprinted in translation with minor revisions with permission of the publisher.

1. On the impulse of Pope Pius XII, the International Catholic Migration Commission was founded in 1951 to promote the rights of people to emigrate, to aid their efforts at integration, and to support all attempts to retain familial unity. The commission also began to publish a monthly journal containing articles on various aspects of migration.

2. The research for this essay was conducted primarily during the summer of 1978. The author would like to thank the Gulbenkian Foundation for so generously supporting the project.

3. For further discussion of this Portugal-France migration, see Brettell 1978, Castles and Kosack 1973, Rocha-Trinidade 1973, Sousa Ferrerira 1976, Sousa Franco 1974.

4. The national census of 1970 reported a total village population of 1,732 (815 men and 917 women) in 368 families and 454 households. It has grown since then. Accurate population figures are often hard to secure. The census itself is taken on December 31, when many emigrants are home visiting. It is therefore unclear to what extent these emigrants are included in census figures.

5. In 1975 records of urban properties in the section of finances in the district seat of Viana do Castelo listed thirty-one new houses. I counted roughly twenty additional houses in the village on my return visit in 1978.

6. This goal is not unique to the Portuguese. Watson (1975), for example, refers to the "sterling houses" of Man Chinese emigrants in London.

7. These *casas franceses* were also discussed in chapter 3.

8. The difference in "religiosity" between northern and southern Portugal has historical roots which date back to the time of the Moslem conquest of the south. The northwest remained a Christian stronghold throughout this period. Furthermore, the seat of the Portuguese Catholic Church is in Braga, a city central to this region.

9. Portugal has experienced several periods of anticlericalism. The first major attack on the authority of the Portuguese church came in the eighteenth century,. during the "reign" of the Marquis de Pombal, King José's secretary of state. With the death of D. José and Pombal's fall from power, anticlericalism waned, but it was revived fifty years later during the 1830s struggle between absolutism and liberalism. In 1834 church property was expropriated and convents, monasteries, and hospices were dissolved. Only during the last decade of the 1890s were these orders restored and seminaries reestablished. Anticlericalism swept the country again with the downfall of the Portuguese monarchy in 1910. Religion came under state control, church property was nationalized, religious orders were closed, and restrictions were placed on worship after sunset as well as upon processions and funerals. Several historians have pointed to this rabid anticlericalism as one of the major downfalls of the First Portuguese Republic. In Wheeler's words, "what had been intended as religious reform became religious persecution" (1978, 69). The position of the church was subsequently restored under Salazar. For an

excellent discussion of the Portuguese church in the early twentieth century and under Salazar, see Cerqueira 1973. See also Robinson (1977) and Wheeler (1978). See Brettell (1990a), Cutileiro (1971), and Riegelhaupt (1973) for discussions of "folk" anticlericalism. Fortunato de Almeida (1910) has written the most complete history of the Portuguese Catholic Church.

10. The PPD became the PSD—Partido Social Democrático.

11. The first mass, the *missa de manhã* (mass of the morning) is at 7 a.m. and is well attended. Most of the women go at this time, so they will be free afterward to prepare the noon meal. The second mass, the *missa de dia* (mass of the day), at 9 a.m. is for the *preguisosos* (the lazy ones) the villagers say. Young couples, young men, and children frequent this mass.

12. The five *confrarias* are: Confraria of Senhor dos Necessidades, Confraria das Almas, Confraria de Nossa Senhora do Rosaria, Confraria do Coração de Jesus, Confraria de Santo António. As a member of the *confraria,* an individual is entitled to a certain number of masses after his death; the number varies from one *confraria* to the next. Annual dues are minimal but also vary from *confraria* to *confraria.* In some there are also different membership categories with different dues. For example, the categories of membership and the dues for the Confraria of Senhor dos Necessidades are as follows:

	Común	Benfeitor	Benemérito	Grande Benemérito
Diploma	—	50$00	50$00	50$00
Quota	50$00	30$00	50$00	100$00
Admissão	50$00	50$00	100$00	150$00
Annual Dues	10$00	30$00	50$00	100$00
Total Membership 1978	491	28	7	4

Note: 100$00 = $2.20 (in 1978). *Escudos* are no longer the currency in Portugal, as of January 2001; the country now uses the Euro.

13. This chapel was purchased a few years ago by the brother of the village priest, who is an emigrant living and working as a landscape gardener in the New York area. It has been renamed in honor of the emigrants, and for a while there was an attempt to collect money to have it restored. No work has been done as yet, although some funds were collected.

14. Other villages in the region also have parish newspapers that are sent to villagers abroad. Although many Portuguese parish priests have traveled to visit their parishioners abroad (Rocha-Trinidade 1973), the priest of Lanheses has not. The newspaper is therefore his main vehicle of communication with them. After the revolution of 1974, several issues of the *Notícias de Lanheses* were devoted to a discussion of political events.

15. This reference is to a stone image that is now located in a niche on the façade of the chapel. The wooden image of Senhor dos Necessidades came later. Some oral historical accounts I collected claim that the wooden image was made in Lan-

heses itself. I was not successful in documenting the precise history of the image. I owe much of the historical background of the chapel and the *confraria* to the work of Gabriel Gonçalves (1935) who taught primary school in Lanheses in the 1930s, 1940s, and 1950s. Sr. Gonçalves has published several small articles on the monuments of Lanheses in the *Arquivo do Alto Minho*.

16. This is the name of an ancient festival of the church related to finding and venerating pieces of the cross of Jesus.

17. See Gonçalves (1935).

18. In 1976, according to several informants, a similar event occurred. It had been a dry year and the invited preacher in his sermon for the *festa* asked for rain. All of a sudden the skies opened, and it poured for forty-five minutes. No one could leave the church. The day then cleared up for the procession during the afternoon. Apparently it only rained on Lanheses and not on other villages in the region. The priest commented to me that "it was probably just coincidental, but enough to make the people believe."

19. See note 12 for current membership in the Confraria of Senhor dos Necessidades. The priest is a native Lanhesan with a great deal of village pride. Hence his own interest in restoring traditions of the past.

20. According to José Crespo, who wrote extensively on the province of Minho: "The *romarias* are fairs in part, and fairs have the happy noise of *romarias*. This active and restless population demonstrates as much of the religious as the commercial. Does it have a Phoenician origin? . . . Renan, the enthusiastic historian of the privileged races, who found the true God in the melancholic countryside of Palestine, says that the Semitic soul reunites ardently in itself the two antagonistic sentiments: that of the love of God and of the love of lucre. At root are not these two aspects of human nature one and the same: the representation of our egotism? Why do we love God: because he promises us the fruition of eternal life. Why do we love Gold? Because it guarantees us enjoyment of terrestrial life" (Crespo 1951, 78).

21. The program for the *festa*, summer 1978, was as follows:

Saturday	7 a.m.	Mass, confession
	2 p.m.	Entrance of the band and music all afternoon
	9 p.m.	Mass and general communion
	10 p.m.	Music until midnight, followed by fireworks
Sunday	7 a.m.	Mass
	9 a.m.	Arrival of the band
	10 a.m.	Solemn mass with the band in the choir
	3 p.m.	Sermon in honor of Senhor dos Necessidades, arrival of the trumpeteers, the Guarda Nacional, and the procession following

22. One man in the region spends his life moving from village to village, decorating the litters for various religious *festas* throughout the year. His father was in the business before he was. He considers himself to be an artist and has great pride in his work.

23. The value of one *escudo* in 1978 was 2.2 cents; in 1975 it was approximately 4 cents.

24. In Lanheses there is an enobled family and a manor house that was built in the eighteenth century. The old Conde died in the spring of 1978, and his son, who works for the Sacor oil company, is now the head of the family. Several young girls from the village have found employment in the service of this family, both in the village and in Porto and Lisbon.

25. Some older people lament the fact that this criterion of selection has been somewhat relaxed at the present time, as part of a general relaxation in "moral conduct."

26. These candles are still used in the annual *festa* in a town on the outskirts of Viana do Castelo, a *festa* that is supported by the government as a major tourist attraction during the summer season.

27. Each saint is believed to be the protector of a particular part of the body and therefore the curer of a particular group of ailments. Sto. Tocata for lameness, Sto. Amaro for rheumatism, Sto. Braz for the throat, Sta. Luzia for sight, Sta. Ovidia for hearing, Sta. Marta for women, and Sto. Antão for animal diseases.

28. Portugal entered a colonial war in the African colonies in 1961, and the period of military service was soon extended from eighteen months to as much as four years. The war was only ended after the 1974 revolution and the process of decolonization.

29. I owe this information to Ernesto Veiga de Oliveira of the Museo Ethnológio in Lisbon, who has made a film about the *romaria* of S. João d'Arga.

30. Sanchis (1976, 69) mentions that in fact many clerics are trying to reduce the importance of sacrificial promises by asking for monetary contributions in the newspapers at various important sanctuaries.

31. See Martins (1971) for a more complete discussion.

32. Watson (1975) also describes the preservation of public prestige activities by emigrants.

33. This is the phrase given most often by emigrants to the question "Why did you emigrate?"

34. Both Gonçalves (1952) and Sanchis (1976) refer to this function. Sanchis notes that, to a certain extent, the social hierarchy of a village is presented in the context of the *festa*. He also alludes to the context that the *festas* provide for courtship. Indeed, displaying the wealth of a family so overtly could be part of a marriage market carried on by emigrants and is worth further exploration. Gonçalves notes that the *mordomas* and the *anjinhos* (the children who walk in the procession dressed as religious figures) signify the "richness or credit of a person." "And the peasants watching are mentally making their calculations as to the value of the chains and bracelets and donations and establishing the credit of the father or godfather or young girl for the first deal they have to make over a pine tree or potatoes" (Gonçalves 1952, 43).

35. These comments are based on research conducted among Rhode Island Portuguese immigrants during the summer of 1971 and among Portuguese immigrants in the city of Toronto during the summer of 1972. The research for both

projects was funded with a small grant from the department of anthropology, Brown University.

36. Trips to places such as Lourdes, Rome, and Jerusalem have been organized on occasion for Portuguese immigrants living in Paris—a continuation of the tradition of voyaging to holy places.

37. During the final week of July in 1978, Portuguese newspapers reported 2,000 entrances a day at the major border points of returning emigrants.

38. I owe this information to Padre Domingos Fernandes, an official with the Secretariado Arquidiocesano and priest in the parish of Terroso, Povoa de Varzim.

39. I refer largely to gossip about the sexuality of clerics. See Keefe et al. (1977). See also Almeida (1910, 226).

40. This points to an age-old conflict between popular Catholicism and formal Catholicism (Riegelhaupt 1973). In the Pastoral on *festas* published in 1943, D. Agostinho de Jesus e Sousa emphasized the necessity of solemnity and called for the prohibition of all nocturnal festivity (*arraial*) and dancing, "especially in proximity of the church or chapel where the *festa* is being held." The conflict is further enhanced by the religious philosophy of recent Portuguese seminary graduates, who emphasize personal devotion and who find religious *festas* anathema. For further discussion see Brettell (1990a).

III

CITIES, IMMIGRANT COMMUNITIES, AND ETHNIC IDENTITY

The chapters in this section take up a number of issues, both specific and general, of importance in the study of immigration. Broadly speaking, they address how the immigrant experience is shaped by different urban contexts, what is the nature of an immigrant community and by extension an ethnic enclave, and what are the institutional mechanisms for maintaining ethnic boundaries and ethnic identity or, conversely, for facilitating incorporation into a new society and culture.

Chapter 5 is based on research among Portuguese immigrants in two different field sites, Toronto and Paris. It poses a question about the inevitability of a geographically bounded urban immigrant community, where people of the same ethnic background live together. For more than a century, these ethnic neighborhoods have been an important part of the American urban landscape, the supreme examples being Chinatown in San Francisco and the Lower East Side of Manhattan.[1] The chapter outlines reasons why such a community, the Kensington Market area, existed for the Portuguese in Toronto but not in Paris. Recently I have returned to and expanded this topic in an essay titled "Bringing the City Back In: Cities as Contexts for Immigrant Incorporation" (Brettell 2003). This more recent essay explores differences in the historical, structural, and cultural characteristics of various cities and how these shape the immigrant experience and the process of incorporation.[2] Some cities have a deep history of dealing with newcomers, while for other cities this history is much more shallow. Some cities self-consciously identify themselves as multicultural; other cities do not. Some cities are divided by conflicts between or among different racial groups that in turn influence how newcomers find a place for themselves and shape their own group identity. In other

101

cities these conflicts are not so intense, and hence outcomes for immigrant groups may differ. Some cities are dominated by a single immigrant population, as Miami is by Cubans and Los Angeles by Mexicans; others, such as Washington, D.C., have received newcomers from various countries such that no single group predominates.

Cities differ in the structure of their labor markets and hence in the economic niches into which newcomers can and do enter. That the issues raised by the chapter comparing Toronto and Paris as distinct contexts for the reception of Portuguese immigrants are still important is evidenced by the development of the Metropolis project, coordinated by the Carnegie Endowment for International Peace and the Canadian Department of Citizenship and Immigration and by the Emerging Gateways project currently emerging under the auspices of the Brookings Institution. The chapter also lends support to the significance of cross-national comparisons, something that has yet to see full elucidation in the study of immigration (Green 1990).

In the early 1970s Toronto was a self-consciously multiethnic city; it has become even more so today, with the foreign-born comprising approximately 42 percent of the total population (Abley 2002). I captured the Portuguese in Toronto during their early phase of arrival in Canada. In the 1960s and 1970s they moved to the central downtown core, an area that had traditionally received newcomers. Indeed, in her novel about postwar immigrant Jews in Toronto, *Fugitive Pieces*, Anne Michaels writes in the voice of her character Ben about the Kensington neighborhood: "When my parents came to Toronto, they saw that most of their fellow immigrants settled in the same downtown district: a rough square of streets from Spadina to Bathurst, Dundas to College, with waves of the more established rippling northward towards Bloor Street. My father would not make the same mistake. 'They wouldn't even have the trouble of rounding us up.'" (Michaels 1998, 243). But it was precisely in this neighborhood that the Portuguese settled, establishing businesses, sprucing up houses, planting vegetable gardens in their small front yards, and occasionally setting out a piece of religious statuary. In my field notes for the summer of 1972 I wrote about Senhor Maia, who owned the Iberica Bakery located on Augusta Street in the heart of the Kensington neighborhood.

> The bakery, which Sr. Maia purchased in 1962, is open from 9 a.m. to 9 p.m. In the back rooms he employs people who need not be bilingual, but at the counters he uses bilingual girls who can deal in both languages. He employs young Portuguese workers either full-time or part-time after school and talks to them a lot about staying in school and then getting other kinds of vocational training. Increasingly, he told me, Canadians are coming into the Kensington area to do their purchasing.

Gradually, as the next generation grew to maturity, the Portuguese began moving into the suburbs of Toronto. And yet, even in the 1990s, one scholar noted that although the community was more dispersed, the heart (core) remained. "The Portuguese return to Kensington to do their weekly shopping, go to church, and participate in cultural events; and some of the first generation still reside there, in a place where they feel comfortable and where they can live in Canada the Portuguese way" (Teixeira 1995, 69).

The gradual dispersal of the Portuguese population reflects the traditional concentric ring model of urban settlement first formulated by Chicago School theorists in the 1920s. They described rundown "slums" and "immigrant enclaves" located somewhere between the central business district and the working-class and second-generation immigrant settlements that spread out in concentric circles to the suburbs. Social and economic mobility, changes in family structure, and other factors associated with immigrant incorporation (assimilation and acculturation were, of course, the concepts used at the time) were directly correlated with progressive distance from downtown. As members of an immigrant group ascended the socioeconomic ladder, they were able to move out of the central core into higher status and more ethnically mixed neighborhoods.

In many North American cities, including Toronto, this pattern has now changed (Frisken et al. 2000). Many immigrants arrive and immediately take up residence in the suburbs rather than in the urban core. The anthropologist Sarah Mahler (1995), in a study of Salvadorans on Long Island, was one of the first to emphasize this trend, and it has been further described by sociologist Richard Alba and his colleagues (Alba et al. 1999; see also Li 1998). This new pattern of settlement reflects a major transformation in the postindustrial city. Suburbs are no longer simply bedroom communities but rather are "dynamic growth poles of employment, consumption, leisure, culture, and public administration" (Manning 1998, 342). Demographer William Frey (2000), drawing on early data from the 2000 census, observes that minorities accounted for most suburban growth in 65 of the 102 largest metropolitan areas. He went on to note that more than half of Asian Americans in large metropolitan areas live in the suburbs, as do half of Hispanics, but only 39 percent of blacks. Even in 1990 more than seven times as many immigrants lived in the Maryland and Virginia suburbs than in Washington, D.C. proper (Singer and Brown 2001, 976), a trend that continued throughout the decade of the 1990s.

What one now finds in cities throughout North America are not necessarily urban enclaves, where immigrants live, work, and shop in ethnic stores, but suburban malls that are devoted to one ethnic group or another and that offer an alternative gathering place on weekends for those of particular countries of origin. Krauss (2002) recently reported on the vibrant

Chinese community in Toronto and on the Pacific Mall, the largest of sixty Chinese street malls and shopping centers that are redefining the greater Toronto area. Perhaps the lesson is that cities are as much transformed by immigration as immigration transforms individuals who migrate. At the moment there is a good deal of emphasis on the second generation of post-1965 immigration to the United States and Canada (Portes 1996; Portes and Rumbaut 2001) but equal emphasis should be placed on the evolution of cities over time, as they incorporate diverse populations. Certainly this is what anthropologist Nancy Foner (2000b) attempts to do in her comparative analysis of New York City during the third wave of immigration at the end of the nineteenth century.

Comparisons over time should be complemented by comparisons across space, something that has recently drawn the attention of a range of social scientists working on immigration (Mollenkopf 1999; Reitz 1998; Waldinger 2001). As chapter 5 indicates, compared to Toronto, Paris offered a very different urban landscape into which the Portuguese moved and settled in the late 1960s and early 1970s. There, as in many other European cities, the middle class has not deserted the city centers for the suburbs as extensively as in North American cities (Body-Gendrot and Martiniello 2000). Furthermore, the city offered a different kind of housing stock than was available in many North American cities.

In Paris, Portuguese immigrants were dispersed from the start, whether as a result of the nature of employment or as a result of a concerted policy on the part of the French government to avoid anything equivalent to American urban ghettoes.[3] The French built public housing in the suburbs beyond the perimeter boulevard of Paris (the *péripherique*) and many immigrants, including the Portuguese, moved into these complexes. Further, a set of laws made it difficult for immigrants to open shops that catered specifically to an immigrant community. It is such shops that often provide the central focus of the ethnic enclave—a place where newcomers both live and work. Only in 1981 did France change laws that had made it difficult for immigrant communities to develop their own voluntary associations. While the Portuguese in Paris in the 1970s worshipped in the side chapels of Catholic Churches that were supported by a broad French population, the Portuguese in Toronto, in keeping with the tradition of the immigrant church in North America, worshipped in their own parishes located close to their places of residence.

As chapter 5 concludes, the ethnic community is not inevitable, but the question still remains significant in more recent studies of immigration. For example, Margolis emphasizes that Brazilians in New York City have no physical community (a distinctly Brazilian neighborhood or shopping district) and hence have no social community or *esprit de corps*.

Even Astoria in Queens, the primary Brazilian residential area, lacks outward signs of the Brazilian presence. "Moreover, because the Brazilian business sector is so circumscribed, newly arrived immigrants from Brazil, in contrast to their Chinese, Indian, Pakistani, Korean, and Greek counterparts, have no ready source of jobs within their own community. They have no economic basis of ethnic solidarity" (Margolis 1994, 197).

Margolis emphasizes the importance of the ethnic economy within physically delimited ethnic communities or ethnic enclaves. This topic is the object of intense debate in social science literature. The key disagreement focuses on whether these enclaves are a stepping stone or a deterrent to social integration (Bun and Hui 1995; Fong and Ooka 2002; Logan, Alba, and McNulty 1994; Zhou 1992). A central issue in these debates is the role of the business enterprises that employ coethnics. Do these enterprises offer new immigrants opportunities in the face of linguistic and other skill limitations, or do they foster economic exploitation? While Alejandro Portes and his colleagues argue the former, based on their work in the Cuban enclave of Miami (Portes 1987; Portes and Manning 1986), Kwong (1997, 366) suggests that, within the Chinese community in New York, ethnic solidarity "has increasingly been manufactured by the economic elite . . . to gain better control over their coethnic employees." Employers convince their employees, many of whom are illegal immigrants, that the larger society is hostile and racist. In what he views as a form of class exploitation, these coethnic elites control the boundaries of the ethnic community and promote ethnic identity to serve their own ends.

The literature on ethnic or immigrant entrepreneurship is extensive (Aldrich and Waldinger 1990; Light and Bhachu 1993) and most fully developed in the discipline of sociology. This literature explores variations in the types of entrepreneurial businesses with which immigrants become involved—those serving the coethnic market (for example, an Indian sari store); those characterized by low economies of scale that serve a broader community (for example, Vietnamese nail salons); those that emerge in underserved markets (for example, Korean liquor or grocery stores in ghetto areas); and those that are left vacant by the mainstream population because they require long hours (convenience stores, motels). This literature also focuses on why particular immigrant populations are characterized by a high degree of self-employment and entrepreneurship, while others are not. Explanations for these variations emphasize motivations, values, and other individual and premigration community traits, including the willingness to take risks and the desire for independence (Bonacich 1973; Cheng and Espiritu 1989; Fawcett and Gardner 1994). Other explanations focus on the labor structure and constraints of the host society or on the particular qualifications and skills of immigrants (Boissevain and

Grotenberg 1986, 1989; Evans 1989; Nee, Sanders, and Sernau 1994). Many of these studies draw on a concept of ethnic resources to argue that people of your own group can provide capital, labor, and clientele, thereby emphasizing the strong relationship between ethnicity and entrepreneurship (Chan and Cheung 1985; Yoon 1991; Zimmer and Aldrich 1987).

While the travel agencies, bookstores, and other businesses that I describe in chapter 6 fall into the category of immigrant enterprises within an ethnic economy, I give entrepreneurship in this essay a different and, I would argue, a more anthropological meaning. I emphasize the ethnic side of entrepreneurship, drawing especially on the literature of cultural brokers to describe these entrepreneurs not just as the "owners and operators of business enterprises" (Aldrich and Waldinger 1990, 113) but also as important mediators of the boundary that exists between new immigrants and the host society. This chapter also addresses the issue of integration, but from a somewhat different perspective, one that emphasizes culture, social relations, and ethnicity more than it emphasizes economic integration.

Anthropologists have perhaps been most attentive to the question of ethnicity in studies of immigration, although it is certainly a question that sociologists also address. "At the heart of current anthropological concerns with transnationalism, identity politics, migration, and human rights," Michael Kearney (1995, 559) writes, "is the persistence, resurgence, or de novo emergence of ethnicity at a time when, according to modernization theory, it was to have been attenuated by robust nation states." Kearney links the growing interest in the concept of identity and by extension ethnicity to the "implosion" of the concept of culture. Anthropological consideration of ethnicity has been characterized by three distinct theoretical approaches. The primordialist approach, which prevailed until the 1960s, argues that ethnic identity is the result of deep-rooted attachments to group and culture; the instrumentalist approach focuses on ethnicity as a political strategy that is pursued for pragmatic interests; and the situational approach, emerging from the theoretical work of Frederik Barth (1969), emphasizes the fluidity and contingency of ethnic identity, which is constructed in specific historical and social contexts (Banks 1996).

The latter two approaches have attracted the most attention in anthropological studies of migration, not only because they suit the more emergent and interactive understanding of culture and the poststructuralist emphasis on the multiple and shifting basis of self-representation (Gupta and Ferguson 1997), but also because the act of migration brings populations of different backgrounds into contact with one another and hence creates boundaries. At the heart of ethnicity is the negotiation across such boundaries, which are themselves constantly shifting. Ethnicity is a strategic response, invoked in particular situations (Durham 1989). It is within this theoretical framework emphasizing boundaries that I have formulated my discussion of ethnic entrepreneurs. How, I ask, is ethnic identity sustained through the creation of ethnic enterprises, such as a travel agency, and by individuals, such as the parish priest?

Two final observations are probably worth making. First, at the time that I began this research, there was a great deal of interest in the study of ethnic voluntary associations, emerging largely from the work of the first generation of urban anthropologists who worked in Africa (for example, Little 1957). But this interest waned. I believe that it has now reemerged, as social scientists examine closely aspects of immigrant communities in a range of host societies across the globe. For example, the question of whether an ethnic community can exist without propinquity through the mechanisms of heterolocalism (associations as well as the use of modern modes of communication) has been recently addressed by Zelinsky and Lee (1998). Second, while I do not discuss it outright in chapter 6, it is important to note that, at least in the Portuguese case, the Portuguese state has had and continues to have a role in supporting these organizations. Under Salazar it was a way to oversee communities of nationals abroad and to retain their attachment to the homeland and hence their economic remittances. Today it is a way to support the idea of the Portuguese diaspora. Certainly there are lessons here for other immigrant populations and the organizations that emerge from among them.

Notes

1. Hasia Diner (2000) has recently argued that, while Jews no longer live on the Lower East Side, the area still resonates in the minds of the Jews in America as the symbolic locus of their identity and the space through which they can reconnect with an imagined past. Today the Lower East Side is associated with a vibrant Chinatown that is home to a host of new immigrants, many from a single province in China (Kwong 1996).

2. The concept of "city as context" was first outlined by Jack Rollwagen (1975) and others in a special issue of *Urban Anthropology*. It received little attention until revived by Foner (1987, 2001a).

3. Despite this effort, Paris does contain some distinctly ethnic neighborhoods; indeed even at the time that I carried out my first field work in France, other ethnic groups (particularly those of North African origin) had the beginnings of such neighborhoods, the Goutte d'Or of the eighteenth *arrondissement* being the prime example. But the Portuguese were then and still remain dispersed in the Parisian urban landscape.

5

Is the Ethnic Community Inevitable?

A Comparison of the Settlement Patterns of Portuguese Immigrants in Toronto and Paris

As ethnologists have turned from the study of small, relatively homogeneous, and isolated rural or tribal villages to concentrate upon the complexities of urban societies and urban living, they have laid bare the problems of the so-called community-study method (Arensberg 1957). This method, based upon the delineation of small-scale and easily bounded geographical (and thereby cultural) units of study, results too often in tautology. One chooses a community to find or prove community. The assumptions become the conclusion.[1]

The development of the concept of social networks (Bott 1957; Epstein 1961; Mitchell 1969; Boissevain and Mitchell 1973), with its emphasis upon the individual at the nexus of an ever-expanding and ever-changing web of affiliations, has been one of the major results of this methodological soul searching on the part of urban ethnologists. The study of social networks moves us away from a preoccupation with geographically or sociologically static systems. It allows us to find a "sense of community" even where the members do not live in proximity. In many parts of America, there are communities held together by virtue of an ethnic social network or state of mind common to people spread out over a wide area (Krickus 1976, 357).

Still, many of these network theorists, especially those interested in the problem of ethnicity, assume that networks based on common origins will inevitably emerge. This concept of the urban ethnic community—in both the geographical and the network senses—needs careful scrutiny, especially since community, in one or both senses, is not necessarily inevitable and cannot simply be assumed.

The focus for this chapter emerges out of a comparison of two different personal field research experiences with Portuguese immigrants, one in the city of Toronto, Canada, the other in Paris, France.[2] When I arrived in Toronto to conduct my research, I brought with me all the baggage of traditional participant-observation anthropology. I looked for an ethnic neighborhood, and my search was rewarded by the Kensington Market area in downtown Toronto. In Kensington, Portuguese stores, a Portuguese church, Portuguese restaurants, and Portuguese families are all clustered together. I had found my Little Portugal, just as Gans (1962) and Whyte (1943) had found their Little Italies and others their Chinatowns and Cabbage Towns. But when I arrived in Paris, I found no Little Portugal that had carved out its own social niche within the great French metropolis. Not only was I forced to adopt new methods of research, but I also had to revise my entire theoretical perspective on immigration and on the patterns of settlement of foreigners in cities. I had to come to terms with the urban structures themselves as they influence the lives of newcomers. I also had to view the formation of a community, be it a geographical community or one based on social networks, as a strategy appropriate in some situations and inappropriate in others. Individuals choose to associate or identify themselves with one another. What factors make such a choice advantageous? What social institutions make it possible or likely?

Portuguese Immigration to Canada and France

Until the publication of Grace Anderson's book *Networks of Contact* (1974), the Portuguese immigrant population in Canada remained relatively unstudied, although the program sponsored by the Canadian government to recruit Portuguese immigrant laborers began in 1952.[3] During the decade of the 1950s, the annual immigration rate of Portuguese nationals to Canada remained relatively low, ranging from approximately 1,300 in 1954 to approximately 4,300 in 1959. In the 1960s the numbers increased, averaging roughly 6,500 per year, and by 1971 there were approximately 97,000 Portuguese immigrants in Canada (table 5.1). While continental Portuguese as well as natives of the island of Madeira can be found among the total population of Portuguese immigrants in Canada, the majority originate from the Azores. Most have settled in the cities of Montreal and Toronto, the latter city having the densest concentration. According to Anderson and Higgs (1976), the Toronto community was established in June 1953, with the arrival in the city of Portuguese immigrants who had been working in rural farming areas or on railroad gangs elsewhere in Canada: "The immigrants were drawn to the center of the metropolis

Table 5.1.   Portuguese Immigration to Canada, 1946–1973

Years	Number of Immigrants
1946–1950	108
1951–1957	8,115
1958–1962	16,731
1963–1967	32,473
1968–1973	54,199
1946–1973	111,626

Source: Anderson and Higgs (1976, 24), based on immigration and population statistics from the Green Paper on Immigration, Vol. 3 (Ottawa: Manpower and Immigration, 1974), p. 32.

where older housing was available at reasonable prices. Rumors of highly paid jobs spread rapidly to clusters of Portuguese immigrants scattered throughout the country. As the word spread, the men dropped their jobs and set off for the big city. It was a newer version of the gold rush, but this time the trend was southward" (Anderson and Higgs, 1976, 69).

Portuguese emigration to France is also largely a post–World War II phenomenon. However, it is almost entirely an emigration of continental Portuguese and is more massive in scale, due both to the proximity of Portugal to France and to the high level of clandestine emigration as opposed to contract labor emigration.[4] In the decade of the 1950s, the annual rate of Portuguese immigration to France varied between 1,000 and 5,000. In the succeeding decade, this rate increased dramatically (to about 40,000 per year), and by 1974 there were approximately 578,000 legal Portuguese immigrants in France (table 5.2).[5] The Region Parisienne (the city of Paris and the seven administrative départements surrounding it) has received

Table 5.2.   Portuguese Immigration to France, 1946–1979

Years	Permanent Workers	Families
1946–1950	72	328
1951–1957	8,170	2,162
1958–1962	32,032	12,794
1963–1967	195,542	69,444
1968–1974	341,545	244,659
1975–1979	11,979	56,034
1946–1979	589,340	385,421

Source: Office National d'Immigration, Statistiques de l'Immigration, 1979.

more than a third of all Portuguese immigrants to France. Outside this region, Portuguese immigrants can be found in significant numbers in the north, near the city of Lille, and in the Rhone valley, near the cities of Lyon and Clermont-Ferrand.[6]

Settlement Patterns and the Structure of the City

Lieberson (1963) has emphasized that new immigrants must adapt to the structure and order of the city into which they enter. Clearly the urban anthropologist must come to terms with the fact that the form of the city differs from one culture to another. Certain aspects of the city's growth, of the place of the city vis-à-vis the nation of which it is a part, of the level of industrialization and the location of labor markets, and of the nature of housing and the social composition of city residents are clearly among the important variables that distinguish one city from the next and that may also lead to differential patterns of settlements among immigrants.

The city of Toronto is built on a grid pattern around a central business district.[7] It possesses an urban structure similar to that of other North American cities which were formed during the nineteenth century, when the old centers became increasingly devoted to business and industry. The neighborhoods bordering on this central business district were abandoned by local inhabitants and taken over by waves of immigrants from Europe.

In the 1971 Canadian census, 34 percent of the total population of metropolitan Toronto was reported as foreign-born and, of these, 83 percent had immigrated since 1945. The spatial distribution of foreign-born populations by census tracts indicates that they are residentially concentrated in a single central region of the city. Although census data are not available for the Portuguese immigrant group per se, table 5.3 provides a more detailed picture of residential concentration by various other ethnic groups, the Asians and Italians being more recent immigrants than the Poles and the Germans. Clearly clusters of families of similar ethnic origins reside in certain small neighborhood areas: Asians to the east in what is recognized as Toronto's Chinatown (census tracts 32 to 37), Poles farther west (census tracts 44 to 55), and Italians (by far the largest ethnic group in Toronto) to the north (census tracts 93 to 105 and 158 to 163).

The Kensington Market area is to the immediate west of Toronto's central business district and coincides approximately with census tract 38. In 1971, 67 percent of the population in the area was foreign-born and, of these, 93 percent had immigrated since 1945. Although the area is not exclusively inhabited by Portuguese, they are the most significant and the most recent in a series of successive waves of immigrants who have lived

Table 5.3. Foreign-Born Population of Metropolitan Toronto and Some Proximate Suburbs, 1971

Census Tracts	Total Population	Born Outside Canada	Immigrated after 1975	Percent Asian	Italian	German	Polish
Metropolitan Toronto							
22–26	30,715	29.2	20.8	2.1	3.3	4.1	1.0
27–31	31,310	26.8	21.5	7.7	2.6	2.3	2.6
32–37	21,530	40.6	29.3	24.7	1.4	3.0	0.5
38–43	35,530	61.6	55.3	4.3	7.4	1.2	2.8
44–50	46,805	47.7	40.5	3.4	5.7	4.2	11.9
51–55	30,025	50.8	45.1	4.2	11.2	3.8	11.4
56–60	28,630	64.9	60.7	7.8	28.2	1.6	1.6
61–66	31,225	40.9	34.7	10.8	1.6	4.3	1.4
67–71	25,375	40.1	33.4	9.3	4.1	3.6	1.1
72–80	52,970	35.3	28.1	3.2	11.1	2.8	0.1
81–85	24,410	49.0	42.3	3.5	13.8	2.8	0.7
86–92	34,120	39.5	33.2	5.3	2.1	5.3	1.7
93–98	46,435	57.5	53.0	2.9	39.3	1.9	1.8
99–105	41,135	47.5	40.4	2.8	3.9	5.4	8.2
106–113	42,135	58.1	53.2	0.9	53.4	1.4	1.2
114–119	26,835	48.9	40.7	2.1	2.4	3.9	1.5
120–126	26,540	30.4	22.3	2.1	1.4	4.8	1.3
127–131	32,675	33.1	24.3	3.4	1.6	3.8	0.8
132–136	28,595	28.3	26.4	2.5	2.3	3.3	1.3
137–142	34,545	29.8	20.4	2.6	1.9	3.8	0.8

(continued)

Table 5.3. Foreign-Born Population of Metropolitan Toronto and Some Proximate Suburbs, 1971 (continued)

Census Tracts	Total Population	Born Outside Canada	Immigrated after 1975	Percent			
				Asian	Italian	German	Polish
York							
150–157	39,990	40.4	33.2	1.8	12.2	5.1	3.9
158–163	38,410	54.7	45.2	1.3	42.3	1.1	0.5
164–168	34,105	52.1	43.4	1.6	25.8	2.6	1.1
169–176	34,775	40.1	33.0	2.1	21.6	2.9	1.2
East York							
180–186	53,240	39.3	29.3	2.9	9.7	3.2	0.9
187–190	18,285	34.5	17.5	3.7	4.8	4.6	0.9
191–196	33,110	32.1	22.1	4.5	1.5	4.1	0.9
Part of North York							
275–281	49,485	32.5	31.0	2.4	17.7	3.3	1.1
282–287	40,230	42.0	36.3	1.7	29.9	2.9	1.5
288–293	37,715	40.9	34.6	1.5	26.4	3.2	1.1
294–298	34,005	40.2	32.4	1.1	21.6	2.8	0.9

Source: 1971 Census or Canada, Toronto: 33⅓ percent sample.

in the vicinity. They have replaced Italian and Eastern European ethnic businesses and institutions with their own.

Kensington is an area of several blocks characterized by two- and three-story row houses, which the Portuguese newcomers have purchased and painted in bright Mediterranean hues. The little gardens out front are well-tended and occasionally furnished with an image of the Virgin Mary or some other piece of religious statuary. Anderson and Higgs comment on the process of buying these homes, which provide Portuguese immigrants with a sense of security and belonging: "After a few months of hard saving, small groups of men were able to pool their resources and make a small down payment (often $500) on a house in Alexandra Park or Kensington Market area of Toronto. Frequently relatives lent money and were promised an inexpensive bed in the new home" (Anderson and Higgs, 1976, 69). While some Portuguese businesses are interspersed with these houses, the majority are concentrated along the *avenida principal* of Kensington—Augusta Street.

Areas like Kensington are preferred by immigrants, not only because they provide low-cost housing but also because they are close to the sources of unskilled employment. Most Portuguese men in Toronto are employed in construction. When they first arrived in the city, they found their jobs not far away, because Toronto's building boom, beginning with the construction of the new City Hall in the 1960s, was directed initially to a face-lifting of the central business district itself. Portuguese women are employed in textile and clothing factories to the immediate south and west of Kensington and on the housekeeping staffs of hotels, hospitals, and other public buildings in downtown Toronto. Often several Portuguese women work together in the same hotel or factory. Similarly, many Portuguese men work together and return to the neighborhood in a group from their place of employment.

The Kensington Market area has served Portuguese immigrants (as it did other immigrant groups before them) as a transitional zone, where newcomers can begin to learn the new language and the new patterns of behavior appropriate to their country of adoption. Residential segregation in areas like Kensington is both voluntary and involuntary (Yuan 1970). Once a Portuguese family has established itself, a decision is often taken to move out of the traditional zone into the suburbs. However, even after the move, many continue to return to Kensington to do their weekly shopping or to meet with compatriots in the local cafés, restaurants, and clubs.

Besides being many centuries older than Toronto, Paris is primarily an administrative and cultural city rather than an industrial and business city. A large residential area with small business sections catering to each of the twenty *arrondissements* (administrative districts) surrounds an administrative core located in the vicinity of the Ile de la Cité, under the shadows of Notre Dame Cathedral. Building and industrial expansions have taken place in the suburbs of Paris beyond the limits of the peripheral boulevard, which rings the city on the old nineteenth-century walls. For twelve to fifteen miles in any direction out of the center of the city, one sees massive low-income housing projects, built to shelter the growing Parisian population. By contrast, central Paris inside the peripheral boulevard has remained relatively unchanged, and only the Eiffel tower and the more modern Montparnasse tower dominate the otherwise conservative skyline of six-story Second-Empire apartment buildings.

Although there is a general east-west division that splits the city between working class and bourgeois, there are no neighborhoods in Paris that have formed along ethnic lines, except perhaps the special case of the historic Jewish ghetto in the Marais. Table 5.4, which shows the 1975 distribution of foreign population in Paris by arrondissement and by major ethnic group, supports this assertion.

The foreign-born population is fairly evenly scattered throughout the urban fabric of the French capital city, although there is a slightly higher concentration in the second and third *arrondissements*. In the Portuguese case, in particular, the employment of women and the nature of urban housing in Paris explain their dispersion. Portuguese women in Paris work as private domestics (*bonne à tout faire*), as cleaning ladies (*femme de menage*), or as *concierges*. In the first two cases, they are often provided with a maid's room on the sixth floor of one of the Parisian apartment buildings for free or in return for several hours of work per week. In the case of the *concierge*, the Portuguese family lives in the one- or two-room quarters on the first floor of the building. While we might call Toronto a horizontally stratified city with distinct socioeconomically and ethnically differentiated neighborhoods, Paris is vertically stratified.[8] As a result of both the pattern of urban stratification and of the employment of Portuguese women in Paris, Portuguese immigrants frequently come into greater contact with middle- and upper-class French families than with lower- or working-class French families, or for that matter with other Portuguese immigrants beyond their own kinsmen. A very small percentage of Algerians live in the eighth and sixteenth *arrondissements*, where the well-to-do native Parisians live, in contrast to the much higher percentages of Spanish and Portuguese immigrants who live there. Table 5.5 clearly shows that much of this difference is due to the presence of Portuguese and Spanish women, many of whom are single and working as private maids.

The world of Portuguese immigrant women in Paris is often confined to a small geographical area where they work and live. The fact that they

Table 5.4. Distribution of the Foreign Population of Paris, by *Arrondissement*, 1975

Arrondissement	Total Population	Foreign	Algerian[a]	Algerian[b]	Spanish[a]	Spanish[b]	Portuguese[a]	Portuguese[b]
1	22,350	14.9	1.5	10.2	4.2	27.9	3.1	20.9
2	26,225	22.3	3.3	15.0	5.1	22.8	1.4	6.5
3	42,265	20.5	5.8	28.1	3.7	18.2	2.2	10.6
4	49,210	11.7	1.6	13.9	1.3	11.0	1.5	12.8
5	67,500	12.6	1.6	12.6	2.1	16.9	1.3	10.4
6	56,135	12.1	0.4	3.5	3.1	25.5	1.3	10.9
7	73,935	12.9	0.4	3.4	3.9	29.9	1.9	14.7
8	53,595	17.1	0.7	4.1	5.5	32.0	3.4	20.2
9	70,180	14.5	1.1	7.4	3.4	23.2	2.0	13.9
10	93,325	16.0	1.8	11.3	1.8	18.5	2.1	13.5
11	158,540	17.8	3.0	16.7	2.5	14.3	2.3	13.0
12	140,565	10.0	1.8	18.6	1.3	13.5	1.3	12.7
13	163,735	10.0	2.3	23.7	1.1	10.9	1.1	11.4
14	149,495	12.4	1.9	15.3	0.7	5.6	2.0	16.3
15	230,835	9.6	1.6	16.2	1.6	16.9	1.5	15.4
16	193,745	14.9	6.5	3.5	3.9	26.1	2.5	16.6
17	185,410	12.4	1.3	10.8	2.7	21.9	1.9	15.6
18	209,000	14.7	3.3	22.2	1.8	12.3	2.2	14.8
19	143,660	14.3	3.8	26.5	1.7	11.6	1.5	10.8
20	175,455	15.0	3.7	29.3	1.7	10.3	1.9	12.0
Total	2,305,160		49,080		52,910		43,355	

a. Percent of total population
b. Percent of foreign population

Source: French National Census, 1975, 20-percent sample.

Table 5.5. Distribution of Portuguese Immigrants in Paris, by Sex and
Arrondissement, 1975

	Male		Female	
Arrondissement	Total	Active	Total	Active
1	350	265	350	205
2	270	185	275	195
3	535	400	385	250
4	360	220	380	195
5	450	290	440	285
6	340	255	405	295
7	635	435	765	615
8	830	635	1,020	715
9	705	515	705	445
10	1,035	635	980	575
11	1,945	1,395	1,735	975
12	970	615	815	475
13	955	700	915	455
14	1,700	1,195	1,330	770
15	1,815	1,370	1,610	1,060
16	2,095	1,620	2,685	1,900
17	1,730	1,370	1,865	1,270
18	2,400	1,740	2,140	1,145
19	1,220	930	1,015	540
20	1,805	1,300	1,565	910
Total	22,145	16,070	20,380	13,275

Source: French National Census, 1975.

work alone makes it more difficult for them to meet other Portuguese immigrant women. Portuguese men who work in construction or in one of
the automobile factories (Citroën, Renault) located on the outskirts of Paris
commute to their jobs. Workplace and home place are consequently segregated for them by the geographical distance between them; a Portuguese
man therefore rarely socializes during leisure hours with those from his
place of work. In short, each immigrant family in Paris contracts on an individual basis with French society, rather than through the filter of a buffer
zone provided by segregated ethnic communities, as in North American
cities like Toronto. With respect to residential concentration, a geographically based Portuguese immigrant community does not exist in Paris as it
does in Toronto, and one explanation for this difference is the varying
structures of the two urban centers and the varying patterns of employment, particularly for women, within these different urban systems.

Ethnic Community and National Immigration Policy

A second factor that must be considered, when trying to explain the absence of a geographically or network-based ethnic community in Paris in contrast with Toronto, is the receiving country's political and cultural ideology toward immigration, as it is rooted in national immigration policy. In Canada the emphasis is upon pluralism or, to put it in post-Canadian centennial terms, multiculturalism.[9] This means that all immigrant groups have the right to retain their language and their culture—their ethnic distinctiveness. In fact, they are encouraged to do so. The composite of these various languages and cultures make up Canadian society and culture. Integration is the preferred concept.

"The integration of immigrants into the life of the country, with the help of its institutions, is surely the road to their self-fulfillment. But in adopting fully the Canadian way of life, sharing its advantages and disadvantages, those whose origin is neither French nor British do not have to cast off or hide their own culture. It may happen that, in their determination to express their desire to live fully in this mode, their culture may conflict with the customs of their adopted society. But Canadian society, open and modern, should be able to integrate heterogeneous elements into a harmonious system, to achieve unity in diversity." (Commission on Bilingualism and Biculturalism 1969, 7)

Furthermore, as in the United States, being "ethnic" carries political force. One can use one's "Portugueseness" or "Italianness" as leverage in political bargaining. Canadian politicians, like their American counterparts, are concerned about the "ethnic vote" in those areas of the country where particular groups are predominant. Ethnic groups are interest groups, and ethnicity itself is an important principle of social organization.

Among immigrant groups in Canada, as in the United States, certain voluntary associations and local clubs have sprung up to represent the "ethnic voice" to the larger society. They give individuals an arena in which to gain social prominence within the community, thereby acting as leaders and spokesmen. In Toronto, Portuguese immigrants can belong to three such clubs. These clubs serve not only as political arenas but also as mutual aid societies. They help to ease the adaptation of newcomers to the urban and foreign milieu (Little 1957), and they sponsor social activities directed specifically to the Portuguese community.

In contrast, the pervasive ideology in France favors "becoming French" rather than promoting ethnic distinctiveness.[10] "Persuaded by the 'civilizing' and generous role of their country, the French only accept foreign cultures with paternalism, at best. Their attraction is exotic and simply for distraction" (Minces 1973, 407).

The politics of immigration in France has followed a complicated course, sometimes to the point of being paradoxical. On the one hand, familial immigration has been favored and linked to efforts to promote population growth in a country that has considered itself underpopulated for several centuries. On the other hand, immigration from southern Europe to northern Europe began as a migration of temporary wage labor rather than permanent migration. A temporary and unstable work force would help to keep wages low and social investments minimal, thereby facilitating economic expansion and development, the raison d'être for importation of migrant labor in the first place.[11]

In short, the choice for an immigrant is either to return home after a short stay abroad (and in this case it is primarily an immigration of male heads of households or, at most, wage-earning couples) or to settle permanently in France and to sever ties with Portugal. In the latter case, the emphasis is upon assimilation, particularly upon the education of immigrant children in French language and culture. In order to facilitate this process of assimilation, it is important that immigrant families are dispersed throughout the fabric of French society rather than concentrated into ethnic neighborhoods, which only hinder that process. This desire is expressed in the general distaste that the French have for the ghetto à l'americaine.[12]

But, most important, ethnicity as yet carries no powers of political persuasion in France. The voluntary associations and local clubs that are so characteristic of immigrant groups of most nationalities in North America are generally and therefore more noticeably absent in France. Furthermore, foreign associations are severely controlled in France. Their creation requires the authorization of the minister of the interior, and they can only have a French citizen at their head. In short, the cultural-political ideology toward immigrants in France creates a situation where individual family interests surmount collective group interests, and consequently the degree of social, political, and communal interaction among unrelated families of the same nationality is comparatively low.

The Institutions of the Ethnic Community

The absence of a pluralistic ideology in France has many ramifications, particularly as it affects the low level of what Breton (1964) has called the "institutional completeness" of North American ethnic communities.[13] Driedger and Church (1974) have argued that residential segregation is, in fact, a prerequisite to such institutional completeness. Community, or community relations, implies a set of institutions or organizations within which context social interaction can occur or with which group membership can be identified. We have already mentioned the voluntary associations and clubs, but there are other institutions—churches, special schools, commercial establishments—that also serve to provide such a context for social interaction. Unlike the Toronto Portuguese community, where several Portuguese newspapers are produced by and for the community, in Paris such publications are issued by French organizations— the national unions and SITA (the interdiocesan Catholic Council). The restaurants, small stores, and travel agencies that are ethnic domains in America (Brettell 1977a) remain French in France, as a result of a long-standing law prohibiting non-French citizens from opening and operating such establishments and as a result of the traditionally heavy concentration of Frenchmen themselves in the tertiary sector of French economy and society.

The most important of such institutions is, of course, the church. The church performed a vital role in the development of immigrant groups in America. The ethnic parish soon became part of the American scene and the Catholic Church of America an essentially immigrant institution (Krickus 1976, 83). A society with no religion as the official religion provides a context wherein "denominational affiliations can be a means for defining oneself against others" (Greeley 1971, 83). Some churches, such as the Ukrainian "minority church" described by Millett, became "hives of political activity" (1971, 57). It is not uncommon to find native priests working among their own kind.

Two Portuguese parishes serve the larger Kensington market area in Toronto. During the summer there are *festas* and religious processions, similar to processions one can see annually in most villages throughout continental and island Portugal. There are masses every Sunday, but the church is open day and night to help immigrants with any problems they might have in adapting to the new society. The social service sector of one Portuguese parish helps immigrants find jobs, arrange for naturalization papers, and get married by proxy. In short, the Portuguese church in Toronto, like most North American immigrant churches, is a rallying point for the formation of "ethnic group interests."[14] As Vallee has emphasized, an "ethnic group relies upon geographically defined multifunctional institutions like parishes to engage people in the ethnic category" (1971, 157).

In Paris, on the other hand, the number of Portuguese priests who work among their brethren is still minimal, although the immigration itself is as old as that to Canada. The Catholic Church in France is French; therefore, French priests are delegated the responsibility for Portuguese immigrants. There are virtually no strictly Portuguese parishes. In some parts of Paris there are Portuguese masses every two weeks and in others once a month.[15] As a result, interest in the church is minimal. It hardly serves as an institution around which dispersed and estranged families can reorganize themselves and establish strong extrafamilial and communal ties. Information that immigrants can obtain from the social service section of the Portuguese parishes in Toronto is largely acquired from kinsmen in France, and the annual religious festivals are celebrated with fellow villagers during summer visits to Portugal, not on the streets of Paris.

Conclusion

Essentially, what I have tried to argue is that "community" in either a geographical sense or in an ethnic network sense does not exist for Portuguese immigrants in Paris as it does among Portuguese immigrants in Toronto. In Paris certain structural, ideological, and political factors make it difficult to establish a community and the ethnic institutions that are traditionally associated with ethnic communities in Canada and elsewhere in North America. Furthermore the French policy toward foreigners does not even make it advantageous for Portuguese immigrants to develop liaisons and community organizations among themselves. So far, there is little to be gained by "interest group" behavior in France, as there is in North America. Social networks among Portuguese immigrants in France are weak because they serve no strategic purpose. However, this does not mean that no social network or community exists at all.

One concluding comparison seems appropriate. Trans-Atlantic migrations are, by necessity, more permanent moves, despite the fact that some immigrants in North America do eventually return to their homeland or think of doing so (Cerase 1974). By contrast, intra-European migration has had a more temporary character, because movement back and forth between the country of origin and the country of destination is facilitated by geographical proximity. Furthermore, although the French promoted familial immigration between 1968 and 1974 to stimulate the more permanent settlement of immigrants in France, such promotion has remained largely at the level of policy than activated through the implementation of social programs. Indeed, once the frontiers were closed in the mid-1970s, one plan was developed to provide monetary incentives to encourage foreigners to return to their homelands. As a result many Portuguese immigrants in France, even if they intend to remain abroad for some time, retain a homeland orientation. Their "community of identification" is not in the host society—France as a nation or a Portuguese ethnic subculture within that nation—but in Portugal itself, in the village they left. This community is sustained by a long-distance social network. News of their home villages reaches them through village newspapers sent by the parish priest (the cleric with whom they really identify) (Rocha-Trindade 1973) or through fellow villagers who come to visit or to find work. Immigrants often help fellow villagers during their initial period of immigration, but, after the newcomers are settled, social ties are frequently dissolved. There is neither time nor reason to continue acquaintances. Rather, such friendships are renewed annually during summer vacation, which the majority of Portuguese immigrants in France spend in Portugal. This is sometimes equally true of kinsmen, who often view the geographical distances in Paris as greater than those between Paris and Portugal. They see each other once a year on vacation.

Unlike Portuguese immigrants in Toronto, who save to make a downpayment on a house in Canada or to open a business in the Kensington area, Portuguese immigrants in Paris save to build in the village. This goal in itself has altered the character of the countryside of northern Portugal in the last decade. New houses have sprung up in most villages. These houses symbolize the fact that Portuguese immigrants in France, in contrast to Portuguese immigrants in Toronto, are not looking for upward mobility in the country of immigration but rather within the Portuguese village they left temporarily, even if temporary means fifteen years or a working lifetime. It is in the village back home that they seek social recognition and social status, not within a new foreign society where they become part of a massive foreign proletariat.

Notes

This chapter was originally published in the *Journal of Ethnic Studies* 9 (1981): 1–17. It is reprinted with minor changes by permission of the publisher.

1. Part of the confusion derives, as Arensberg (1957) notes, from the failure to analytically distinguish the community study method, which explores a theoretical problem in a given locale, from the study of community, which tries to understand a community as a social group.

2. The research in Toronto was conducted during the summer of 1972 with the help of a training grant from the department of anthropology, Brown University. The research in Paris and in Portugal was conducted between July 1974 and January 1976 with the assistance of the Canada Council and the Social Science Research Council of New York. The author would like to express kind thanks to these and also to the Institute of Emigration in Lisbon for its assistance with the final preparation of this article.

3. See Anderson (1974) for a more complete discussion of the Portuguese in Toronto; Anderson and Higgs (1976) for a broader study of the Portuguese communities throughout Canada; and Alpalhão and Pereira da Rosa (1979) for a detailed discussion of the Portuguese in Quebec.

4. See Brettell (1978) and Rocha (1962) for a discussion of clandestine emigration. Many young men emigrated clandestinely in order to avoid military service in Africa which, by the mid-1960s, was as long as four years. Others left clandestinely because they did not want to wait for a passport or because they were ineligible to receive one.

5. These are the official figures provided by the Office National d'Immigration. Most figures for the total number of Portuguese immigrants in France can only be estimates because of the high degree of clandestine immigration.

6. The bibliography on Portuguese migration to France is quite extensive. For a starting bibliography, see Brettell (1977a).

7. The concept of the central business district was developed by the Chicago School of sociology in the 1930s in conjunction with the concentric zone model of cities.

8. David Pinkney, in his book *Napoleon the Third and the Rebuilding of Paris*, includes an illustration of the cross-section of a Parisian apartment building, showing the vertical stratification of classes. Middle- and upper class families are sandwiched between lower-class families on the first floor and the servants on the sixth floor (1958, plate 23).

9. Grace Anderson has characterized the fever of multiculturalism quite well in her description of the ethnic "caravan" held annually in Toronto. Ever since Canada's Centennial year, 1967, the Dominion Day holiday weekend in metropolitan Toronto has been celebrated by an ethnic caravan. Each ethnic group in the metropolis is invited to display traditional cultural features to all interested persons who purchase a caravan passport. This showcase of ethnic culture continues for several days. Torontonians and visitors alike tour the city by bus to eat in ethnic restaurants and clubs, watch folk dancing, listen to musical groups, and peruse and purchase crafts displayed in improvised stalls (Anderson 1974, 163).

10. In the late 1970s an attempt was made to change this policy and to stimulate more interest in the cultural heritage of the various immigrant groups in France. There has also been some discussion of establishing maternal language classes in French schools. The contrast is apparent, because such language classes have been in operation for more than a decade in Toronto.

11. For a discussion of this economic background to contemporary intra-European migration, see Castles and Kosack (1973).

12. Several of these traditional attitudes toward immigrants are discussed in Girard's classic study (1954).

13. Institutional completeness refers to the presence or absence of formal organizations in the ethnic community. According to Breton, ethnic communities can vary enormously in their degree of institutional completeness. Some are at one extreme, where the ethnic community performs all services required by its members, while others are at another extreme, where no services are provided by the ethnic community.

14. Gans (1962, 111) claims that it gives people a chance to socialize though they have no real identification with the parish.

15. The importance of the church as a central institution for the formation of "community identification" is evident in one area of Paris, where I did find such activities organized around a church and a priest. In Neuilly, just to the west of the city proper, and an area where many single Portuguese women live and work because it is one of the wealthiest neighborhoods of the Paris region, there was a young Portuguese priest who had come to France to study. He was in charge of the Portuguese population in the parish and said a mass every Sunday. On a good day a hundred people often attended, men and women. The group also organized excursions and occasionally an afternoon of entertainment in the church hall. Much of the activity depended on the personality of the priest himself. When I returned to the parish in 1980, there was a new priest, also Portuguese, but the spirit of the group as I knew it in 1975 no longer existed.

6

Ethnicity and Entrepreneurs
Portuguese Immigrants in a Canadian City

In his analysis of Hausa migrants in lbadan, Cohen (1969) concludes that ethnicity is basically a political and not a cultural phenomenon. This particular understanding of ethnicity pervades the literature, both scholarly and popular, on the place of ethnicity in American political life (cf. Bailey and Katz 1969; Fuchs 1968; Litt 1970; Parenti 1967; Wolfinger 1965). Ethnic groups are catered to by politicians, who champion their grievances to win election to public office. The politician may at times have to mobilize ethnic sentiment and organize the group himself to be assured of strong collective support. In either case, the politician is an entrepreneur working for the profits he can gain by identifying himself with ethnic pride or ethnic issues.

I wish to suggest here, in light of research I conducted among Portuguese immigrants in Toronto, Canada,[1] that the politician is only one kind of entrepreneur attempting to organize people on the basis of ethnicity. A variety of other individuals, whom I shall call ethnic entrepreneurs, employ ethnic symbols to establish themselves as mediators between those who share an identity and others in the society.[2] I shall discuss here how these ethnic entrepreneurs can be said to play the roles of both patron and broker.

Though concepts such as "mediator," "cultural broker," "hinge," and "patron" are familiar in anthropological literature, they have rarely been applied to the study of social interaction, or the lack of it, in urban society. In a review of these concepts, Paine has suggested a rigorous distinction between patron and broker in particular. Though the former "recruits followers by his power to dispense favors," the latter "is a middle man attracting followers who believe him able to influence the persons who control the favors" (Paine 1971a, 19). Despite this analytical separation, Paine acknowledges that these roles are often combined in a single individual, especially where "patrons assume a broker role in order to buttress their positions as patrons" (p. 21). It is just this combination that characterizes the ethnic entrepreneur. Emphasis on the manipulation of ethnic symbols to maintain ethnic boundaries is contrasted with the more customary approach to the study of ethnic persistence.

Ethnic groups have usually been considered readily isolatable and easily bounded "culture-bearing units," acting in unison according to shared customs and norms for behavior. This approach is characteristic of anthropological studies of urban life that focus upon geographically delimited and residentially segregated ethnic enclaves and "urban villages" (Gans 1962; Glazer and Moynihan, 1963), as well as studies of closely knit networks of regular communication and interaction that constitute "functional little communities within the city" (Ablon 1971, 76).[3]

This approach is contrasted with the work of Barth and his colleagues (1969) which, although significant in turning our emphasis away from the study of ethnic groups as culture-bearing units, nevertheless relies upon boundaries that circumscribe separate ethnic *groups* occupying distinct niches. In short, Barth tends to ignore the distinction between ethnicity and ethnic group.[4] An ethnic boundary can exist without necessarily circumscribing a group. It is this boundary line that the ethnic entrepreneur often mediates.

History of Migration

The idea [of emigration] resides in the breast of each man like an implacable parasite against even our most steadfast feelings for the homeland. It comes from our great grandfather, from farther still; they inherited it and passed it on to their descendants. All generations are born with this innate ambition and it makes a nuisance of itself when not satisfied. It always lurks around a corner in the mind, to be brought out like a talisman in moments of challenge to fate, or used as a prop in times when desperate remedies are needed (Ferreira de Castro 1928, 32–33).[5]

The Portuguese have always been an emigrating people, looking out over the Atlantic to territories that lie beyond their horizons. Although actual ties between Portugal and Canada date back to the late fifteenth and early sixteenth centuries, when Portuguese explorers and fishermen set foot on the eastern seaboard of Newfoundland, immigration in significant proportions is a post–World War II phenomenon. In 1953, during a period of zealous economic development, the government of Canada brought the first boatload of immigrants from Portugal. At first a quota of 500 per year was set, but the response by immigrants was so favorable that this figure was soon increased. Most of these early immigrants were sent to work on farms and railroads. As recently as the 1950s the immigrant gang, so much a part of the history of the growth and development of the Canadian nation, could be observed at work.

> And on the rock ballast and gravel and steel of the line for 200 yards, machines clattered and stuttered and foremen stood watching the rising and falling backs of 150 Portuguese, gritty and strong and sweaty, with eloquent eyes and dark skins and no English, performing the harsh duties of the steel gang . . . . These Portuguese are strangers here, so they seldom make the first advance. But if you catch one's eye and smile or nod, his smile is quick and flashing. In other words they are like any man away from home. They have snapshots: this man, but cleanly dressed, a dark unsmiling wife, sober clean children (Young 1957).

However, the drift to the cities soon began, particularly as more and more immigrants arrived. Between 1957 and 1967 approximately 58,000 people of Portuguese birth came to Canada, and in the next five years the average was about 8,500 per year. Of these, 60 to 70 percent came from the Azores.[6] The majority of immigrants settled either in Toronto or Montreal, the former city containing more than three times as many Portuguese as the latter.[7] In Toronto the densest concentration is in the Kensington Market area, a traditionally low-cost housing area similar to "Cabbage Town" in the east end of the city, where Irish immigrants and their descendants have long been established. The houses in Kensington are painted in a panoply of bright Mediterranean hues. The small flower and vegetable gardens in front are carefully tended and sometimes adorned with religious statuary. Traditionally residence here has been transitional, the Portuguese being the most recent in a series of successive waves of immigrants.[8] This flow of population is clearly indicated by the number of signs for rooms or flats for rent and houses for sale that appear and disappear daily. Beyond the few blocks immediately surrounding the outdoor market, the population is ethnically mixed. Family and friends of those living in the market area may live several blocks to the west or northwest or even in the suburbs.

Augusta Street is the main marketing thoroughfare. It is lined with produce stalls, fish stores, Portuguese bakeries, dry goods stores, and other businesses catering to a Portuguese clientele. As early as 8 a.m. young boys are busy washing lettuce and arranging fruit baskets in preparation for the day's business. The street is normally congested, particularly on Fridays and Saturdays, when Anglos (as the Portuguese refer to all English-speaking Canadians) also come to do their weekly shopping.

The Portuguese have emigrated to Canada for a variety of reasons—
to join family already in Canada,[9] to provide better educational opportunities for their children, to escape military conscription, to find
"adventure"—best summed up as the search for a "better way of life"
(*melhor nível da vida*). A few traditional sectors of the urban economy employ immigrants. Many Portuguese hold construction jobs; others are occupied in gardening and landscaping or are employed as cleaners in
public buildings or as private domestics. The Kensington area is close to
the factory district, and many immigrants, especially women, hold jobs in
the textile and clothing industries. In some cases several members of the
same family can be found working for one company. Individuals often
hold more than one job to meet the mortgage payments on a house or to
build savings with which they hope someday to return to Portugal. However, the proportion of those who do return is fairly small. Those remaining in Canada admit that they become too accustomed to the amenities of
Canadian life and also find it difficult to extricate their children, who
come to speak English better than Portuguese.

The Travel Agent as Patron and Broker

One of the most obvious features of the Kensington Market area to anyone entering for the first time is the number of Portuguese travel agencies
clustered in close proximity. Although extensive travel might seem unlikely among a lower economic class (to which the majority of Portuguese
immigrants belong), some Portuguese manage to make occasional trips to
Portugal. Yet this alone would not explain why these agencies are busy
every day.

For several reasons, the travel agent can be interpreted as both an entrepreneurial patron building up a clientele and as a broker between the
immigrant and larger Canadian society and with the Portuguese world
overseas. As an entrepreneur, the travel agent establishes and mediates a
boundary between Portuguese immigrants and Canadian society. This
boundary is an ethnic one, in the sense that the entrepreneur employs the
idiom of ethnicity to maintain a degree of ethnic isolation and to enhance
identification with the Portuguese nation. In the first case, he can distinguish himself from non-Portuguese travel agents and thereby be assured
of attracting Portuguese clients; in the second, he ensures his own success
in the travel business. Keeping a watchful eye like Janus (Wolf 1956, 1076)
the ethnic entrepreneur is simultaneously "a communication line and a
barrier to communication" (Murphy 1964, 849).

The agent provides a multitude of services that make it unnecessary
for the immigrant to have much contact with other Canadians and conse-

quently make it unnecessary for him to learn a new language and fend for himself in a foreign milieu. The agent is first of all a translator. Immigrants come in with a bundle of official but unread mail that they have saved up for weeks; they may need help writing letters or placing telephone calls to inquire about jobs. Even if they know enough English for these tasks, they seem to prefer to work through a middleman. Men who have been unemployed for months will come regularly, every two weeks, to have the agent fill out their unemployment insurance cards, a procedure that, after initial assistance, they could manage themselves. The agent helps fill out income tax forms, applications for unemployment insurance or medicare, sponsorship forms for the immigration department, or forms to arrange for marriage by proxy. Individuals sometimes use a travel agency as a mailing address. The agent sometimes acts as a legal adviser at the Immigration Appeals Board or as a witness at a civil marriage ceremony.

One of the reasons Portuguese immigrants rely so heavily on the assistance of the travel agent may be that they find it hard to adjust to the specialization and division of services in the city. Many have come from rural villages where a single individual, for example, the priest[10] or the local *cacique* (local political boss), performs a variety of roles and offers a multitude of services, "being for his clients at once the economic, political, social, and ideological link to a larger society" (Silverman 1965, 181).[11] The travel agent thus fits a preconceived image of a man of many parts. Moreover, it is equally to the agent's advantage to perform some or all of these functions himself; therefore he does not encourage his clients to consult insurance agents, tax consultants, or marriage brokers. The agent has "a fund of assets which he dispenses, especially while establishing himself with a client; he uses the fund to promote the client's dependence on him" (Paine 1971a, 16). Providing these services has become a competitive game of entrepreneurship.

Initially there was a charge for most services, but several years ago the most prosperous agent began to offer many of them free, forcing other agents to do likewise to remain in business. Despite their lack of monetary profit, providing this kind of service helps the travel business, which still remains their primary concern. The agent increases his clients, whom he hopes will return to him later when they buy tickets to travel to Portugal or bring their relatives over to visit. Travel, particularly in the summer months and at Christmas, "is a million dollar business." The agent sponsors group and charter flights. To compete with other agents he organizes package deals that may include, for example, transportation to the airport in the price of the ticket. Thus not only is the role of patron assumed by the travel agent in the interest of entrepreneurial competition, but the two kinds of services he provides embody his brokerage role with respect to Canadian society as well as to the Portuguese homeland.

As the number of travel agencies increases, individual agents look to other means for maintaining their economic foothold. In most cases they continue to use the ethnic idiom. They may either open another business alone or in partnership with others (in at least three known cases this has been a driving school) catering to Portuguese immigrants. This doubling of activities is illustrated by an immigrant from mainland Portugal:

> In 1970 a friend of mine working at another agency wanted to open up one of his own and become so good as to run the others out. I decided to go into partnership with him. After a few months he became tired of it. I decided to keep it. I enjoy the work, but also it serves my purpose. It is not really what I want to do, but it helps me to establish contacts. I work for a real estate agent in the afternoons but in a week I will be getting my broker's license. Then I want to set up my own business in real estate.

Another agent in the late 1960s began a Portuguese television show, which continues to be popular. Guests on the show include representatives from various Canadian government institutions or knowledgeable individuals from the Portuguese Canadian community itself. Discussion focuses on problems of adjustment and integration. Half the show is devoted to documentary travelogues of Portugal. Throughout the hour the name of the travel agency slips periodically across the bottom of the screen. The link with the homeland is emphasized, information about the new nation of which the immigrant is now a part is filtered down, and the economic position of the agent is enhanced. The roles of patron and broker are combined and reinforced, and ethnic identification is maintained through the television show.

Other Ethnic Entrepreneurs

The history of the travel agents' success is the history of many other successful entrepreneurs—bakers, watchmakers, restaurant owners, photographers, tailors, and barbers, all of whom cater to Portuguese tastes. Clustered together near the Kensington Market, they focus identification for the Portuguese people and establish an area with which the Portuguese can be identified by other Canadians.[12] The Portuguese who live within the city limits are not the only ones who shop in Kensington. Portuguese living in suburban areas know of and identify with Augusta Street. They frequently travel half an hour to do their shopping and to meet friends in the area.

Occasionally these new proprietors, like the travel agents, build up a clientele by providing one kind of service, which they then expand into more serious entrepreneurial endeavors. For example, during the month of June 1971, a takeout chicken (*frango no espeto*) store opened in the heart of Kensington. I discovered later that the owner is also self-employed in bringing Portuguese entertainers to the Toronto community; for the past three years he had organized a Miss Portugal of Canada contest. Tickets for these events are sold in his new store and at other stores in the area. When he books an act, he travels with it to communities of Portuguese immigrants throughout North America. Since he began in 1965, at least two other entrepreneurs have become involved in capitalizing on ethnicity. Through his takeout chicken business he can extend his range of contacts and his clientele in the face of increasing competition. His connections with Portuguese entertainers make him a special kind of broker with the Portuguese nation. Furthermore, the fact that he travels throughout North America to other communities of Portuguese immigrants makes the Portuguese aware of their fellow countrymen in other areas, thereby reinforcing the idea of a Portuguese "community," as well as Portuguese ethnicity.

A second example of an ethnic entrepreneur is the bookstore owner who was cofounder and, at the time of my fieldwork, vice president of the First Portuguese-Canadian Club. Most of the travel agents are members of this club and many have, at one time, been its president. The primary activities of the club are the promotion of a local soccer team and the operation of a Portuguese language school. Tickets for the soccer games are sold primarily at the bookstore, which is located near the clubhouse in the market area. On Sunday mornings soccer games from Portugal are broadcast over a shortwave radio owned by the proprietor of the bookstore, and as many as 100 men gather on the street in front of the store every week to hear the game. Because of its popularity in Portugal, soccer has become an ethnic symbol around which the Portuguese can rally.

Besides his involvement in soccer, the bookstore proprietor also provides books for the club's Portuguese language school. A few years ago the owner of this store and the owner of the only other Portuguese bookstore in Toronto were battling, each accusing the other of using the club to promote his own business. In short, the involvement of the bookstore owners and the travel agents in the First Portuguese-Canadian Club offers support for Parkin's thesis (1969a) that economic and entrepreneurial interests motivate individuals to seek positions of leadership in ethnic associations. The ethnic entrepreneurs described so far use their membership and offices in the Portuguese-Canadian Club (and use the activities the club sponsors) to further their own political and economic interests. One of my informants, the owner of a Portuguese bakery, admitted that he belongs to some of the Portuguese clubs and organizations because it is good for business, "especially when they put on *festas* for which they require Portuguese delicacies." However, no matter what their motives, their support of the club and its activities promotes ethnic distinctiveness.

The editors of the three Portuguese-language newspapers are also new proprietors and ethnic entrepreneurs. They work through the institution of the ethnic press, and therefore with symbols of ethnicity, to establish their roles as patrons and brokers and, as a result, gain firm economic footing in the Portuguese community. The first Portuguese paper began publishing in 1963. At that time it contained primarily news from Portugal, but gradually Canadian news (particularly from the Portuguese-Canadian communities) has taken over and now makes up about 75 percent of each issue. These newspapers compete with each other for financial support and subscribers. In 1971 a dispute between a priest (for whom one of the papers, which he helps to finance, is a mouthpiece) and the editor of another paper was carried out in print. This internecine battle remained a subject of conversation and gossip more than a year after it began. At the time, people bought the papers with great interest so they could keep up with the exchange of invective. The publisher of the third paper attempted to remain uninvolved but, as he reported, was ultimately "forced into it by the state of fierce competition within the community." He summarized the conflict: "Anywhere where business is involved there is competition. It is the same with the papers. They fight each other. The result is that no one can be better. No one can come out on top." This fight between the newspapers is important not only because it demonstrates the competition among ethnic entrepreneurs but also because, as a subject of gossip, it enables people to identify themselves as part of an "in-group." Gluckman (1968) has argued that gossip and scandal maintain the unity, morals, and values of social groups. The right to gossip marks off one group from another.[13]

Thus, like the travel agents, the newspaper editors are entrepreneurs employing symbols of ethnic identity and are establishing themselves as brokers to stabilize their own positions. From their standing among Portuguese immigrants in Toronto, they mediate the boundaries between both the Portuguese nation and the Canadian nation, in terms of the material they print. The newspaper itself becomes a symbol of Portuguese identity.

The Portuguese parish priests are ethnic entrepreneurs not only in their activities outside the church but in their clerical roles, as well.[14] The city of Toronto has three Portuguese parishes, and the priests compete to build up a clientele of parishioners. More people means more money, more power, more prestige. As one recent immigrant commented, "The church is very strong here. The priests are leaders of a sort. The people do everything the priest says. If he says dump your pockets, they will. The church is very rich here."

Like the travel agent, the priest is a broker between the Portuguese community and the larger Canadian society. In Canadian society he is looked upon as a Portuguese leader. One priest was approached by municipal officials to take charge of the Portuguese booth for Caravan, an annual citywide international fair. Another permitted local politicians to speak at the opening festivities of the annual feast of Nosso Senhor da Pedra. In the Portuguese community, each church has a parish center, where social services and advice are available. Competition between the parishes is most obvious in the organization of traditional processions. Each parish, encouraged by its priest, tries to top the others. In some cases immigrants from communities in the United States are invited to attend. Such contacts are the mark of a powerful patron with a wealth of resources at his command.

In short, an analysis of the travel agencies, the church, the press, and other ethnic businesses from the perspective of the immigrant presents a more complicated picture than what might be revealed simply by identifying these institutions as physical markers of an ethnic group. The ethnic entrepreneurs I have described, who are themselves immigrants, employ ethnic symbols to establish and secure their own prestige and their political and economic power. Their combined roles of patron and broker create and sustain an ethnic boundary between the Portuguese immigrants in Toronto and other groups in Canadian society. This boundary can exist whether or not the Portuguese act as a corporate group or live in geographic isolation.

Conclusion

The literature on patronage and brokerage focuses on the ways in which the gap between "moderns" and "traditionals" is narrowed by the roles that mediate these two systems. I have argued here that these two concepts can be useful in the study of immigrants in urban settings. Mediation occurs not only when there are visible physical boundaries between a little community and the larger community or society (for example, when a rural village establishes contacts with an urban center), but also when such boundaries are not immediately apparent (that is, they do not circumscribe a "group") or are defined in a completely different way. This latter case describes the situation of migrants and immigrants to the city and the persistence of an ethnic boundary between these newcomers and others. In discussions of the adjustment of these immigrants to a new society, the concepts of patron and broker, as they have been used here, are particularly apposite. The ethnic entrepreneur, acting as a broker, transmits the values of the larger society (Paine, 1971b) to the newcomers and expresses concern and interest in the question of their integration. Through patronage, on the other hand, he furthers his own goals by his ability to dispense favors to the immigrants. His values or goals "cannot necessarily be predicted from those of either of these groups [between which he stands], but can be achieved by the actor through the manipulation of the goals, the resources, and restrictions of both groups" (Paine, 1971b, 99). Ethnicity is partially sustained in urban areas as a good business venture.

Silverman (1965) has suggested that when alternative links become available, mediators (as a group) lose their exclusive roles as gatekeepers and therefore cease to be mediators. In the early 1970s Portuguese immigration to Canada was occurring at an average rate of 8,500 per year. This stimulated the maintenance of the brokerage roles described above. In the future, particularly with the maturation of the second and third generations and the possible slowing of immigration, ethnic entrepreneurs may have to look elsewhere for the clientele needed to sustain their positions. The preceding analysis demonstrates that they are capable of such a shift and suggests that emphasis will be placed less upon new immigrants and increasingly upon a more general sense of "Portugueseness." The political arena, in which the Portuguese were unrepresented in the 1970s, is a focus for the patron-broker; his skills can be turned toward mobilizing ethnicity. The relationship between the immigrants and the national society will, in this case, be slowly altered, and the boundary that distinguishes the Portuguese from others in the society will actually circumscribe a "group," organized collectively to defend its political and ethnic interests.

Notes

This chapter was originally published in *Ethnic Encounters: Identities and Contexts*, eds. George L. Hicks and Philip E. Leis (Belmont, Calif.: Wadsworth, 1977). It is published here with minor changes.

1. The fieldwork on which this paper is based was financed by the department of anthropology, Brown University. It was part of a 1972 summer training program under the direction of Professor Philip Leis.

2. Breton (1964) uses the term *social entrepreneur* to refer to the individual who tries to organize something for immigrants, seeing in it an opportunity for himself. Although Breton does not develop this concept as a central theme of his article, he does suggest that the social entrepreneur strengthens ethnic identity to maintain a large potential public.

3. See Parkin (1969b). Cronin's criticism (1970, 10–11) of this approach is particularly forceful.

4. Crissman elucidates this distinction: "Whether a given ethnic community is a corporate group, a group, or a quasigroup is a matter of empirical verification. The fact that all ethnic communities are, in addition, categories based on ethnic criteria is important because it provides the basis for stereotyped treatment of members by outsiders. In so far as identification with the community is consciously held by the members it is a quasigroup. When this identification is acknowledged and acted upon the community is a group. The community is a corporate group if it endures over time despite changes in membership, has internal organization and leadership, and its members exercise rights and have duties as members in respect to different members. The same ethnic community can be a quasigroup, a group, or a corporate group and in respect to any particular member it can change its character with time" (Crissman 1967, 188).

5. My translation.

6. Most of the immigrants from the Azores come from the largest island, São Miguel. The Portuguese community in the town of Hull, Ontario, is settled primarily by immigrants from one village in São Miguel. Certain patterns of Portuguese immigration (in terms of place of destination) can be discerned. Unlike the cities of Providence, R.I., and New Bedford, Mass., Toronto has no Cape Verdeans. Those people in Toronto who originate from the islands of Madeira have generally come after spending several years in South America (Venezuela and Brazil). Canada is often a second stopping place. For example, in 1970, 8,700 Portuguese citizens registered with the Department of Immigration; 35 came from Bermuda, 60 from Brazil, 32 from Great Britain, 19 from China, 506 from France, 33 from Germany, 10 from the Netherlands, 16 from the United States, and 9 from the West Indies. Although people from the Azorean islands of Terceira, Faial, and Graçiosa can be found in Toronto, I was told that emigrants from these islands are found in greater numbers in the Portuguese communities of California.

7. In the early 1970s, about 52,000 Portuguese resided in metropolitan Toronto and about 25,000 more in surrounding towns of Ontario.

8. The Kensington Market was originally established in 1905 as a Jewish market. In the 1940s (as these first Jews slowly moved out), Italians, Hungarians, Ukrainians, and a new group of Rumanian Jews moved in. Gradually this second wave of immigrants acquired more wealth and abandoned the area as well, leaving a shuttered synagogue and only a few unsold shops and delicatessens (many now employing Portuguese people) behind. They were replaced by increasing numbers of Portuguese immigrants. Most recently some Chinese families, displaced from the downtown area by the new city hall, have moved to the market area along with a few West Indians and East Indians.

9. Canada's sponsorship program makes it possible for unskilled laborers to enter the country. Any member of a family can sponsor the immigration of other members of his family to Canada. He is responsible for them for one year. One couple, during twenty years, sponsored her twelve siblings and his four, together with their spouses and families.

10. Boissevain (1965, 122) comments on the village priests of Malta: "The patronage of the parish priest has traditionally been important. Not only are all villagers his spiritual clients but he is also a source of charity and assistance in many fields. He serves his parishioners individually in the capacity of legal adviser, character reference, and often also as letter-writer and banker. He frequently argues their claims against the government. He also represents the interest of the community at large, and attempts, often successfully, to obtain improved public amenities such as new roads and street lighting."

11. Compare also Boissevain (1965), Geertz (1960), Heath (1973), Kenny (1960), and Pitt-Rivers (1954).

12. Discussing the fact that a substantial portion of a cultural group is employed in serving the wants of that group, the report of Canada's Royal Commission on Bilingualism and Biculturalism, *The Cultural Contribution of Other Ethnic Groups* (1970), points out that "ethnic enterprises . . . require a sufficiently large group to serve in order to survive, but they do not necessarily require residential concentration, as long as the business and institutional centre of the group is known and accessible."

13. For an alternative view, see the responses of Paine (1967) and Gluckman (1968). See also Bailey (1971b) on the importance of gossip in European peasant communities in general.

14. Two of the Portuguese priests have their own radio programs.

IV

GENDER AND MIGRATION

Despite E. G. Ravenstein's (1885) claim more than a century ago that women dominated short-distance population movements, women were not a focus of migration studies until quite recently. As chapter 8 notes, if women were considered at all in studies of migration, it was generally as dependents and passive followers of the initiating male migrant, their movement often encompassed under the category of family reunification. Alternatively, women were the ones who waited in the countryside, assuming many of the responsibilities that once had been in the hands of men (Levine 1966). Chapter 7 takes up this latter issue by examining the impact of extensive male emigration on the lives of women left behind, looking particularly at household structure and the way women "live" in families.

Portugal is a country with a deep-rooted history of migrating men and waiting women (Brettell 1986). Nunes (2000, 29) reports that, in the passport registers of the 1790s, of 146 passports issued to Rio de Janeiro, only 34 were to women. The men who left were often young and unmarried. One result of this skewed migration pattern of single men was that Portuguese daughters were often favored with the third share of parental property, the share that could be allocated at the discretion of parents before the rest of the property was divided equally among all offspring. In exchange for this special bequest it was often a daughter who married into her parents' household, lived with them, and took care of them in their old age. Such bequests often created multigeneration households or compounds of kin-related households based on female kinship ties. These kinship ties were important, because in the absence of men it was groups of women who farmed the fields together and who shared in the responsibilities of raising children. If the village square and village café were the arenas for social interaction among men, the neighboring households of female kin provided women with their social arena. This domestic social arena was often populated by so-called "widows of the living" (*viuvas dos vivos*) who put on the black garb of a widow on the day their husbands emigrated and kept it on until he returned, if he returned.

The core of chapter 7 presents data drawn from the historical records from one Portuguese village in the period between 1850 and 1920, when emigration to Brazil was at its height. Engel (1986) offers another historical example, that of nineteenth-century Russia. When men left the villages of Kostroma province for Russian cities, women took over complete responsibility for agricultural work and moved in to live with in-laws. When the men returned to the village, Engel writes, "they often lived there like guests, doing no work around the house or yard" (p. 262). Not only did the extent of male migration help to keep female migration low, it also limited it almost entirely to "nonmarriageable" women. Engel argues that women had more work to do, but their lives were also freer, because they had fewer children, were more self-reliant, and assumed the places of their husbands on the village assembly.

The Russian and Portuguese cases suggest a deep past to a gendered division of labor that spanned the divide between city and country or even nation and nation. An additional example is offered by Nelson writing about Kenya. "The agricultural peoples of central and western Kenya . . . have historically manifested gender power systems with certain shared characteristics. The gender division of labour was such that women were farmers, childcarers, and reproducers, while men were long-distance traders, politicians, and religious specialists." Nelson then notes that the colonial era intensified these patterns "resulting in an established economic pattern of male labour migration and female farm management" (1992, 112). Many men left their communities in order to earn the cash to pay for the ever-increasing taxes levied on them by the British. "In the period of 1902–23, the number of male Africans in the migrant wage-earning economy rose from 5,000 to 120,000. . . . Leys (1975, 31) estimated that 50 percent of the men of the two largest groups in Kenya (the Gikuyu and the Luo) were working away from home. This number grew slowly throughout the 1930s, despite the depression. All workers, even domestic workers, were men" (Nelson 1992, 117). Nelson acknowledges that the literature of the colonial period in Kenya reveals little about the impact of male out-migration on the lives of women. While it is clear, she argues, that their workload intensified, it is not clear whether the absence of husbands yielded greater social power. Certainly she suggests that, although women did become effective farm managers, they were also transformed from independent cultivators to dependent laborers in the subsistence zone.

Chapter 7 and the other work I have discussed here offer a solid historical foundation to more contemporary work on the impact of migration on the gendered division of labor between sending and receiving societies. Scholars are beginning to suggest that this historical perspective is essential to a broader understanding of population movements within or across boundaries that may or may not have defined nation-states. A comparative approach to migration must account not only for spatial similarities and differences but also for temporal similarities and differences.

The pattern of leaving women in charge of the house and fields persisted in Portugal into the post–World War II period and the early phase of migrations to northern Europe, particularly France. It is equally characteristic of other migration streams around the world. For example, Hammam (1986, 171) estimates that in the mid-1980s households that were, de facto, headed by women represented 16 percent of all households in the Middle East and North Africa, and Petra Weyland describes a village in Egypt where the feminization of agriculture has become an aspect of everyday life. She cites the comments of a fifty-year-old male peasant:

> The roles of women in agriculture are no longer the same as in the 1960s, when women restricted themselves to the house and to bringing up children. Since the inhabitants of the village are leaving for the Arab States, the woman carries the full responsibility for the house, the field, and she has to look after the family affairs inside and outside the house. She also is responsible for anything concerning agriculture—for example, contacts with the cooperative, the bank, or with the daily wage laborers, and among the most important characteristics is that she works in the field. (Weyland 1993, 182)

How resonant this is of the Portuguese case of a century earlier!

When anthropologists have turned their attention to the women left behind in these more contemporary migration streams, they have asked whether the migration of men is disempowering or empowering to women, and whether changes in gender roles bring changes in gender ideology and gender hierarchies in the sending society (Curry-Rodriguez 1988; Grimes 1998; Hondagneu-Sotelo 1992). Research results are mixed. Writing about the impact of the absence of men on women in towns in the province of Guanacasteco in Costa Rica, Chant (1992, 63) notes that women were accorded "greater decision-making power and more personal freedom than they might otherwise have, even if they remain subject to the influence of husbands when they are away." But she also claims that there is no great change in the division of productive and reproductive roles; men are the chief breadwinners, while women keep the households and material assets intact. When men migrate, women become de facto heads of households and are required to deal with short-term crises. Their domestic chores are reduced because they do not need to cater to a husband on a daily basis and they are not constantly pregnant. They can spend more time with extended kin, something a present husband might not allow. But, Chant cautions, if the separation is long, mistrust can enter a relationship, or a woman may be required to seek a job to support her household needs. Based on her research on the impact of seasonal male migration on the lives of Mafa women of the Cameroons who remain behind, Schaafsma (2000, 44–45) offers a complicated argument for the emergence of a new type of complementary gender balance. In the absence of men, the workload of women increases as they become "the principal defenders of their husbands' home interests," and men's status is therefore "contingent on the way their wives safeguard their compound." But equally, women's status within the community becomes more dependent on their husbands, because it is the money and clothing that their husbands send to them that earns them respect.

Some researchers have shown that migrating men tend to leave other male relatives in charge of their households, resulting therefore in little change in the power or authority of women (Levine 1979; Ross and Weisner 1977; Weyland 1993). Nelson (1992, 123) suggests that in Africa this pattern is most characteristic of groups like the Luo/Luyia, who have sustained their strong patrilineages. But she also cautions that even in a single place there is enormous variation in household arrangements, some of it linked to the level of employment of the husband, the distance between the rural home and the place of the husband's employment, and the amount of land at the family's disposal. Similarly some newly married young men among the Mafa of the Cameroon defer setting up an independent household compound and instead leave their wives in the households and under the authority of their parents or brothers (Schaafsma 2000, 45).

Still another body of research has tended to emphasize that any gains that women have in the absence of their husbands is temporary at best and that when men return they reassume the roles they had prior to departure. This is what Sandra Bever (1999) argues in a study that focuses on two villages in the Yucatan Peninsula that have been affected by male out-migration to Cancun. Women assume the responsibilities for household decisions in the absence of men and yield them when the men return. She suggests that if there are changes in gender roles, they are not necessarily accompanied by changes in gender ideology. Conversely,

Peggy Levitt has argued, based on her research in sending communities in the Dominican Republic, that the "social remittances" that flow back ("the ideas, behaviors, and social capital that flow from receiving to sending communities" [Levitt 2001a, 11; see also Levitt 1998b]) encourage women to experiment with new gender roles and new political ideas.[1] "The Miraflorena woman who tries to establish a more equitable relationship with her husband does so not only because Dominican women in general are gaining more independence, but because she is inspired by the kind of marriage her migrant sister has with her husband" (Levitt 2001a, 14).

Finally, some studies suggest that in certain instances women see increasing burdens, as they have to take over productive activities in addition to their reproductive activities (the rural equivalent of the double day, identified among urban women in the sociological literature). Hammam describes modifications in property relations in rural areas of the Middle East that result from male out-migration. These induce changes in the division of labor within the household. "Depending on the amount of remittances a family or household receives, on its regularity, and its investment, the out-migration of males has relieved some women of the necessity to work either as family producers and/or for a wage at the same time that it compels others to assume increased work loads. Thus, acquisition of land or expansion of landholdings may accentuate dependence on family labor, or it may increase the options of the household: to rent out the land and/or to hire day laborers. . . . In some areas of Upper Egypt, for instance, where male out-migration, mainly to Kuwait, is high . . . labor scarcity and the concomitant rise in the price of hired labor has accentuated dependence on the unpaid family labor for women and children" (Hammam 1986, 169–170).

In its most extreme form these increased responsibilities placed on the shoulders of women can result in extreme psychosocial distress, something that a student of mine, Barbara Lomonoco, found in her study of the women left behind on the island of Thyrrisia, off the coast of Santorini in Greece (Lomonaco 1993). Women feel overburdened by their responsibilities and fearful that their husbands will abandon them. Levine (1979) documented similar sentiments among the Gusii in Kenya. In addition, while some studies argue that the economic remittances sent back by migrant husbands make life easier for the women left behind, other research suggests that this in fact causes women to become even more dependent on their husbands, relying on the cash sent back rather than their own productivity (Griffith 1985).

All these more contemporary studies of women left behind can shed further light on research such as mine in Portugal, which examines the problem in historical populations. But it is equally significant to notice how deeply rooted the international division of labor really is. The issues that these contemporary researchers are looking at were characteristic of Portuguese and Russian households more than century ago. It is also true that more than a century ago there were unmarried Portuguese women who themselves migrated, sometimes to the local provincial town or to the capital city of Lisbon to work in domestic service for an upper-middle-class or elite household, and other times to join a father, brother or, if they were married, a husband who had established himself in Brazil. But these women were never the majority of migrants. This is equally true of other international migration streams.

In the world of the late twentieth and early twenty-first centuries, migration patterns have changed. Not only are women often the first to migrate (sometimes they receive the initial job contract), but in some international migration streams they outnumber men. This is the case among Caribbean immigrants to the United States (Donato 1992; Ho 1993; Momsen 1992; United Nations 1995) and Filipino immigrants in several parts of the world (Chang 1997; Constable 1997, 1999; Groves and Chang 1999; Ong and Azores 1994; Tyner 1999). The Philippines, according to Choy (2000, 113) "has become the world's largest exporter of nurses, with significant numbers of Filipino nurses working in the Middle East, Germany, and Canada, as well as the United States." The increasing numbers of women involved in both internal and international population flows has recently led some scholars to speak of the feminization of migration. Indeed, in their book *The Age of Migration* (1993), Stephen Castles and Mark Miller describe this process as one of the four tendencies characterizing migration in the twentieth century, along with the globalization of migration, the acceleration of migration, and the differentiation of migration (into various types within any one flow). These female migrants have become domestic workers in households as far afield as Washington, D.C., Los Angeles, Italy, Kuwait, and Malaysia (Chang 2000; Chin 1997; Hondagneu-Sotelo 2001; Neale and Neale 1987; O'Neill 2001; Parreñas 2001; Repak 1995; Sanjek and Colen 1990; Truong 2000). They have become factory workers on the global assembly lines located along the United States–Mexican border and throughout Asia and Southeast Asia—that is, working for multinational industries that are especially dependent on a mobile female labor force (Fernandez-Kelly 1983; Wolf 1990). They have become garment workers in the gateway cities of the United States (Fernandez-Kelly 1990; Louie 2001). And migrant women, some of them very young, have become prostitutes in the cities of both the developed and developing world, part of the growth of the global sex industry (Kempadoo and Doezema 1998; Pettman 1996; Psimmenos 2000; Simon 2000).[2]

The literature on women immigrants has grown rapidly since the 1980s (Willis and Yeoh 2000; Kelson and DeLaet 1999), particularly in the disciplines of history (Friedman-Kasaba 1996; Gabaccia 1994; Weinberg 1992), sociology (Anthias and Lazaridis 2000; Pedraza 1991; Simon 1992; Kofman 1999), and anthropology (Brettell and deBerjeois 1992; Knörr and Meier 2000; Pessar 1999a, 1999b). Theoretically, immigration scholars from this range of disciplines have shown that gender is important in the decision to migrate (when, where, and who) as well as in the process of settlement in the receiving society. It is apparent that, while some women still move as dependents (as wives, daughters, mothers), there are many who are labor migrants moving in search of economic opportunities that are sometimes distinct from those for men (Pedraza 1991).

While early research tended to emphasize a household strategy of migration involving consensus between husband and wife about male departure, recent research (Hondagneu-Sotelo 1994) has presented a more complex picture. In some cases women are left out of the decision-making process precisely because of gendered hierarchies of power in the home community. Whether migration is an individual or a household decision is clearly an empirical question that varies from one context to another and requires an ethnographic knowledge of gender roles and relations in the sending society. In Portugal the departure of men was something that both husband and wife expected. It has been a recognized stage in the male life course, just as working in the fields was expected of women both before and after marriage (Brettell 2002b). In northern Portuguese rural households, husbands and wives consider themselves as a team, as *os donos da casa* (the bosses of the household) and hence share decisions and responsibilities (Pina-Cabral 1986).

The importance of understanding gender relations in the sending society in order to understand the different experiences of men and women as immigrants is apparent in Mary Beth Mills's research on rural-urban migration in Thailand (Mills 1997, 1998). Both young men and young women leave their homes in Thai villages in search of the excitement of urban life, the independence of work in the export-oriented manufacturing zones of Bangkok, and a *thansamay*, or up-to-date self identity. But gender hierarchies and gendered sexual ideologies shape the experience of young men and women differently. A son's departure is consistent with norms of masculine behavior, while it is counter to expectations for a daughter. If they do migrate, daughters are expected to remit more to their parents than are sons; this action will define them as "good daughters." Of significance in this case, and it is one that is similar to northern Portugal, is the matrilocal residence preferences that tie more young women to the parental home after marriage.

In Thailand, as in northern Portugal, daughters often inherit more land than sons, something I note in chapter 7.

In Thailand, migration is more risky for daughters, while for sons the expectation is that they will engage in a range of sexual experiences for which they need not assume much responsibility. Daughters must work to uphold their reputations, especially in the context of the widely lucrative and significant sex trade in Bangkok. Being a migrant can stigmatize a woman. Stalker (2000, 71–72) cites a report from an export-processing zone near the airport in Sri Lanka that found that "women's chances of marriage were damaged because women who went on their own to the city were deemed sexually promiscuous." Virginia, whose story opens chapter 8, faced similar stigma. It was equally true of Ricardina, a Portuguese woman about whom I wrote in my book *We Have Already Cried Many Tears*. Ricardina spent several years in the provincial town near her village, working as a domestic servant. When she returned to her village, young men gossiped about her, suggesting that she had lost her virginity while she was away. It was this gossip and her loss of reputation that drove her to leave for France.

Anthropologists have been at the forefront in theorizing about the significance of gendered migration (Brettell and deBerjeois 1992; Buijs 1996; Pessar 1995, 1999b; Pessar and Mahler 2001). Much of their research has focused on the role and experiences of men and women in migration and on the changes that occur in gender and kin relations as a result of migration (Chai 1987a, 1987b; Eastmond 1996; Goodson-Lawes 1993; Holtzman 2000; Kibria 1993; Pessar 1984, 1999b; Grasmuck and Pessar 1991). This work can be situated in relation to analytical models that are at the heart of feminist anthropology. One is the domestic-public model, which explores the relative status of men and women in relation to different spheres of activity; the other is the model emerging from a Marxist-feminist position, which addresses the interrelationship between production and reproduction. Some of the questions that anthropologists address are: whether wage earning serves to enhance the power and status of immigrant women within their households; whether greater sharing of household activities emerges as a result of the work obligations of women; how changes in employment, family structure, and lifestyle affect women's public activities as well as their own assessments of their well-being; and how gender ideologies play out for the second generation (Bhachu 1988; Chavira-Prado 1992; Das Gupta 1997; Giles 2002; Groves and Chang 1999; Hirsch 1999; Ui 1991).

The research on the impact of immigrant women's employment on the division of labor and gender relations in the immigrant household has yielded mixed results. In some cases scholars have documented greater independence for women and more equity in the family, something that is certainly suggested in the research on Portuguese immigrant families that I discuss in chapter 8. By contrast, other scholars have argued that even when immigrant women earn more than their spouses do, this does not necessarily result in greater decision-making power within the household or greater autonomy outside it. For example, in her work on Central American immigrant families in California, Menjívar (1999) describes a significant cultural difference between indigenous households, where traditional gender relations were relatively egalitarian, and *mestizo/ladino* (those of mixed or European (nonindigenous) background) households, where gender relations were inegalitarian. In the immigrant context, indigenous men welcome the extra earnings of their wives, while *mestizo/ladino* men feel threatened by it.

Menjívar further documents the differential exposure of immigrant men and women to gender relations in the United States through their employment, something I also noted among Portuguese families in France (Brettell 1995). Women who are employed in domestic service have greater access to host society families than do their husbands, who tend to work in occupational niches with other immigrant men. The women see more sharing of domestic responsibilities, and they try, sometimes successfully and sometimes not, to introduce a similar pattern into their own families.[3] In other words, changes in gender relations within immigrant families may be the result of processes other than "simply . . . earning a wage" (Menjívar 1999, 602), and while the division of labor and patterns of household decision-making may change, gender ideology or gender role constructs may remain unchanged. In some cases, and Kibria's work on Vietnamese families offers a good example, women walk "an ideological tightrope—struggling to take advantage of their new resources but also to protect the structure and sanctity of the traditional family system" (1993, 109).

The lesson of all this research, including my work on the Portuguese, is that the cultural context must be considered: What is the nature of the "traditional family system" for one group in comparison with another? In Portugal a long history of spousal separation had already created a family system that accorded domestic power to women, and thus they faced less of an ideological tightrope in the immigrant context. Hondagneu-Sotelo (1992) has also identified lengthy spousal separation as the cause of altered patterns of patriarchal authority and traditional gendered household division of labor among Mexican families, resulting in more egalitarian conjugal relations upon settlement in United States.

Whether immigration actually improves the lives of women also varies from one group to another. Writing about Puerto Rican women,

Alicea (1997, 601) concludes that "immigrant women, while gaining some forms of freedom because of their paid work, still have the primary responsibility for the subsistence work that sustains their families and communities. Thus, women must work the double shift of paid work and household work. Furthermore, with the decline of traditionally male manufacturing and service sector jobs, some immigrant women find themselves working more steadily and earning more money than their husbands. Men who feel that their status and identity as primary wage earners and providers are threatened because of their wives' paid work will at times be abusive toward their spouses." The ambivalence that women themselves feel about being an immigrant is perhaps best captured by the comment made by a *ladina* Guatemalan to Cecilia Menjívar: "Here we are equal, we both work [for an income] so we both have to do stuff at home, there's no way around it. But I can't really say that it's better here or there, because there I didn't work [outside the home] this much. Here I earn more, but there I worked less" (1999, 609)

While Menjívar argues persuasively that differences in ethnic background lead to different outcomes where changes in gender relations are concerned, Espiritu (1999) suggests that class background should equally be considered. Among Asian immigrants she documents variations for three different occupational categories: salaried professionals, self-employed entrepreneurs, and wage laborers. Among professional families, the bulk of research shows a greater sharing of domestic responsibilities. But both men and women are confronted by racism in the workplace that puts undue stress on the family. This sometimes leads Asian professional women to "accept certain components of the traditional patriarchal system because they need their husbands' incomes and because they desire a strong and intact family—an important bastion of resistance to oppression" (p. 635). Women employed in the small-business sector make choices based on their exclusion from well-paying jobs in the general labor market. But whereas self-employed Asian men "benefit economically and socially from the unpaid or underpaid female labor, women bear the added burden of the double work day. . . . The ethnic economy is both a thriving center and a source of hardship and exploitation for Asian immigrant women" (p. 638). It is among wage laborers, Espiritu argues, that gender role reversals are most pronounced. Women often have greater employment opportunities and become the primary breadwinners. Yet here too women also work "to preserve the traditional family system—albeit in a tempered form—because they value the promise of male economic protection. Although migration may have equalized or reversed the economic resources of working-class men and women, women's earnings continue to be too meager to sustain their economic independence from men" (p. 642).

Yet another perspective that complicates the picture is offered by Kurien (1999), who argues that, to understand gender relations within the Asian Indian community, analytical distinctions must be drawn between the household, the local ethnic community, and the pan-Indian umbrella organizations. Within the first two spheres, women are active and able "to reinterpret the patriarchal images more in their favor and construct a model of gender that emphasizes the importance of male responsibilities." By contrast, the pan-Indian umbrella organizations are dominated by wealthy Indian males. "Few women obtain leadership positions in such organizations. Faced with the pressures of racism and assimilation, Indian immigrants construct an 'exemplary public face' to locate themselves as a 'model minority' group. Gender and class are central to this construction. . . . The Hindu Indian woman is constructed as a virtuous and self-sacrificing homemaker, enabling the professional success of her husband and the academic achievements of her children through her unselfish actions on their behalf (p. 650). Kurien distinguishes between the informal roles of women as ethnic architects in the household and community spheres and the formal and more public roles of men in the pan-Indian organizations. This is an important analytical distinction within feminist anthropology itself, first formulated by Rogers (1975). It clearly helps to illuminate what is going on in this particular community.

Another approach that takes into account this balance between the domestic and the public spheres is found in Hirsch's work on Mexican immigrants in Atlanta. Hirsch writes about relative uses of space among Mexican immigrants in Atlanta. "Mexican men do not 'own' the street in Atlanta; they are well aware they are just visiting. Women's widespread participation in the formal labor market in Atlanta further neutralizes the street's gendered aspects. Going to and from work gives women as much justification as men to be outside. Women use the ideology of family progress . . . to justify their embrace of other previously masculine privileges, such as driving and owning a car. . . . For migrant women, mobility is power" (Hirsch 1999, 1378). Hirsch describes other changes as well—priests have less control over family life, especially in relation to contraception, and men cannot hit their wives without expecting government interference. I too noted a change in how domestic and public spaces were used among Portuguese immigrant families in Paris. As chapter 8 notes, Portuguese immigrant couples commented that they did more together, because in Paris there was no equivalent to the village square, where Portuguese men could gather together and "hang out." Kurien (1999, 657) records a similar pattern among Asian-Indians: "In India, men and women generally have separate social networks and thus receive most of their social support from members of their own sex. The loss of this social network forces Indian immigrant couples to depend much more on each other for companionship and emotional intimacy than they would have in India." Kurien, like Hirsch, also comments on the greater independence and spatial mobility of Indian women in the United States by comparison with India. But while all these are examples of the emergence of more companionship for immigrant couples, there are equally examples of the maintenance of separation and the isolation of immigrant women, as, for example, among Palestinians in Berlin (Abdulrahim 1996) and Bangladeshis in Britain (Summerfield 1996). These differences are evidence of how important it is to consider closely the gender ideology of the sending society and the economic and social activities in the receiving society in order to fully understand if and how gender relations change.

The question of distinct social networks among immigrant men and women in local, national, and transnational contexts is something that has captured the attention of other ethnographers (Alicea 1997; Hagan 1998; Hondagenu-Sotelo 1994; Menjívar 2000; O'Connor 1990). So have varying attitudes between men and women toward return to the home country, something I discuss briefly in chapter 8. I also discuss some aspects of Portuguese immigrant women's involvement in political activities and their interactions with other groups, something that is perhaps not as well developed in the literature as it should be (see, however, Groves and Chang 1999; Louie 2001; Ong 1987; Salzinger 1991; Ui 1991). Some of this research on women's political action is informed by broader thinking within feminist anthropology on formal and informal strategies of resistance that is itself influenced by the work of James Scott and by Anthony Gidden's theory of agency (Giddens 1984; Scott 1985; see also Abu-Lughod 1990; Moore 1994; Ortner 1995). It also challenges widely accepted notions that cultural constraints and a tight-knit ethnic enclave preclude immigrant women from engaging in political and leadership activities within and on behalf of their communities.

There is much to be learned from understanding how Portuguese women have interfaced with the migration process, whether as movers or as stayers. And, as this introduction has tried to suggest, there is much to be learned from a broad comparative perspective that situates one group in relation to a host of other groups.

Notes

1. Levitt moves us beyond the emphasis on economic ties and economic remittances about which many scholars, anthropologists and others, have written (Chevannes and Ricketts 1997; Guarnizo 1997a; Massey and Parrado 1994; Menjívar et al. 1998).

2. Lin writes about the Asian-run houses of prostitution in the Philadelphia area, which are full of young women from Thailand, Korea, and other countries of Asia and southeast Asia. "Most of the trafficked women in the United States come from Asia, Russia, central Europe, and Mexico. . . . In Europe, Albanian women have been kidnapped to work as prostitutes in Italy" (Lin 2000, 7). This pattern is not unique to cities in the developed world but also occurs within the developing world. According to a report released by the nongovernmental organization Action Aid Pakistan in 2001, 200,000 women and girls between the ages of twelve and thirty were trafficked from Bangladesh to Pakistan during the 1990s. Reference to this report can be found at www.irinnews.org/report.asp?ReportID= 5002&SelectRegion=Central_Asia.

3. However, Hagan (1998, 61) also observes that immigrant women who work "long and unpredictable hours in the confines of an employer's house" are isolated from coethnics and "uprooted from the social relations of exchange and reciprocity that characterize working-class urban families." For the case that she studied, Mayans from Guatemala living in Houston, she argues that in fact immigrant women become increasingly dependent on and controlled by their *patronas* (employers). By comparison with the men who live and work together, pool rides, and meet for soccer matches on weekends, women have weaker social networks.

7

Emigration and Household Structure in a Portuguese Parish, 1850–1920

During the late nineteenth and the early twentieth centuries, Portugal sent thousands of emigrants abroad, primarily to Brazil and to a lesser extent to Spain, on a seasonal or temporary basis. Between 1888, when slavery was abolished in Brazil, and 1929, the annual rate of emigration from Portugal was approximately 15,000. The most dramatic years of outflow were those immediately preceding World War I; 59,000 left in 1911, 87,000 in 1912, and 77,000 in 1913. These figures were not reached again until the late 1960s, when emigration to France was at its height (Brettell 1984, 1995). The bulk of this emigration originated in the northern half of the country, among the landless or small-scale landowning populations. It was primarily an emigration of men. Whether as fiancées waiting for their boyfriends to return from Brazil with money that would facilitate a marriage or as wives in the limbo status of "widows of the living" (the Portuguese expression is *viuvas dos vivos*), women carried on the life of the villages. The feminine character of the rural countryside of northern Portugal was something noted repeatedly by travelers to the region in the late nineteenth and early twentieth centuries. "To tramp behind the plough, to hoe the fields, and to perform all the ordinary tasks of the agricultural laborer. . . . Such are the normal duties of women here, for the men of the district, possessed with an unconquerable aversion for this form of labor, are well content to leave the soil to their wives and daughters while they, for their part, go out into the world and adopt the less strenuous callings of carpenters, masons, and waiters" (Koebel 1909, 230).

In more recent times, several ethnographers have noted the continuity of this tradition of women remaining behind while their sons and husbands emigrated (Callier 1966; Goldey 1981; Pina-Cabral 1984a; Wall 1984), although, with the post-1960 migrations to France, Portuguese women have entered into the migration process in numbers that surpass any previous generation (Brettell 1995).

The important economic role of women in northwestern Portuguese rural society was one of the factors that the French sociologist Paul Descamps (1935) cited in his characterization of this region as matriarchal. The other two factors he noted were the emphasis on succession through the female line and the frequent transmission of names, including nicknames, through the mother. Whereas the term *matriarchal is* not really appropriate, the matricentric characteristics that Descamps noted are indeed a fundamental aspect of the way of life in northwestern Portugal and are, to a large extent, the result of a longstanding regional tradition of male emigration.

Focusing in particular on the residence patterns of women over the life course, this chapter explores the impact of this predominantly male pattern of migration on the formation and structure of households in a parish in northwestern Portugal between 1850 and 1920. It will demonstrate the way in which patterns of coresidence and bonds of kinship manifest the matricentric bias in this region. Because there are neither census manuscripts nor population registers available, the household data are derived from a series of household lists (Róis da Desobriga) kept by the parish priest to keep track of Easter duties. These lists record all residents in the parish by household and by relationship to the first person listed in each household. Marital status is generally provided, and servants are listed as such. Beginning with the 1881 list, ages are also provided.[1] Where possible, these have been compared to parish register data. In addition, the *róis* contain notations of presence or absence in the parish at the time that the list was made. It is not fully clear how rigorous successive village priests were in recording these absences, and the *róis* are a once-a-year census. Thus the absences noted on them should be taken as an estimate of migration rather than as an accurate enumeration.

The Setting: The Parish of Santa Eulália de Lanheses

The parish of Santa Eulália de Lanheses is located on the Lima River in the northwestern province of Minho, fourteen kilometers from the Atlantic coast. Covering an area of approximately eleven square kilometers, the parish is divided into twenty-five residential hamlets (*lugares*) spread out over land that varies from wet marshlands by the river's edge to forested mountain plots. Before the turn of the century, much of this mountain acreage was communal property, but it is now divided up among parish families.

The province of Minho is the most densely settled region of Portugal and has been since the founding of the nation in the twelfth century. It is a region characterized by subsistence-oriented, polycultural, small-scale farming on plots of land averaging from one to three hectares in size. While most families own or rent some land, there is an important population of day laborers, who earn their livelihood working the lands of the larger landowners, including several ennobled and military families who owned substantial farms (*quintas*) in the parish over the course of its history. Men of the parish have also been involved in various artisan activities, many of these, such as that of stonemason (*pedreiro*), associated with the experience of emigration.

In 1864, according to the first national census of Portugal, Lanheses had a de facto or actual population of 1,207 individuals living in 243 households. By 1900 the actual population had declined to 1,029, although the number of households had increased to 270; and by 1920 there were 1,083 individuals in 269 households. These figures correspond roughly with those on the Easter rolls for the same or close years. That the village was affected by emigration to Brazil in the late nineteenth and early twentieth centuries is apparent not only in differences between the de facto and the de jure population figures included in the census but also in the sex ratios of the populations of both married and single men and women. In 1878 there were 67 single men per 100 single women and 90 married men per 100 married women; in 1890 corresponding ratios of single and married men per 100 women were 53 and 78; in 1900, 64 and 97; in 1911, 64 and 72; and in 1920, 66 and 80. The significance of the disproportions among the married population in particular will become apparent later in the discussion.

The parish of Santa Eulália de Lanheses was characterized in the late nineteenth and early twentieth centuries by late marriage ages for both men and women. In the 1850s the mean age at marriage was twenty-nine for men and twenty-eight for women; in the 1870s the mean was thirty-one for men and thirty for women. During the first decade of the twentieth century, men were marrying on average at twenty-eight and women at twenty-seven; and by the 1920s the corresponding figure for both men and women was twenty-six. As might be expected, given these mean ages at marriage, rates of permanent celibacy, especially for women, were also high. In the 1860s, 34 percent of women dying over fifty were single and 10 percent of men; in the 1900s, corresponding proportions were 34 percent women and 9 percent men; and in the 1920s they were 37 percent women and 4 percent men. Finally, ratios of illegitimacy in late nineteenth- and early twentieth-century Lanheses were also high. Illegitimate births represented 13 percent of all births in the 1860s and

1870s, and again in the 1900s and 1910s.[2] All these phenomena—late marriage, high illegitimacy, and female spinsterhood—are integral to an understanding of household structure.

Overall Household Composition: Temporal Changes and Normative Ideology

In several recent discussions of household and family structure in Portugal (Feijó and Nunes 1986; Rowland 1981, 1984, 1985), the northern half of the country is described as a region where complex households, and particularly the stem family (a household composed of a parental generation, one married offspring, and the grandchildren) predominate. Whereas it is certainly true that complex households are more common in the north than in the south, the simple dichotomous characterization by region obscures both intraregional variation and temporal flexibility. Callier-Boisvert (1968, 96), for example, notes a distinction by socioeconomic group within the northern region, suggesting that whereas patriarchal extended families are common among the middle- and large-scale property owners of the countryside and the urban middle classes, nuclear families are prevalent among the "popular sectors" of the city and the country. More recently, Nunes (1985, 1986) has noted some important variations in an area where subsistence-oriented agriculture is combined with market-oriented industry.

In addition to some awareness of distinctions by socioeconomic group, it is also important to question whether a high incidence of complex households in northwestern Portugal has any relationship to a rule or preference for the stem family form of household organization as it exists elsewhere in southern Europe. This is a region characterized by partible inheritance, and although a single heir was frequently favored with a third share that generally included the parental house, the designation of favored heir was more often a matter of choice than of any form of systematic primogeniture or ultimogeniture. In fact, gender is generally more important than birth order in the designation of any single individual as the recipient of the third share, and more commonly female offspring are chosen over male offspring. In testaments of the eighteenth and nineteenth centuries, the most frequently cited criterion for choosing the favored heir was the nurturance extended by a child to his or her parents. Notions of the necessity to preserve a family patrimony were rarely mentioned. Although Lanhesans today say that it is best to have at least one child at home, this child can be equally a spinster daughter as a married son or daughter.

Coincident with the notion that one child should stay at home, there is in this region a strong ideological preference for a separate nuclear family household. This preference is embodied in the often-quoted phrase *quem casa, quer casa* (whoever marries wants a house). Thus the major reason that a contemporary Portuguese emigrant gives for his departure is to earn money to build a house for himself and his family back in his native village. This preference for independent households and the way in which it motivated the emigration process is deeply embedded in the culture of northwestern Portugal. In the late nineteenth century the fanciful houses built by emigrants returned from Brazil gained the epithet of *casas brasileiras*. These *casas* were described by numerous Portuguese writers, among them novelist Camillo Castello Branco, who writes of "tiled extravaganzas with columns painted in green and walls with yellow bases and scarlet vertexes" (1966, 24). Another writer, Luíz de Magalhães, suggests that these houses "represented the necessity to shout, to publicize through unusual forms and bright and ridiculous colors, a vital energy which explains the fiat of the emigratory movement" (1886, 76).[3]

These descriptions could equally be applied to the houses that have cropped up throughout the north of Portugal during the past twenty years, houses that are referred to as *casas franceses* (houses of Portuguese emigrants in France) or *casas estilo maison* (houses in the *maison* style). Many of these new dwellings are covered in colorful tiles and fronted with complex wrought iron balconies. In the past twenty years, the construction of these emigrant houses has changed the face of northern rural Portugal and demonstrates the success with which recent emigrants have been able to achieve the ideal of a separate nuclear family household. But what of their fathers and grandfathers? To what extent were Lanhesan couples of the late nineteenth and early twentieth centuries able to establish their own households?

Table 7.1 delineates the types of households that existed in Lanheses between 1850 and 1920. The classification follows that of Hammel and Laslett (1974), with some major additions or modifications (see key) that are necessary for a proper understanding of the northwestern Portuguese case.[4] For example, the sex of single persons living alone is specified, and a category of single mothers living alone with their illegitimate offspring has been created. In the multiple family household category, links through the bride (patriuxorilocal) versus the groom (patrivirilocal) are differentiated, as are multiple households headed by married couples as opposed to those headed by a widow or widower. The significance of most of these subcategories will be discussed later in the chapter.

Key to Household Type Classifications for Lanheses Data (Table 7.1)

Solitaries

1a Widow or widower living alone
1b Unmarried man or woman living alone
Note: Above two differentiated by sex.

Coresident Singles

2a Coresident siblings
2b Coresident relatives of other kinds
2c Coresident singles of unknown relationship

Simple Family Households

3a Married couple living alone
3b Married couple with children (nuclear family)
3c Widower with children
3d Widow with children
3e Single mother with offspring
3f Single mother with offspring and one or more of her siblings

Extended Family Households

4a Extended upward through parent or parent-in-law of head
4b Extended upward through other relative of head
4c Extended downward through grandchild of head
4d Extended downward through other relative of head
4e Extended laterally through sibling or sibling-in-law of head
4f Any combination of above

Multiple Family Households

5a Secondary couple extended up
5b Secondary couple extended down through male line, both
spouses in both generations alive

5c Secondary couple extended down through male line, widow or widower in senior generation
5d Secondary couple extended down through female line, both spouses in both generations alive
5e Secondary couple extended down through female line, widow or widower in senior generation
5f *Fréreches* (groups of brothers and their wives)
5g Other multiples
5h Single mother, married illegitimate offspring with spouse and children
5i Widow or widower, widowed child, and widowed child's offspring

Others

6a Unclassifiable

In broad terms, this table demonstrates that, throughout the late nineteenth and early twentieth centuries, complex households (extended and multiple) made up a significant proportion of the households in Lanheses. With the exception of 1870 and 1881, extended and multiple family households together comprised over 25 percent of all households in the parish until 1920, when the proportion dropped to 20 percent. Conversely, with the same exceptions in 1870 and 1881, simple family households hovered around 50 percent.

What is of most interest to explain is the short-term decline in the proportion of complex households sometime in the 1850s or 1860s (it is unfortunate that no Róis da Desobriga for the 1860s exists), and the persistence of this trend into the early 1880s. That this period may be particularly exceptional is also evident when one considers the growth in the total number of households in the parish between the sixteenth and the twentieth centuries. Between 1527 and 1712, an average of one new household was formed every two and a half years; only three new households were established in the fifty-five years between 1712 and 1767, whereas one new household was established every other year in the thirty-three years between 1767 and the dawn of the nineteenth century. Conversely in the fourteen years between 1864 and 1878, fifty new households were established (an average of 3.6 per year) at a time when the de facto population itself declined by almost 200 individuals, and age at marriage rose.[5]

Table 7.1. Distribution of Household Types in Lanheses, 1850–1920[a]

Type	1850	1870	1881	1887	1892	1899	1907	1913	1920
Solitaries									
1a (M)	0.0	1.4	1.0	1.1	1.9	1.1	1.5	1.5	1.5
1a (F)	1.6	3.4	2.7	1.8	1.1	1.9	1.5	2.7	5.2
1a total	1.6	4.8	3.7	2.9	3.0	3.0	3.0	4.2	6.7
1b (M)	0.6	4.8	5.3[d]	2.2	1.8	1.9	0.7	1.2	1.5
1b (F)	4.8	7.2	6.3	6.2	6.7	7.1	5.2	5.8	3.7
1b total	5.4	12.0	11.6	8.4	8.5	9.0	5.9	7.0	5.2
Coresident Singles									
2a	2.4	4.1	4.0	4.4	4.4	3.0	3.4	1.5	1.1
2b	2.4	0.7	1.3	1.8	0.7	1.5	3.0	3.5	3.7
2c	0.0	0.0	0.0	0.4	0.3	0.0	0.0	0.0	0.4
Simple Family Households									
3a	10.0[b]	14.5[c]	8.6	8.1	7.4	6.7	7.9	6.6	7.5
3b	35.4[b]	36.2[c]	46.2	31.6	33.3	32.1	34.4	33.7	36.2
3c	3.3	3.8	3.0	2.2	1.1	3.0	2.6	1.9	3.3
3d	5.3	9.3	8.6	8.8	6.7	10.4	5.6	9.3	10.1
Total	54.0	63.8	66.4	50.7	48.5	52.2	50.5	51.5	57.1
Single Mothers with Offspring									
3e	4.8	3.8	2.3	3.3	3.3	4.8	4.1	3.1	4.9
3f					0.4				

Extended Family Households									
4a	0.4	0.3	0.3	3.7	6.3	4.1	1.9	1.6	1.5
4b	1.9	0.0	0.0	0.7	1.5	0.4	1.5	0.4	0.0
4c	1.4	2.1	5.0	4.4	3.7	5.2	5.6	4.3	2.6
4d	2.4	1.0	1.3	0.0	0.7	1.5	0.4	2.3	1.5
4e	3.3	3.4	2.3	4.4	5.6	6.0	3.7	5.0	3.7
4f	2.9	1.0	1.0	1.5	3.3	1.8	2.6	1.5	3.4
Total	12.3	7.8	9.9	14.7	21.1	19.0	15.7	15.1	12.7
Multiple Family Households									
5b	1.4	0.3	0.3	2.6	2.6	1.1	1.5	2.7	0.4
5c	4.3	0.0	0.0	3.3	1.1	1.5	1.1	0.8	1.9
5d	5.2	0.3	0.3	2.2	2.9	2.2	4.5	2.7	0.7
5e	3.3	1.7	0.0	4.0	2.2	1.5	4.9	6.2	4.5
Total	14.2	2.3	0.6	12.1	8.8	6.3	12.0	12.4	7.5
Other Multiples and Unclassifiable									
59	0.4			0.3					
5h				0.7	0.7	0.4	0.7	1.2	0.7
5i						0.4	0.4		
6a	2.4	0.7	0.0	0.0		0.4	1.1	0.3	
Total	210	290	301	272	270	268	267	258	268

a. Percent of population. For explanation of classifications, see box.
b. Revised figures (see text) are 3a . . . 6.2%; 3b . . . 38.2%
c. Revised figures (see text) are 3a . . . 10.7%; 3b . . . 39.2%
d. Includes two priests in addition to the parish priest who each year is among the single male households, generally living with servants and in one instance with a sister and therefore classified as 2a.

Source: Róis da Desobriga, Lanheses.

It is possible that the changes in the system of property devolution called for by the new Civil Code of 1867 facilitated the expansion of simple family households in Lanheses, at least in the short term. This code clearly specified strictly egalitarian inheritance, the abolition of all entailed estates (*vínculos*), the registration of all long-term leases (*foros*), and the distribution of common pasture lands. By the 1880s, aggravated by increasing population, the process of land division generated by the new civil code had proceeded to the point of nonviability, such that land for both housing and subsistence farming was no longer readily available. Furthermore, new taxation laws introduced at this time imposed severe burdens on the rural populations of northwestern Portugal. These factors, in addition to stimulating emigration, may have served to halt a temporary process of land and household fragmentation.

Despite this important short-term fluctuation, the long-term picture is one of less dramatic change, although the number of multiple households declined by 50 percent between 1850 and 1920. In light of the short-term decline sometime between 1850 and the early 1880s, does overall decline represent a major change in household organization or a change in a set of external conditions that, during the late nineteenth and early twentieth centuries, made three-generation households either necessary or preferable? I will return to this question later.

In general, the ratio of complex to simple households in Lanheses in the late nineteenth and early twentieth centuries approximates that in other regions of nineteenth-century northern Portugal (Amorím 1983; Rowland 1981), although the proportion of nuclear family households is less than the 70 percent found by Pina-Cabral (1984b, 1986) in two villages of the Alto Minho in the late 1970s. When the Lanheses data are categorized according to the life-course method used by Kertzer (1984) in his study of Bertalia, the proportion of Lanhesans who lived in simple family households during the late nineteenth century is approximately 50 percent of the total population. The proportion living in complex households is around 40 percent. Over time, however, there is variation that parallels the variation that the more static categorization of household types has demonstrated. In 1850, 57 percent of the population lived in simple family households; in 1870, 78 percent; in 1881, 75 percent; in 1892, 50 percent; in 1907, 51 percent; and in 1920, 59 percent. As in Bertalia, living in a complex household is to a large extent a function of age. Children under ten, adults between thirty and thirty-nine, and adults over sixty are most likely to be found living in three-generation households. Between 1887 and 1913, an average of 19 percent of male heads of households who were over fifty headed a three-generation household. Conversely, approximately 77 percent of males between thirty and forty-nine who headed households were heading simple family ones. I will return to some of these life-course issues shortly in discussions of the residence patterns of women, in particular. While the household composition data indicate that complex household organization was fundamental to the Lanhesan way of life in the late nineteenth and early twentieth centuries, it is worth emphasizing that the majority of complex households in this parish, with the exception of the year 1850, were extended family households rather than three-generation multiple households. Although some of this difference may be due to the method of categorization,[6] it also suggests that household complexity cannot be fully explained by a set of rules emerging from clear and precise inheritance practices, as is suggested for other regions of southern Europe. As is demonstrated in the following discussion, a great majority of extended households are formed directly or indirectly as a result of the demographic impact of a male-biased migration pattern.

Solteiras: The Spinster Population

As a result to some extent of the heavy out-migration of single men during the late nineteenth and early twentieth centuries, a high proportion of women in Lanheses were left out of the marriage market. Where did these spinsters live and how did they survive? Table 7.2 delineates the coresidence of single women in Lanheses for selected years by age.[7] Until the 1890s more than 50 percent of all single women lived in simple family households with their parents. The proportion drops slightly below 50 percent during the 1890s, 1900s, and 1910s. The age distribution of single women living in simple family households demonstrates the impact of the late age at marriage in this parish at this time. Rather high proportions of single women in their thirties and forties remained in households with their parents. Most of these women probably worked farming the land their parents either owned or rented or as day laborers for wealthy peasant or aristocratic families in the region. The sheer numbers of these spinster daughters obviously contributed significantly to the high proportion of simple family households and especially of full nuclear families (3b) or widows and widowers with offspring (3c, 3d) as opposed to married couples living alone in an "empty nest" (3a). In addition, Lanhesans today say that it is not good for a young married couple to move into a household where there are still many *solteiras,* especially when it is a groom moving in with his bride's family. Thus, in a household with several children, it was more likely that the eldest children and the first to marry would move out rather than bring their spouses to live with their parents and siblings. This, too, created pressure for the formation of separate family households.

Table 7.2. Coresidence of Single Women, by Age, 1850–1920

Ages	Type of Household[a]						Total	
	Solitaries/NF	Simple	Illegitimate Mothers	Extended	Multiple	Other	n	Percent
1850 (n = 350)								
χ²[b]	22	25	4	25	20	4	110	31
0–9	0	71	0	16	13	0	31	9
10–19	1	76	4	10	9	1	105	30
20–29	4	67	8	9	12	0	67	19
30–39	0	61	9	13	17	0	23	7
40–49	14	14	29	14	29	0	2	1
50–59	0	0	80	20	0	0	5	1
60–69	0	50	50	0	0	2	2	1
Total percent	8	54	7	15	14	2		
1870 (n = 352)								
χ²[b]	26	34	13	22	3	1	76	22
0–9	0	93	0	7	0	0	29	8
10–19	0	91	0	6	3	0	77	22
20–29	5	83	0	9	3	0	76	22
30–39	16	70	4	9	2	0	56	16
40–49	50	33	6	11	0	0	18	5
50–59	64	0	9	18	9	0	11	3
60–69	50	50	0	0	0	1	2	1
Total percent	15	66	5	11	2	1		
1881 (n = 402)								
0–9	0	87	0	10	1	2	102	25
10–19	2	84	1	12	0	1	95	24
20–29	15	68	1	15	0	1	76	19

	(1)	(2)	(3)	(4)	(5)	(6)	(7)	(8)
30–39	20	52	2	25	2	0	56	14
40–49	28	49	10	10	3	0	39	10
50–59	58	17	4	21	0	0	24	6
60–69	78	0	11	11	0	0	9	2
70+	100	0	0	0	1	1	1	0
Total percent	14	68	2	14	1			
1892 (n = 410)								
0–9	1	62	2	19	16	0	122	30
10–19	2	63	1	22	12	0	86	21
20–29	4	57	4	24	11	0	80	20
30–39	9	47	3	22	19	0	32	8
40–49	53	9	9	23	6	0	34	8
50–59	45	7	21	28	0	0	29	7
60–69	48	5	0	38	9	0	21	5
70+	50	0	0	33	17	0	6	1
Total percent	13	48	4	23	12	0		
1907 (n = 440)								
0–9	2	60	3	17	18	0	146	33
10–19	3	64	2	21	9	1	104	24
20–29	1	52	4	22	21	0	68	15
30–39	12	33	6	27	21	0	33	7
40–49	30	21	15	27	6	0	33	7
50–59	47	3	12	25	9	3	32	7
60–69	42	0	0	33	25	0	12	3
70+	33	8	8	17	33	0	12	3
Total percent	10	48	5	21	15	1		

(continued)

Table 7.2. Coresidence of Single Women by Age, 1850–1920 (*continued*)

			Type of Household[a]				Total	
Ages	Solitaries/NF	Simple	Illegitimate Mothers	Extended	Multiple	Other	n	Percent
1920 (n = 434)								
0–9	6	68	1	14	11	0	113	26
10–19	1	75	1	14	10	0	132	30
20–29	8	52	3	22	15	0	73	17
30–39	5	51	13	23	8	0	39	9
40–49	19	33	9	29	9	0	21	5
50–59	45	5	20	20	10	0	20	5
60–69	50	12	12	12	12	0	16	4
70+	35	5	20	20	20	0	20	5
Total percent	10	57	5	17	11			

a. In percentages.
b. Age unknown.

Source: Róis da Desobriga and Parish Registers, Lanheses.

While the greatest proportion of women in their twenties and thirties continued to live with parents in simple family households after age forty and especially after age fifty, a significant number lived alone. Throughout the period between 1850 and 1920, approximately one-quarter of the households were neither complex nor simple family households. Solitaries, particularly unmarried women, made up more than half of the remaining 25 percent. From 1870 to 1899, between 6 and 7 percent of households were composed of spinsters living alone. The proportion declined after the turn of the century, to just under 4 percent by 1920. In 1881, 55 percent of these women living alone were over fifty; in 1899, 74 percent; and in 1920, 75 percent.

In table 7.2, these solitary households are grouped together with no-family households, some of which are households composed of coresident siblings (2a). Cumulating all the households of coresident siblings in the nine rolls analyzed between 1850 and 1920, 35 percent were households composed of two or more spinster sisters living together. Another 14 percent were households headed by a spinster sister who was living with other unwed siblings of both sexes. Forty-eight percent were households headed by an unwed man and his unwed siblings. In general these were households that were headed, in some previous year, by a widowed mother or father. The parent died, and the unwed children were left in the household together. That virtually as many of these households were headed by women as by men is certainly an indication that females were as likely to inherit the paternal household and the adjacent cultivated plots as were males.

The proportion of unwed women who lived in extended households is also significant, and in general the likelihood of a single woman living in an extended household increased with age. Such households (classified as 4e on table 7.1) represented 6 percent of the total in 1899, rising from 3 percent in 1850 and declining again to 3 percent in 1920. There is no question that the increase in these types of households is directly related to the increase in the spinster population in general. Female siblings, either as sisters or sisters-in-law of the head of household, outnumbered male siblings by three to one, a figure that indicates the strength of female kinship ties in particular. The majority of these women were between ages twenty and forty-nine. Whether such households were formed by a spinster sister moving in with a married sibling or a married couple moving in with the spinster after the death of the parental generation is not always clear, unless the move is from one hamlet to another. The rolls are not necessarily recorded in the same order from year to year and therefore cannot be easily linked to precise physical structures within a single hamlet. Residential changes within the parish indicate that both forms of movement occurred. A specific example will illustrate one form of this process. (See table 7.2.)

Maria Nunes was born in 1835. In 1850 she was living in a household in the *lugar* (hamlet) of Roupeiras, headed by her maternal grandmother, Susana Correia, with her widowed father, Caetano, her younger sister, Francisca, her two younger brothers, Manuel and António, and her two unmarried aunts, Luisa (age thirty-one) and Rosa (age eighteen). By 1870 Susana, Caetano, Francisca, and Luisa, who had married in 1856, were all dead. There is no further record of António. Maria, her brother Manuel, and her aunt Rosa were each living in solitary households adjacent to one another in the same *lugar* of Roupeiras. By 1881 Manuel had married and was living in the *lugar* of Santo Antão with his wife and son, Manuel, for whom Maria Nunes was godmother. The aunt Rosa had died, and Maria still lived alone in the house in Roupeiras. By 1887, however, Manuel Nunes's wife had also died, and Maria moved to the household in Santo Antão, presumably to help care for him and for her godson, Manuel. In 1888 Manuel Nunes remarried and in 1892 was living with his new wife and his son in a simple family household (presumably the same physical structure) in Santo Antão. Her domestic services no longer needed, Maria Nunes moved back to a solitary household in Roupieras. In 1899 Maria was still by herself in Roupeiras, Manuel Nunes senior had moved to a house in the lugar of Granja near his wife's kin, and Manuel Nunes junior was married and living with his wife and children in the house in Santo Antão. Presumably Maria Nunes continued to live by herself until her death in 1904.

Whereas the proportion hovers around only 5 percent, the single women living in households that have been classified as 3e—those made up of unwed mothers and their illegitimate offspring—cannot be ignored. These households comprised from 3 to 5 percent of all the households throughout the period. These women appear to be older, in their forties and fifties, and a number of them worked as day laborers. In principle, these households need to be considered in conjunction with the majority of households that are classified as 4c—simple families extended vertically downward by the presence of a grandchild. In general, and especially toward the end of the nineteenth century and the beginning of the twentieth century, such a grandchild was illegitimate. In fact, the proportion of such households increases during the 1890s and early 1900s in conjunction with an increase in the proportion of illegitimate births in the parish. In 1907, 21 percent of all single women in the parish were living in households made up of an unwed mother and her offspring. Elsewhere (Brettell 1985, 1986) I have argued that illegitimacy can also be explained, at least partially, by the extensiveness of male migration, and that the birth of an illegitimate child in some senses bound the mother more firmly to her family of origin. These unwed mothers, like virginal spinsters, provided sustenance and support to the parental generation and in return were recipients of the third share. Neither unwed mothers nor illegitimate offspring were discriminated against in property bequests (Brettell 1986).

Before leaving this discussion of spinsters, a word should be said about servants. While households have been classified according to the major kinship connections that bind the residents together, approximately 7 percent of the households in Lanheses had servants. The lowest proportion was in 1892, when only 4 percent had them; the highest proportion was in 1920 with 11 percent. These proportions are much smaller than the 20 percent calculated by Nunes (1986) for the more industrialized parishes near the town of Guimarães. The majority of these servants were unmarried women, ranging in age from thirteen to over sixty, although the bulk were in their twenties and thirties. When all these households with servants are cumulated, 44 percent were simple family households, 20 percent were solitary or no-family households, 17 percent were multiple family households, and 16 percent were extended family households. Although the data at hand provide no precise evidence about those young women from Lanheses who were in service elsewhere, the absences recorded on the *róis* indicate that this phenomenon was by no means insignificant. In 1870, twenty-two single females were marked absent; in 1887, twenty-nine; in 1899, twenty-seven; in 1907, twenty-four; and in 1920, eighteen. For some unmarried women, service in another household, whether in her home parish or in a neighboring parish or provincial town, was a definite life-course option.

Casadas: Married Women and "Widows of the Living"

In Lanheses during the late nineteenth and early twentieth centuries there was a high rate of village endogamy. Approximately 65 percent of the marriages between 1850 and 1920 were contracted between a young man and a young women who were both natives of the village. When a bride or groom came from another parish, the wedding was always celebrated in the bride's village, and while some brides went to live in their husbands' villages after the marriage, it was more common for the groom to move and live in his bride's village. This again reflects the fact that the bonds of kinship were stronger between a woman and her family of orientation than between a man and his.

Table 7.3 traces the residence patterns of married women through the life course. As we would expect, there is change both through historical time and in individual or life-course time in the coresidence patterns of married women. During the 1860s, 1870s, and early 1880s, the total proportion of married women living in multiple households declined. This was then followed by a sharp increase in the 1890s and 1900s. Over the life cycle, women between the ages of twenty and twenty-nine (and occasionally in their thirties) and women over age sixty were more likely to be found in complex households. In fact a majority of married women at some point in their lives lived in a complex household. For example, of the eighty-one couples who married in the parish between 1830 and 1859 and who appear on three or more successive rolls, fifty-two (64 percent) were at some point part of a complex household. The same proportion emerges from among the marriages contracted between 1890 and 1909 that appear on three or more successive róis.

Although the proportion of married women who live in complex extended households is consistently greater than the proportion living in

Table 7.3. Coresidence of Married Women, by Age, 1850–1920

Ages	Type of Household[a]				Total	
	Simple	Extended	Multiple	Other	n	Percent
1850 (n = 161)						
?[b]	60	5	30	5	20	12
15–19	100	0	0	0	1	1
20–29	53	7	40	0	15	9
30–39	54	15	28	3	39	24
40–49	70	11	20	0	46	29
50–59	74	9	17	0	23	14
60–69	41	12	47	0	17	11
Total percent	61	11	27	1		
1870 (n = 173)						
?[b]	79	14	0	7	14	8
15–19	0	0	1	0	1	1
20–29	58	0	25	17	12	7
30–39	82	12	6	0	34	20
40–49	91	7	2	0	53	31
50–59	83	10	7	0	30	17
60–69	96	4	0	0	24	14
70+	100	0	0	0	5	3
Total percent	85	8	5	2		

Table 7.3. Coresidence of Married Women, by Age, 1850–1920 (*continued*)

Ages	Type of Household[a]				Total	
	Simple	Extended	Multiple	Other	n	Percent
1881 (n = 184)						
10–19	100	0	0	0	1	0
20–29	95	0	0	0	19	10
30–39	87	5	5	3	37	20
40–49	96	4	0	0	49	27
50–59	92	8	0	0	39	21
60–69	77	19	0	4	26	14
70+	69	15	15	0	13	7
Total percent	89	8	2	1		
1892 (n = 197)						
20–29	59	18	23	0	22	11
30–39	43	24	33	0	46	23
40–49	70	24	6	0	46	23
50–59	63	26	10	0	49	25
60–69	50	21	29	0	24	12
70+	50	10	40	0	10	5
Total percent	57	23	20	0		
1907 (n = 191)						
20–29	42	4	50	4	26	14
30–39	68	3	29	0	38	20
40–49	76	14	8	2	49	26
50–59	57	23	20	0	30	16
60–69	57	21	21	0	33	17
70+	20	27	40	13	15	8
Total percent	59	14	25	2		
1920 (n = 172)						
?[b]	50	0	50	0	2	1
15–19	100	0	0	0	1	1
20–29	50	25	25	10	20	12
30–39	65	10	20	4	49	28
40–49	73	9	18	0	44	26
50–59	72	20	8	0	25	14
60–69	74	21	5	0	19	11
70+	50	42	8	0	12	7
Total percent	66	16	15	2		

a. In percentages.
b. Ages unknown.

Source: Róis da Desobriga and Parish Registers, Lanheses.

complex three-generation households, the latter form is not to be ignored. Further, as the data in table 7.1 make apparent, the strength of female kinship ties in particular is reflected in the somewhat greater tendency, even in village endogamous marriages, for multiple-generation households to be formed on the basis of patriuxorilocality (5d, 5e) rather than patrivirilocality (5b, 5c). This is in contrast to other areas of southern Europe—central Italy, for example, where a groom moving in with the bride's family was a much rarer phenomenon (Kertzer 1984).

The heavy emigration of men is, I think, a significant factor explaining this tendency. If married sons and sons-in-law were frequently absent, it was better for the parents to be left to deal with a daughter rather than a daughter-in-law. And, from the bride's perspective, it was preferable to be left alone in a household with her mother and father than with her in-laws. The proportion of such households increases during the late nineteenth and early twentieth centuries, just as the emigration of married men from this region surpasses that of single men.

In 1850, 8 percent of the households in Lanheses were patriuxorilocal compared with 6 percent that were patrivirilocal. In 1907, 9 percent of households were patriuxorilocal compared with 3 percent patrivirilocal; and in 1913 the corresponding proportions were 8 percent and 3 percent. Some of these households were formed through a regroupment process. Young married women, who had been living in simple family households with their husbands and children, moved back in with their parents when their husbands emigrated. A specific example will illustrate some of the dynamics of this process.

Conceição Franco was born in 1884 to a potter named Manuel Dantas and his wife, Maria das Dores Franco. Manuel and Maria das Dores were married in 1883, and in 1887 they were living in the only four-generation household that appeared on any of the *róis* analyzed. The household, located in the *lugar* of Outeiro, was headed by Domingos Afonso, Conceição's great-grandfather. He was seventy-nine years old and a widower. Also present in the household were Domingos's son-in-law, Manuel Gonçalves da Rocha; his married daughter, Maria, who was fifty-four; his granddaughter, Maria das Dores, and her husband, Manuel Dantas; four other grandchildren; and two great-grandchildren.

By 1892 Manuel Dantas and Maria das Dores had moved into a separate but adjacent household, where they lived with their three children. Domingos Afonso was still alive and heading a household composed of his widowed son-in-law, Manuel Gonçalves da Rocha; a married granddaughter, Rosa Maria; three more grandchildren; and one great-grandchild. By 1899 Manuel Dantas, his wife, and their children had moved to the neighboring *lugar* of Romão but were still in a simple family household. Both

Domingos Afonso and Manuel Goncalves da Rocha had died, and the original house in the *lugar* of Outeiro appears to have been occupied by Manuel Rodrigues da Costa and his wife, Maria Rosa Franco, she being another granddaughter of Domingos Afonso. The married granddaughter Rosa Maria had moved out of the Outeiro household to a household in the *lugar* of Romão which she shared with her husband and children. The sister married first was replaced by the sister who married three years later in the paternal household.

In 1904 Conceicão Franco, the eldest daughter of Manuel Dantas and Maria Dores Franco, was married, and in 1907 she was living in a simple family household with her husband, João Fernandes, and her daughter, Rosalina, in the *lugar* of Romão near her parents and her aunt Rosa Maria. By 1913, however, she had moved in with her parents to form a three-generation multiple household which included her husband and three of her children. Her husband, João, however, was marked absent. In 1908 Conceicão's sister Rosalina was married, and in 1913 she was living nearby in a simple family household. Conceicão and Rosalina's brother Alvaro does not appear on the roll for 1913, although he married in the parish in 1919 and in 1920 was living in the *lugar* of Romão with his wife, a brother-in-law, and a sister-in-law, presumably in a house left to his wife, the eldest child, and her as yet unmarried siblings by their widowed mother when she died in 1914. Conceicão's coresidence with her elderly parents was temporary. By 1920 she was back in a simple family household in the *lugar* of Romão. Manuel Dantas and his wife were living alone.

This case suggests that the increase in male, and especially married male, emigration during the late nineteenth and early twentieth centuries may have set a condition for the reemergence of multiple-generation households. In slightly more than a third of the patriuxorilocal households in 1907, the in-marrying sons-in-law were absent; in 1913 the proportion was 40 percent.

The emigration of men affected other household forms as well. Table 7.4 presents the proportion of the total number of households, by household type, that had a male absent, for each year analyzed.[8] With the caveat that the absences marked on the rolls probably only begin to account for men who emigrated on a seasonal or temporary basis, it seems that a number of women remained in simple family households and, as *viuvas dos vivos* (widows of the living), became de facto heads of household. In 1913, at the height of emigration to Brazil, households with a male head of household or a married son or son-in-law absent represented 15 percent of the total. Although these "widows of the living" probably represented the households they headed beyond the domestic sphere in the jural domain of the village, this position was a temporary one. However,

Table 7.4. Simple and Multiple Households with Male Absences, 1850–1920

	Household Type											
	a		b		c		d		e		f	Total
	n	%	n	%	n	%	n	%	n	%	n	%	%
1850	6	2.9	11	5.3	1	.5	6	2.9	0	0	0	0	11.6
1870	2	.7	12	4.1	0	0	0	0	0	0	1	.3	5.1
1881	1	.3	14	4.7	0	0	0	0	0	0	0	0	5.0
1887	3	1.1	22	8.1	4	1.5	4	1.5	0	0	0	0	12.2
1892	3	1.1	15	5.6	1	.4	4	1.5	0	0	0	0	8.6
1899	2	.7	13	4.9	0	0	4	1.5	0	0	0	0	7.1
1907	1	.4	19	7.1	1	.4	9	3.4	1	.4	0	0	11.7
1913	1	.4	28	10.9	2	.8	8	3.1	0	0	0	0	15.2
1920	1	.4	25	9.3	1	.4	1	.4	0	0	0	0	10.5

a=Married head of married couple absent (revised 3a)
b=Married head of nuclear family absent (revised 3b)
c=Multiple family with married son absent (revised 5b, 5c)
d=Multiple family with married son-in-law absent (revised 5d, 5e)
e=Multiple with both head and married son/son-in-law absent
f=Multiple with head absent and married son/son-in-law present
Total=Total percent of all households
Source: Róis da Desobriga, Lanheses.

as the discussion of the *solteira* population above indicated, de jure female-headed households were not at all uncommon in this parish. Similarly, households headed by widows were quite common. It is thus to the widowed population that I now turn.

Viuvas: Women in Real Widowhood

The proportion of female-headed households in Lanheses was 28 percent in 1850 and 1870, 25 percent in 1881, 31 percent in 1887, 1899, and 1907, and then rose to 39 percent by 1920. These figures are high when compared with data from other communities in southern Europe (compare Kertzer 1984). Although some of this high proportion is accounted for by households made up of spinsters living alone and of unwed mothers living with their illegitimate children, a number of simple, extended, and even multiple households are headed by widowed women. Table 7.5 breaks down these widowed and de jure female heads of household by age and household type. Heading a household is clearly more likely for a woman as she gets older. While there is some variation over time in the

Table 7.5. Female-Headed Households, by Age and Type, 1850–1920

By Age, Percentage

	N	?[a]	20–29	30–39	40–49	50–59	60–69	70–79	80–89	90+
1850	60	40	2	3	8	15	13	17	2	0
1870	81	26	2	5	15	16	20	11	5	0
1881	76	0	5	8	12	24	22	26	3	0
1887	86	0	1	12	21	19	22	15	9	1
1892	66	0	1	1	27	32	20	12	5	1
1899	83	0	1	8	19	28	29	12	2	0
1907	84	0	1	4	19	26	18	26	6	0
1913	91	0	3	6	11	16	32	25	7	0
1920	105	0	3	9	8	21	26	22	11	0

By Household Type, Percentage

	Solitaries	Coresidents	Simple	Unwed Mothers	Extended	Multiple	Other
1850	20	12	18	17	10	20	3
1870	37	10	33	12	2	4	1
1881	35	9	34	9	11	0	1
1887	26	14	28	10	6	14	0
1892	29	15	27	15	9	4	0
1899	29	7	34	14	10	4	2
1907	21	15	18	13	12	15	5
1913	26	9	26	9	11	15	3
1920	23	10	31	13	8	12	2

a. Ages unknown.

Source: Róis da Desobriga, Lanheses.

age distribution of these female heads-of-household, no particular year of those analyzed appears to stand out. However, in the distribution of female heads by household type, the year 1907 is somewhat curious. The proportion of women heading solitary and simple family households is relatively low, while the proportions heading extended and multiple family households reach all-time highs. In the case of multiple households, this is related to the fact that in-marrying sons or sons-in-law may have been absent.

Table 7.6 analyzes the coresidence patterns of Lanhesan widows on six rolls between 1850 and 1920. Although a significant proportion of widows live alone, it appears that the older they are the more likely they are to live with some other family member in either a simple or a complex household. In cases where they are living alone, it is likely to be in a household in proximity to offspring. There are also indications of movement precipitated by widowhood or during widowhood. The rolls contain several examples of women widowed at earlier ages who move from a simple family household back in with their parents. Other cases demonstrate widows who circulate among the households of their offspring or who move from a multiple situation to a solitary situation as they get older. One specific example will illustrate aspects of these processes.

Maria Peixoto was married in 1850 and in that year appeared on the roll with her husband in a simple family household in the *lugar* of Romão. In 1870 the household was still a simple family, one made up of Maria, her husband, and four children ranging in age from nineteen to nine. By 1881 the eldest daughter had married, left the household, and was living with her husband and young son in the *lugar* of Feira. Maria was widowed but remained with her three children in the household in Romão. By 1887 the eldest son had also married and was living in the *lugar* of Taboneira in a multiple household headed by his eighty-year-old widowed mother-in-law. His wife and three young children made up the rest of the household. The eldest daughter continued in a simple family household in the *lugar* of Feira, and Maria continued to reside in Romão with her two younger children, Rosa and Luis.

In 1889 the youngest daughter, Rosa, married Francisco Feijó, and in 1892 Francisco was listed as the head of a household composed of his wife, a one-year-old son, his mother-in-law, and his brother-in-law, Luis. However, both Francisco and Luis were marked absent. The son in Taboneira had become the head of a simple family household, and the household in the *lugar* of Feira remained unchanged. By 1899 the son Luis had returned, had married, and was heading a household in Romão composed of his wife, a baby daughter, and his mother-in-law, Maria. The daughter Rosa, a widow, was living in an adjacent household with her three children. The household of the son Pedro in Taboneira remained unchanged in 1899 and 1907. That of the daughter Maria Rosa in Feira was temporarily extended in 1899 by the addition of her husband's eighty-two-year-old father. He died shortly after the roll for that year was recorded, and the household reverted to a simple family one. By 1907 Maria Peixoto had moved in with her widowed daughter Rosa and her children, leaving her son Luis in an adjacent simple family household with his wife and daughter. She remained there until her death in 1914.

Because women inherited, owned, and could bequeath property, and because husbands in general left usufruct rights to their wives upon their deaths, the authority that a widowed woman could maintain over the household was sustained. This is evident in the fact that widowed women who headed simple, extended, and multiple family households generally did so until late in life. However, when individual households are traced through their developmental cycles, in a number of instances we can discern a point at which the authority that accompanied a headship was transferred to a son or son-in-law living in the household. In terms of the categorization used in this analysis, a household that in one year is classified as multiple and headed by a widow (5c, 5e), in another year might be classified as extended vertically upward (4a). The developmental cycle of the household of Ana Maria de Costa provides a concrete example.

Ana Maria was born in 1819 and married in 1848. In 1850 she and her husband were living in a simple family household in the *lugar* of Lamas. Ana Maria was pregnant; her first child was born in June of that year. Although Ana Maria's parents were dead by 1850, her husband's parents were living in Corredoura with several unmarried children. By 1870 Ana was widowed and living in the *lugar* of Lamas with her twenty-year-old daughter, Maria, and her fifteen-year-old son. Eleven years later, the son had disappeared (did he emigrate?) and mother and daughter were alone in the same household. By 1887 the daughter had married and had brought her husband, Manuel Martins, to live with her mother. The household also included two grandchildren and a seventeen-year-old male servant. Ana Maria was age 68 and still listed as the head of household. However by 1892 she had apparently transferred the headship to her son-in-law, Manuel, who by that time was fifty-three. Ana Maria continued in this subordinate status until her death in 1906.

In 1907 the household was composed of Manuel Martins, his wife, Maria, and their recently married son, António. Their daughter, who was married in 1900, was widowed in 1904, and in 1907 was living in a household by herself in a nonproximate *lugar*. In 1913 the three-generation

Table 7.6. Coresidence of Widows, by Age, 1850–1920

| | Type of Household[a] | | | | | Total | |
	Solitary/NF	Simple	Extended	Multiple	Other	n	Percent
1850 (n = 35)							
?b	0	12	38	38	12	8	23
30–39	0	50	0	50	0	2	6
40–49	50	50	0	0	0	2	6
50–59	0	60	0	0	40	5	14
60–69	0	43	14	43	0	7	20
70+	27	18	0	55	0	11	31
Total percent	11	31	11	37	9		
1870 (n = 41)							
?b	29	40	20	0	20	5	12
20–29	100	0	0	0	0	1	2
30–39	0	100	0	0	0	1	2
40–49	29	71	0	0	0	7	17
50–59	0	100	0	0	0	6	15
60–69	20	67	7	7	0	15	37
70+	33	67	0	0	0	6	15
Total percent	22	68	5	2	2		
1881 (n = 45)							
20–29	0	0	0	0	100	1	2
30–39	0	100	0	0	0	1	2
40–49	0	100	0	0	0	1	2
50–59	0	60	40	0	0	10	22
60–69	10	60	30	0	0	10	22
70+	31	55	14	0	0	22	49
Total percent	18	58	22	0	2		

1892 (n = 54)							
30–39	0	0	33	67	0	3	6
40–49	0	44	33	22	0	9	17
50–59	17	83	0	0	0	6	11
60–69	6	37	50	6	0	18	31
70+	6	17	56	22	0	18	35
Total percent	6	35	42	17	0		
1907 (n = 60)							
20–29	0	0	0	100	0	1	2
40–49	12	38	12	12	25	8	13
50–59	0	44	44	11	0	9	15
60–69	15	15	31	31	8	13	22
70+	17	21	35	24	3	29	48
Total percent	13	25	32	23	7		
1920 (n = 72)							
20–29	33	67	0	0	0	3	4
30–39	0	100	0	0	0	2	3
40–49	25	50	25	0	0	4	6
50–59	17	56	22	6	0	18	25
60–69	33	33	11	22	0	18	25
70+	22	26	22	30	0	27	37
Total percentage	24	40	18	18	0		

a. In percentages.
b. Ages unknown.

Source: Róis da Desobriga and Parish Registers, Lanheses.

household was still intact, although António was absent and, according to other sources, never returned. Maria, his wife, by this time had three children. In 1920 the daughter-in-law Maria was in a simple family household in Lamas. Her father-in-law had died in 1916 and, although her mother-in-law survived until 1935, there was no trace of either her or her widowed daughter on the 1920 roll.

Bonds Between Women: Household and Kinship

In the preceding sections, several specific examples were used to illustrate the coresidence patterns of Lanhesan women through the life course and how these were influenced, either directly or indirectly, by extensive male emigration. In the process I referred to the strength of female kinship bonds. What most of the cases demonstrate is a greater tendency, not only for a groom to move in with his bride's family than the reverse, but also for a couple, even if living in a separate household, to take up residence near the bride's kin rather than those of the groom.

This sibling vicinality has previously been noted by Pina-Cabral (1984b, 1986) in his ethnographic study of two villages in the Alto Minho. Clearly the Lanhesan data demonstrate that this tendency has historical depth. The implication, of course, is that despite the fact that at least half the families in Lanheses at any point in time lived in separate nuclear family households, these households were by no means independent. In many senses, this region of Portugal approximates that of Brittany (Segalen 1984). The paradox between a desire for an independent household and an emphasis on intrafamily cooperation is equally strong. Further, given the fact that men (whether sons, brothers, or husbands) were frequently absent, the development of geographically concentrated sets of households linked through females makes perfect sense. It was the women who farmed the fields together and who shared in the responsibilities of raising children. If the village square and village café were the arenas for social interaction among men, the neighboring households of female kin provided women with their social arena. Although I have not fully analyzed the data, it is quite possible that godparents were more frequently chosen among those geographically as well as consanguineously proximate kinsmen. It is certainly true that godparents were more often kin than nonkin, and a child might occasionally (or even for more extended periods) spend time in the household of a godmother, especially a spinster godmother, or of a widowed grandmother living de jure in a household by herself. Living in geographical proximity facilitated such circulation of children.

Conclusion: Is Northwestern Portugal Matrifocal?

Anthropologists have long been interested in the impact of migration on the family. Although more attention has been placed on the immigrant family itself, there is some research on the impact of the emigration of some family members on those left behind. In an early attempt to synthesize the latter material, González (1961) formulates a typology that describes how different forms of migration—seasonal, nonseasonal, recurrent, continuous, and permanent—affect the family. She demonstrates that the length of time that family members are absent, as well as the pattern of migration itself, are essential to an understanding of the kinds of social structures that emerge to cope with absences. Some forms of migrant labor, she argues, appear to have little, if any, effect on the family, regardless of its traditional structure, although they do affect the lives of women in other ways. Other forms (and here she points to recurrent, continuous, and permanent migration) have a more serious impact.

Emerging from this analysis over the years is González's refinement of the concept of matrifocality, which she defines as female role dominance in concrete social structures such as the family, household, neighborhood, and community (González 1970, 243). She places her emphasis not on the labeling of an entire society as matrifocal but on the degree of matrifocality found in each. She also cites several circumstances that tend to enhance this degree, one of which is the frequent absence or numerical shortage of males. In this context matrifocal characteristics emerge—a greater emphasis on mother's rather than father's relatives as godparents and household decisions made by women. The fact that none of these characteristics may have anything to do with the jural domain makes the use of the concept of matrifocality more appropriate than that of matriarchy.

It is difficult to adapt González's migration typology to the Portuguese case, because different men followed different patterns of migration, at different stages in their life cycles. Some returned regularly, even from Brazil, while others were absent for years. What is important in the Portuguese case is that households adjusted to these absences in ways that demonstrate several of the characteristics of matrifocality. The female-headed and patriuxorilocal households found in Lanheses in the late nineteenth and early twentieth centuries are the result of many years of coping, both demographically and socially, with the absence of men. Male migration affected household structure in northwestern Portugal not only directly but also indirectly, through its impact on female spinsterhood and illegitimacy.

To my knowledge, the concept of matrifocality has been used directly in only two other contexts in western Europe—by Lee (1977) in his study of illegitimacy in Bavaria and by Lopreato (1965, 1967) in some of his work on the southern Italian peasantry.[9] Without using the term, Boissevain (1979) alludes to female-centeredness in his analysis of Malta. The "ethics of inheritance" among coastal Galician fishermen in northwestern Spain described by Lison-Tolosana (1976) clearly demonstrate some of the matrifocal characteristics that have been described for northwestern Portugal. In studies of Iberian family and household structure in particular, and of the southern European family more generally, future research might fruitfully devote itself to more rigorous comparative study of these pockets of matrifocality. With this comparative data in hand, scholars will be better able to assess whether the concept of matrifocality, controversial in the Caribbean context where it was first defined, is itself appropriate, or even useful, to describe some European family systems.

Acknowledgements

The author would like to thank the National Institute of Child Health and Human Development and the Wenner-Gren Foundation for supporting the research on which this essay is based.

Notes

This chapter was originally published in *Journal of Family History* 13 (1): 33–57. It is reprinted with minor revisions with the permission of Sage Publications.

1. The extant rolls for this parish are not continuous. Three from 1850, 1851, and 1852 were found. The next one is dated 1870, and the one after that 1881. Although not available annually until after 1900, extant rolls between 1881 and 1900 are more numerous. I chose to analyze these rolls at five-, six-, or seven-year intervals, depending on availability. Because ages do not appear on the 1850 and 1870 rolls, they were determined through linkages with parish register data when possible. In addition, the two early rolls are incomplete, because no children under seven are listed. Where linkages to a reconstituted family could be made, these unlisted children are added for some analyses. For further discussion of these sources, see Brettell (1986).

2. For more detailed discussion of these demographic phenomena, see Brettell (1986).

3. For further discussion, see Brettell (1979, 1986).

4. Nunes (1986) also found it necessary to adapt the Hammel-Laslett typology. The categorizations here are somewhat different from his, although we tend to agree on what variations are important to emphasize.

5. These figures are based on a 1527 census mandated by João III (Freire 1905), a chorography of Portugal compiled by Padre António Carvalho da Costa be-

tween 1706 and 1712, another by Padre Cardosa (1767), Luiz de Pina Manique's 1798 census (1970), and Villas Boas's *cadastre* of the same period (Cruz 1970).

6. Household type was determined by reference to the head of household. In numerous instances, a household is listed in one year with a widowed parent as head (categorized as multiple) and in the following period with the son or son-in-law as head and the widowed parent as a household member (categorized as extended). The possibility that this represents some sort of transfer of authority is discussed later in the essay.

7. The ages of a number of women in 1850 and 1870 cannot be precisely determined. On several tables, they are included in an unknown category, headed with a question mark.

8. Although Nunes (1986) creates a separate subcategory for these households under simple family households, I have chosen to treat all such households as de facto, because on the de jure rolls the name of the husband is included. These households with absent males are broken down into six categories on table 7.4, depending on which male or males are absent.

9. Of course, it is not uncommon for anthropologists of southern Europe to describe the "behind the scenes" power of women in these cultures (Freidl 1967; Riegelhaupt 1967), the strength of mother-son ties (Parsons 1967; Saunders 1981), or the way in which women symbolically represent the nuclear family unit (Giovannini 1981).

8

Women Are Migrants, Too

A Portuguese Perspective

Virginia Fernandes dos Santos Caldas lives in the town of Viana do Castelo in northwestern Portugal. Fourteen kilometers to the east is the rural agricultural village where she was born in 1932. I first met Virginia in Paris in 1974.[1] At that time she was employed as a maid (*bonne à toute faire*) for a bourgeois French family who lived in the posh Parisian suburb of Neuilly. Her work day began before seven in the morning and ended well after nine in the evening. Normally she had a few hours off in the middle of the afternoon. For this work she was paid 1,400 francs a month (at the time about U.S. $350 a month) plus room and board. Although not much by today's standards, it was significantly more than the 150 *escudos* a month (about U.S. $5 in 1970) that she had earned as a maid in Lisbon, Portugal.

In France, Virginia did not work on Sundays. In the mornings she attended mass at a neighborhood church, where a young Portuguese priest administered to the community of Portuguese immigrants who lived in the vicinity. Many of these immigrants were like Virginia—single women who had emigrated to France in the late 1960s and early 1970s. Virginia's dreams were their dreams—to make enough money to buy or build a house or apartment in Portugal, where they could live in peace and security in their old age.

When I first met Virginia she was not married, but she had a son, born out of wedlock in 1954. Soon after his birth, the father left for South America. He wrote periodically but never returned to Portugal. When her son, Joaquim, was three years old, Virginia went to work for a well-to-do family who owned a house in Lisbon as well as a *solar* (manor house and estate) in her natal village. Rather than take Joaquim with her to Lisbon, she left him in the village in the care of her mother and aunts. She saw him on holidays and during the summer, when her employers returned to their *solar*. Virginia remained in the service of this family for eleven years.

Sometime in 1968 she corresponded with Joaquim's father to ask him to send the papers that would allow her son to take his father's name in addition to her own. As a result of this process, she discovered that her son's father, who was by this time living in Brazil, had married another woman. She was devastated. Two years later he wrote to say that his wife had left him and asked Virginia and her son to join him in Brazil. "I was so crazy about him," Virginia told me, "that I quit my job in Lisbon and returned to the village to make preparations for our departure. I even bought a new dress to wear when I arrived. I was very happy, because my dream of marrying him was finally coming true." However, at the last moment the Portuguese government would not give her son a passport, because he was sixteen and approaching the age for obligatory military service. Virginia would not leave without her son. "I was heartbroken, ashamed, and without work."

In the late 1960s Virginia's brother-in-law—the husband of her younger sister, Rosa—had emigrated to France, leaving his wife and four children behind in the village. He had developed a serious stomach ailment and asked his wife to join him in France. Rosa was frightened to go by herself and convinced Virginia to emigrate too, telling her that she had a lot of experience as a maid and would find work easily. Virginia and her sister arrived in France in October of 1971. Virginia was forty years old.

She found a job soon after her arrival and stayed in the same position until her departure in 1977. She had a good relationship with her employers, although she complained at times of having too much work. Everything had to be precise and just right for her *patroa* (mistress of the house). However, they were generous with vacations, and each summer she was able to return to Portugal for a month. Sometimes she also spent Christmas with her family.

In 1977 Virginia received a letter from her son, Joaquim. His father, Manuel, had written from Venezuela and asked him to join him there. Unable to emigrate to France (after 1974 it became increasingly difficult), Joaquim decided to fly across the Atlantic Ocean to meet his father for the first time. His father gave him work, and by the fall of 1977 Joaquim had suggested to his mother that she join them in Venezuela. In December of that year Virginia quit her job in Paris and flew to South America to re-meet, and later marry, the father of her son—a man she had not seen since he abandoned her in 1954.

Virginia, her husband, Manuel, and her son, Joaquim (who married a young woman from a neighboring parish in Portugal) eventually returned to Portugal, but Virginia's marriage (a civil rather than a religious contract) had already failed. Manuel was constantly suspicious of Virginia's years of independence and particularly of her life in France. He started a relationship with his Venezuelan secretary, a woman much younger than he, whom he had brought with him to Portugal. Manuel asked Virginia for a divorce, offering her a small apartment in Viana do Castelo as a place to live. Although not without much emotional and spiritual pain, Virginia finally decided to give him the divorce. She spent a few years living primarily in her natal village, taking care of her aged mother, but when her mother died family differences in the household drove her to the apartment. Although her ex-husband gives her some money each month, it is not enough to get by. Recently Virginia has taken a job caring for an elderly woman five afternoons a week.

Virginia's life has been shaped both by migration and emigration, her own and that of others close to her, to the urban centers of Portugal, northern Europe, and South America. While her life story is uniquely her own, it also reflects many aspects of the roles and experiences of migrant and immigrant women more generally.

In 1974 two American anthropologists, Michelle Rosaldo and Louise Lamphere, published a book titled *Woman, Culture and Society*. This book brought gender as an analytic concept into the mainstream of anthropology. Two years later the journal *Anthropological Quarterly* published a special issue that dealt with the topic of women and migration (Buechler 1976). For the first time the presence of women in migration flows was recognized and considered in a systematic fashion. Prior to this time, in anthropology as in other social science disciplines, the pervasive assumption was that the migrant, and particularly the international migrant, was a young male who left his homeland for economic reasons. This assumption persisted well into the 1980s, despite the fact that by then some migration streams—particularly those to the United States—were dominated by women (Houstoun et al. 1984).[2]

In the research that addresses female migrants, women are portrayed as actors rather than passive followers in the migration process—affected by the forces of capitalism, colonialism, or socialism the same as are men; they are also described as central to the networks of exchange of people, goods, services, and information, by which urban immigrant communities function and survive. The emphasis is on how women understand their lives and the challenges posed by migration; how women's experiences of emigration might differ from those of men; and how geographical mobility, both within and across national boundaries, might alter not only the culturally rooted understandings of what it means to be a woman but also other aspects of culture that individuals and families bring with them as they migrate or emigrate.

I discuss some of these issues here, drawing on the lives and experiences of Portuguese immigrant women like Virginia, who have emigrated to a number of different receiving societies. My discussion centers on a few questions: Are the decisions of women to emigrate any different from those of men? How are women incorporated into the urban labor force in the country of immigration? What is the impact of salaried employment on family roles? Are immigrant women politicized and, if so, how? Do men and women differ in their desire to return to their country of origin?

The Decision to Emigrate

Traditionally it has been assumed that men were the ones who decided to emigrate and that women and children would either follow or remain in the sending country. In the history of Portuguese emigration, this has been true to some extent. Familial emigration has tended to follow a period of emigration heavily dominated by men. And yet, does the fact that women follow men mean that women are only passively involved in the decision to emigrate? The answer to this question must be no. No matter who departs, decisions are generally collective ones, taken by the members of a household. For the most part, wives are fully involved as partners in a domestic enterprise. Not only does the family as a unit decide whether to emigrate, who will emigrate, and for how long, but also what resources will be spent on the process, and what money earned in the city or abroad will be sent back.

Recent emigration streams reveal that many women get jobs abroad prior to their husbands and are, therefore, the first to emigrate. This is the case among Turkish women in Germany and Portuguese women in London (Giles 1991). Furthermore, not all women who are involved in emigration are married. Single women like Virginia often have some of the best opportunities for employment in domestic service in the receiving societies.

The overriding factor leading to a decision to emigrate is economic. And yet, when we delve deeper into the personal stories of female emigrants, especially those who are single, we find that often they are also emigrating to join a family member. Klimt (1992, 86) quotes one Portuguese woman in Hamburg, Germany, who claimed that she "emigrated thinking not only of money, but of the longing and desire to be with [her] sister." Indeed, Klimt found that Portuguese women in Germany, whether single or married, tended to emphasize the familial rather than the material motives, even though they worked for and contributed equally to the new house being built in Portugal. In Virginia's case it was the need to support herself and her son that sent her to Lisbon and the request of her sister that took her to Paris.

Other single women decide to emigrate because they want to change their lives; they are looking for a life different from the one to which they are destined in their home village. In many cases it is not poverty that motivates emigration but an active effort to improve one's life. In Paris I met several Portuguese women like Virginia who were no longer young, who were not directly attached to a man, and who wanted to earn money so that they could settle themselves comfortably in their waning years. Some of these women, like Virginia, have now returned to Portugal and have set themselves up in small apartments in provincial towns. They have independence and financial security and do not have to continue in the backbreaking life of cultivating the fields.

Gender and Labor Force Participation

The great majority of immigrant women, no matter from what country they come or to what country they emigrate, become part of the urban labor force. Portuguese women in France have shown a high level of employment. More than half of Portuguese women in France over age fifteen are actively employed. Like immigrant men, immigrant women are occupationally concentrated. In France the majority of first-generation Portuguese immigrant women find work as private domestics, cleaning ladies, or concierges. Employment for Portuguese immigrant women has often been linked to housing; consequently women could combine their productive and reproductive roles. In more recent times, employment patterns have changed, and more women are working in the secondary sector of the economy—manufacturing. It is also true that the generation of Portuguese born in France have a different employment experience; they are citizens who are bilingual, and many new opportunities are open to them. Whereas twenty years ago you would not have found a Portuguese taxi driver in Paris, today it is common, and women can be found in a range of civil service positions.

Portuguese women in London have moved into the domestic service sector of the economy. Of the Portuguese women interviewed by Giles (1992), 43 percent were employed as waitresses or cleaners in the hotel and catering trade; 18 percent were private domestic cleaners; and 18 percent were on the cleaning staff of hospitals. The remaining 21 percent either worked full time in their homes or were nurses, teachers, or hairdressers. Giles writes of the exploitation to which these women are exposed, particularly in the form of low wages and the fear of deportation.

In addition, they frequently work in isolation and, by the time they get home to face domestic work, they are exhausted.

The high rate of employment among Portuguese immigrant women is equally characteristic of the population in the United States. Lamphere (1986a) found that Portuguese men in Rhode Island were more likely to encourage their wives to work than Colombian men, who thought that having a wife who worked cast doubts on their role as the male provider. Portuguese men thought that what their wives could earn was necessary to the survival of the household. In Rhode Island, some Portuguese women work as domestics, but greater numbers are employed in the garment industry. Lamphere's study encompasses a historical approach; she argues that in the past the women working in the textile mills were daughters of French-Canadian, Irish, English, and Polish immigrants. Today these working daughters have been replaced by the working wives of Portuguese and Colombian immigrants.

Gender, Work, and Family

How does this high rate of employment affect gender roles within the household and family? While many immigrant women, like gainfully employed women in general, are as exposed to the so-called "second shift" or double day, most research documents a definite change in the division of labor and gender relations within the household, by comparison with the sending society.

Among first-generation Portuguese immigrant families in France, the absence of kin networks, combined with the fact that many couples left children with maternal grandparents in Portugal, resulted in a greater sharing of roles between husband and wife. Among couples with coresident children, women worked as concierges or did occasional cleaning, and in these cases husbands participated less in domestic chores. In both cases, husbands and wives spent more leisure time together in France—a definite change from Portugal. Men were deprived of the kind of male public space that exists in the village squares of northern Portugal.

In her work among Portuguese immigrant women in Montreal, Meintel (1987) found that Portuguese women with young children tended to turn to work as hourly cleaning women or to home piecework, because the conditions of work are both more flexible and less stressful. This strategy allows for the combination of productive and reproductive roles. Meintel observes, however, that such an option is possible only if women are in stable marital relationships with partners who earn a good income. Piecework and hourly cleaning are not excessively lucrative!

Among Portuguese women in Rhode Island (Lamphere 1987) a somewhat different option has been pursued. Given the constraints of the local economy, wives and mothers are forced into the productive sphere of waged work in textile factories. As a result, reproductive labor within the household is reallocated, and husbands take on many household chores that are normally defined as female tasks. In addition, husbands and wives work different shifts in order to accommodate child care. As in France, waged employment for Portuguese immigrant women in Rhode Island has also had the effect of drawing nuclear families closer together, while ties to extended families and friends have become less important.

In Hamburg, Germany, Klimt (1992) found that Portuguese women face for the first time the demands of balancing shift work with caring for the family. They are helped by husbands who understand the value of teamwork and actively participate in household chores, grocery shopping, cooking, and child care. Klimt documents the judgment passed by Portuguese immigrant women on arrogant husbands "who did not participate in housework; [on] weak-willed wives who let them get away with it; [on] women who were *escravas* (slaves) and had to ask their husbands permission to make purchases or leave the house; and also [on] wives who controlled the finances and never allowed husbands adequate spending money" (Klimt 1992, 202–03). It should be noted that these Portuguese women in Germany differ from their counterparts in Montreal. The Montreal Portuguese women studied by Meintel hold on to the belief that the male should remain the head of household, and few of them leave the house without consulting or asking permission of their husbands.

Women's Politicization and Encounters with "the Other"

Scant research has been done on the political activity of immigrant women in general and of Portuguese immigrant women in particular. It seems that it takes time for political consciousness to emerge. Immigrant women have little time for anything beyond their work and their domestic chores. What leisure time they do enjoy is spent with family or friends. Where there is evidence of political activity, it has generally emerged from a problem that immediately affects their working or domestic lives. Giles (1991, 1992) has described labor disputes in the London hotel and catering industry in which Portuguese immigrant women took part. These women were also involved in a six-year struggle to protest poor housing conditions. The women attended meetings with the housing council, an activity that required them to take off time from work or rearrange their schedule. Interestingly Giles observes that the involvement of women in a protest movement was quite different from what they claim would have happened in Portugal: Men would have attended the meetings. The implication is that the situation can be different abroad, such that the kind of public activities representing the interests of the household that would have been the purview of men in Portugal become the responsibility of women. However, Giles also notes that the movement that these Portuguese immigrant women initiated soon became bureaucratized, and progressively they lost control and became more silent.

The strategies of resistance described by Lamphere (1985) are much more subtle. In her study of a New England apparel plant, she found some resentment between older (Italian, Irish, French-Canadian) and newer (Portuguese, Latin American) female immigrants. Most of it centered on accusations of "rate busting." The perception is that new immigrants work too fast, and the piece rate is lowered, such that all workers have to increase their output to make the same pay. However, despite these divisions and tensions, there is also a culture of resistance that crosses ethnic lines and that develops when unions base their organizational activities on the informal networks that are established among women who bring their social and familial roles to the workplace. Women humanize the work culture, and this provides a powerful basis for collective action when confrontation with management is necessary.

Klimt (1992) has written about the encounter between social workers and Portuguese immigrant women and the varying concepts of gender, family, and good citizenship that each group holds. Her study focuses on a Portuguese women's group in Hamburg that was organized by professional German social workers. Klimt draws our attention to an evolutionist model underlying German attitudes, embodied in the expectation that migrants will change from being an uneducated conservative peasantry to an enlightened and engaged urban proletariat. She tells us that German social science literature about foreign workers portrays peasant women as dominated by their menfolk and excluded from familial decision-making. In German eyes, migration (and, by extension, urbanization) makes immigrants more sophisticated. Alternatively, there is an image of immigrant women as exploited and oppressed. In Germany both these images derive to a large extent from observations of Turkish families, but they are applied to all immigrants. As a result of these images, the courses offered to immigrant women stress personal health and hygiene, cooking, and child-rearing. They do not address issues such as union organizing, financial planning, or job training, even though, at least in the case of Portuguese women in Germany, the large majority of women work in heavy industry or the service sector and manage or comanage family finances. In other words, classes are aimed at making immigrant women conscious of themselves as women, wives, mothers, and domestic consumers (p. 216). In addition they socialize immigrant women, Portuguese and others, to the German way of doing business—arriving on time, holding orderly meetings, and not talking all at once.

Klimt notes that the Portuguese women with whom she worked attended these classes because they were fun, a break from their normal routine. However, their goals were not those of their German instructors. They wanted to become *senhoras* (ladies) in Portugal. They did not want to become part of a more liberated and proletarian German working class. Portuguese immigrant women and the German social workers agreed that Portugal was backward. But for the Portuguese women to focus on homemaking, on feminine forms of leisure, and on family life was not a way to become more German but to become better than the women who remained behind in the villages of Portugal. The women who were the subjects of Klimt's research "positioned themselves somewhere between Turkish women, whom they imagined to be totally submissive and powerless, and German women, whose life styles they thought of as unacceptably loose" (Klimt 1992, 220).

Returning Home

Klimt's observation that Portuguese immigrant women in Germany assess themselves and formulate their goals in relation to the country they have left behind leads me to the final issue—the temporariness or permanence of emigration. One of the reasons why I went to conduct research among Portuguese immigrants in France was because I wanted to study a population that had more opportunity to move back and forth between the country of emigration and the country of immigration. I was interested in the relationship between distance and the perception of permanence of emigration. I indeed found that the Portuguese I knew in France had a powerful return orientation which was essentially absent among the Portuguese I had previously worked with in Toronto or Providence.

This difference is also reflected among the Hamburg Portuguese families studied by Klimt. She writes about a couple named Adelina and Jose, who framed their future in terms of a return to Portugal. They lived modestly in Germany in order to live well in Portugal. In fact, there is an ethic of self-restraint and denial among the Portuguese of Hamburg. Any excessive consumerism abroad draws the criticism of compatriots. Adelina and Jose argued not about whether or not to return to Portugal but about when and under what circumstances. Their daughter felt the same way.

But Jose had a sister and brother-in-law in New Jersey who decided to settle permanently there. While Adelina and Jose built a nice new house in their natal village, the couple in New Jersey have not and only return to visit each summer.

Jose and Adelina, like other Portuguese couples in Hamburg, act in unison to achieve their goal to return to Portugal and are equally involved in making it happen. The only gender difference occurs when children wish to remain abroad; in this case wives tend to argue for remaining longer in Germany to stay near children. However, even this position does not mean giving up the commitment to return to Portugal some day. It may mean separation from children, but in some sense this is the nature of the Portuguese family, in a country that has experienced emigration for centuries.

In other contexts, husbands and wives do not always share the same ideas about returning to Portugal. Among couples I studied in France, I found that the women were sometimes more reluctant to think about returning than were their husbands. To some extent this was a function of the kind of work women did. They were well integrated into French life as domestics and concierges, while their spouses worked with other immigrants in a factory environment and were consequently more alienated from their host society.

Giles (1991), by contrast, found that among the Portuguese families living in London the women were more interested in returning to their homeland. There was a difference, however, between single and married women. The former enjoyed the social and economic independence of their life in London and were more reluctant to consider return to Portugal. Certainly attitudes about returning to Portugal are affected by the attitudes of the host society toward immigrant groups, by work laws, by the susceptibility to exploitation, and by the fear of expulsion.

As Klimt (1992) has observed, the return orientation is a powerful mechanism that liberates migrants from the need to measure their worth in German terms. A Portuguese chambermaid in Germany can be a successful property owner with sophisticated tastes in Portugal. We can never say with certainty that all those immigrants who say they will return to Portugal, and plan for it by buying land and building houses, will do so. But it is important that they operate with this future in mind.

Conclusion

In this chapter I have outlined some aspects of the experience of Portuguese immigrant women in a number of host societies. Those experiences can certainly be shaped differently by the particularities of the occupational structure and immigration policy in the receiving country. But there are also experiences that Portuguese women, and migrant and immigrant women in general, share no matter where they go. They share these experiences because they are women who must juggle the pressures of domestic life with those of their job. This juggling act is particularly difficult in an urban environment, because work lives and home lives generally take place in separate spheres. In some cases women have found the kind of work that brings the domestic and wage-labor activities back together—home piecework or concierge work, for example. What is certain is that migration profoundly impacts both the public and private lives of women and that looking at this impact is as important as the study of the classic male migrant, who has so long served as a prototype for all migrants.

Notes

This chapter was originally published in Gmelch and Zenner, *Urban Life*. It is reprinted with minor changes by permission of Waveland Press.

1. See Brettell (1995) for a more detailed discussion of Virginia's life as an emigrant.

2. By the mid-1980s a new awareness of the role of women in migration led to the publication of numerous anthologies and case studies dealing particularly with female migration and immigration, both in the past and at present. See, for example, Simon and Brettell 1986, Gabaccia 1992, Gilad 1989, Diner 1983, Ewen 1985, Weatherford 1986. For an analysis of the anthropology of immigrant women in particular, see Brettell and deBerjeois 1992.

9
Conclusion
Toward a Comparative Understanding of Migration

In this book I have explored a range of concepts and theoretical issues that are germane to the anthropology of migration but also to migration studies more broadly conceived. I have drawn on some of my ethnographic and historical work on Portuguese emigration and Portuguese immigrants to illustrate how these concepts and theories illuminate and are illuminated by a case that has generally not been integral to recent historical and social scientific debates within migration studies. In my view, knowledge of the Portuguese case, a case of great historical depth and geographic breadth, adds an important dimension to the comparative understanding of the migration process and suggests that patterns that we may think are unprecedented in fact have occurred at other times and in other places, albeit often with a unique contextual twist. My own empirical research, spanning the period from the 1970s to the 1990s, has been in mainland Portugal and among Portuguese immigrants in the United States, Canada, and France. But one could easily add to these receiving contexts Germany, England, Luxembourg, Australia, Venezuela, and all the former Portuguese colonies—Brazil, Angola, Mozambique, Guinea, Macao, Goa, Timor. Colonization and emigration, two of the more important global processes of the capitalist world system, have created a Portuguese diaspora of extensive proportions. If the Portuguese state has recently been reterritorialized and Europeanized, the deterritorialized Portuguese-speaking world remains.

Underlying my efforts to introduce the Portuguese case into broader discussion of global migrations is the suggestion that we move with urgency toward more comparisons across space and time, letting the past inform and be informed by the present, and letting the experience of

197

immigrants in Europe, Canada, Australia, and elsewhere inform and be informed by that of immigrants to the United States.[1] Research on specific immigrant populations is still quite nationalist in orientation; conversation across borders and oceans is still limited.[2] This seems at odds with the reality of diasporic families, such as those featured in the migration stories presented in this volume.

I have also suggested that we make the comparative study of cities a focus of our attention, looking, for example, at how the same immigrant group is incorporated in two urban contexts, as I did in my comparative analysis of the Portuguese in Toronto and Paris. In addition, what is implicit in the anthropological study of migration—working at both ends of migration streams, in both sending and receiving contexts—should be more explicit across the range of disciplines that address the topic of migration. And finally, although my work is rooted in ethnography and history, it is informed by the contributions of scholars in other disciplines—sociology, political science, economics, and geography. Migration studies of the twenty-first century must be an interdisciplinary enterprise.[3] Perhaps within a rigorous interdisciplinary context a more nuanced understanding of the relationship between structure and agency, or what Patricia Pessar (1999b) has called "contingent agency," can be worked out.

There are dimensions of the Portuguese case that remain unaddressed or underaddressed here but that are particularly germane to the field of migration studies. For example, the literature on Caribbean immigrants in the United States raises significant theoretical questions about the relationship between race and immigration and particularly about how "blackness" has been renegotiated in an increasingly complex and multiethnic black America (Foner 2001b; Stepick 1998). Clearly these discussions will be informed by emerging research on immigrants from Africa, who must also confront racism in the United States. Within the Portuguese immigrant population are people from the Cape Verde Islands who have settled in New Bedford, Massachusetts, and the surrounding area. Their relationship with the larger community of white Portuguese from the Azores is tenuous, at best. Their case should be brought into the larger discussion of race and immigration, and this discussion should then be extended back to the homeland, where issues of race are at the center of the "immigration problem" in mainland Portugal. This question also merits broad cross-national consideration. Race is problematic in England and France as well, and in all three cases it is in part associated with decolonization. Such comparisons also might move us to an understanding of how race intersects with religion, certainly an issue of contention in France and some other countries in Europe.[4]

Issues of race are closely related to issues of ethnicity and identity. Here too the Portuguese case raises some challenging research questions.

How do Portuguese immigrants situate themselves in relation to the hegemonic discourse on Hispanics in the United States? How do they interact, particularly in the New York/New Jersey area, with the significant Brazilian population? How meaningful is a shared language? Certainly new work on Hispanics and Latinos is beginning to demonstrate that Salvadorans, Guatemalans, Nicaraguans, and others want to differentiate themselves from the massive Mexican immigrant group and think of *Hispanic* as a label imposed from the outside. How do the Portuguese in the United States confront these issues, particularly in comparison with those in Canada or France, where there is no strong Hispanic or Brazilian presence?

The Portuguese immigrant population is also interesting because it represents an important European migration stream to the United States in a post-1965 period that has been characterized as the age of immigration from Asia and Latin America. More work should be done to bring together, in a comparative context, these European-origin populations— Poles, Bosnians, Portuguese. Is there anything distinctive about their experiences by comparison with the non-European origin populations? If, as I found in my work in France, groups like the Portuguese are considered "highly assimilable," has this occurred and is it occurring in other receiving contexts where the mix of immigrant populations is different. Of special importance is the experience of the second generation, something I have not captured in my own work. Do European-origin second-generation immigrants in the United States experience the kind of segmented assimilation that has been described for other groups (Portes and Zhou 1993; Zhou 1999)? Research on the second generation has proliferated in recent years (Perlmann and Waldinger 1997, 1999; Portes 1996; Portes and Rumbaut 2001) but to date there is little research on the second generation of Portuguese in Canada, France, Germany, the United States, and Australia. This is yet another area crying out for more comparative research. For example, the European context offers the added dimension of a European identity above that of being French (or German) or of Portuguese heritage. Does this matter? Does it lead to different outcomes?

Finally, the Lusophone world of the twenty-first century is different from that of the two previous centuries. Brazil has moved from being a receiving country for immigrants to being a sending country, even sending some of its citizens to "mother Portugal." Portugal has moved from being a sending country to a receiving country. Clearly there is much to be done in looking at this process of immigration in Portugal itself and comparing it with what is happening in other countries of southern Europe and to prior experience in countries of northern Europe in the post–World War II period.[5]

Notes

1. Certainly the book by Massey et al. (1998) begins this comparative discussion. However, we equally need more fine-tuned ethnographic and historical comparisons that address some of the subtleties of the migration experience. Recently, Lucassen (2002) has addressed the relevance of debates in U.S. immigration history for European immigration history. Jan Rath has used the theoretical literature on immigrant entrepreneurship in the United States to frame research questions for the European context (Rath 2002; Rath and Kloosterman 2000).

2. One exception is the fascinating work of Irene Bloemraad, a young political scientist. She compares political incorporation and citizenship among Portuguese immigrants in the United States and Canada (Bloemraad 2002, 2003). She has found that the Portuguese in Canada are more likely to acquire citizenship than those in the United States and explains the difference in relation to differences in federal policy and state support for ethnic organizations. One external reviewer to this manuscript has noted that presently there is more back and forth movement between Portuguese immigrants in the United States and their home communities than I described for Canada in the mid 1970s. While this may also be characteristic of Portuguese immigrants in Canada today as opposed to thirty years ago, Bloemraad's research suggests that the differences between these two receiving contexts may be very real. Certainly these are fascinating questions, worthy of much more rigorous consideration.

3. The calls for such interdisciplinarity are more than a decade old (Morawska 1990; Pedraza 1990, Massey et al. 1994), and yet the canyons dividing disciplines are still wide (Lucassen and Lucassen 1997). Even my attempt with James Hollifield (Brettell and Hollifield 2000) has been criticized for not fully succeeding in having scholars talk across disciplines (see the review by Russell King in the *Journal of Ethnic and Migration Studies* 27 (4) (2001): 749–50).

4. Of course it has become more important in the United States after September 11, 2001. Suddenly the spotlight was turned on Muslims in America.

5. This research is beginning to emerge, spearheaded by Portuguese scholars such as Maria Baganha (1997).

References

Abdulrahim, Dima. 1996. "Defining Gender in a Second Exile: Palestinian Women in West Berlin." Pp. 55–82 in *Migrant Women: Crossing Boundaries and Changing Identities*, ed. Gina Buijs. Oxford: Berg Publishers.

Abley, Mark. 2002. "Toronto Is a Magnet That's Hard to Resist." *The Gazette* (Toronto) (September 26).

Ablon, Joan. 1971. "The Social Organization of an Urban Samoan Community." *Southwestern Journal of Anthropology* 27: 75–96.

Abu-Lughod, Lila. 1990. "The Romance of Resistance: Tracing Transformations of Power through Bedouin Women." *American Ethnologist* 17: 41–55.

———. 1991. "Writing Against Culture." Pp. 137–62 in *Recapturing Anthropology: Working in the Present*, ed. Richard G. Fox. Santa Fe: School of American Research Press.

Alba, Richard D., John R. Logan, Brian J. Stults, Gilbert Marzan, and Wenquan Zhang. 1999. "Immigrant Groups in the Suburbs: A Reexamination of Suburbanization and Spatial Assimilation." *American Sociological Review* 64: 446–60.

Aldrich, Howard E., and Roger Waldinger. 1990. "Ethnicity and Entrepreneurship." *Annual Review of Sociology* 16: 111–35.

Alicea, Marixsa. 1997. "A Chambered Nautilus: The Contradictory Nature of Puerto Rican Women's Role in the Social Construction of a Transnational Community." *Gender and Society* 11: 597–626.

Almeida, Fortunato de. 1910–22. *História da Igreja em Portugal.* Coimbra: Imprensa Acadêmica.

Alpalhão, J. António, and Victor M. Pereira da Rosa. 1979. *Les Portugais du Québec. Éléments d'analyse socio-culturelle.* Ottawa: University of Ottawa Press.

Amorím, Norberta Bettencourt. 1983. *Exploração de Róis de Confessados duma Paróquia de Guimarães (1734–1760).* Guimarães.

Anderson, Benedict. 1983. *Imagined Communities: Reflections on the Origin and Spread of Nationalism.* London: Verso.

Anderson, Grace. 1974. *Networks of Contact: The Portuguese and Toronto.* Waterloo: Wilfrid Laurier University.

Anderson, Grace M., and David Higgs. 1976. *A Future to Inherit: The Portuguese Communities of Canada.* Toronto: McClelland and Stewart Ltd.

Angrosino, Michael. 1976. "The Use of Autobiography as Life History: The Case of Albert Gomes." *Ethos* 4: 133–54.

———. 1989. *Documents of Interaction: Biography, Autobiography, and Life History in Social Science Perspective.* University of Florida Monographs in Social Sciences 74. Gainesville: University of Florida Press.

Anthias, Floya, and Gabriella Lazaridis, eds. 2000. *Gender and Migration in Southern Europe: Women on the Move.* Oxford: Berg Publishers.

Antunes, M. L. Marinho. 1970. "Vinte Anos de Emigração Portuguesa: Alguns Dados e Commentários." *Análise Social* 8: 299–385.

Araujo, José Rosa de. 1957. "A Serra de Arga." *Arquivo do Alto Minho* 7: 89–110.

Arensberg, Conrad M. 1957. "Discussion of R. A. Manners' Methods of Community Analysis." Pp. 44 ff. in *Caribbean Studies: A Symposium,* ed. Vera Rubin. Jamaica. Institute of Social and Economic Research.

Baganha, Maria Ioannis Benis. 1988. "Social Marginalization, Government Policies and Emigrants' Remittances, Portugal 1870–1930." Pp. 431–50 in *Estudos e Ensaios em Homenagem a Vitorino Magalhães Godinho.* Lisbon: Livraria Sá da Costa Editora.

———. 1990. *Portuguese Emigration to the United States, 1820–1930.* New York: Garland Publishing.

———. 1995. "Unbroken Links: Portuguese Emigration to the USA." Pp. 91–96 in *The Cambridge Survey of World Migration,* ed. Robin Cohen. Cambridge: Cambridge University Press.

———. 1997. *Immigration in Southern Europe.* Oeiras: Celta Editora.

Baganha, Maria Ioannis B., José Carlos Marques, and Graça Fonseca. 2000. *Is an Ethclass Emerging in Europe? The Portuguese Case.* Lisbon: Luso-American Foundation.

Bailey, F. G. 1971a. "Gifts and Poison." Pp. 1–25 in *Gifts and Poison,* ed. F. G. Bailey. New York: Schocken Books.

———. 1971b. *Gifts and Poison: The Politics of Reputation.* New York: Oxford University Press.

Bailey, Harris, and Ellis Katz, eds. 1969. *Ethnic Group Politics.* Columbus, Ohio: C. Merrill.

Banfield, Edward. 1958. *The Moral Basis of Backward Society.* New York: Free Press.

Banks, Marcus. 1996. *Ethnicity: Anthropological Constructions.* New York: Routledge.

Barnes, J. A. 1954. "Class and Committees in a Norwegian Island Parish." *Human Relations* 7: 39–58.

Barrett, Richard. 1972. "Social Hierarchy and Intimacy in a Spanish Town." *Ethnology* 7: 386–98.

Barth, Frederik, ed. 1969. *Ethnic Groups and Boundaries: The Social Organization of Cultural Difference.* London: George Allen and Unwin.

Basch, Linda, Nina Glick Schiller, and Cristina Szanton Blanc. 1994. *Nations Unbound: Transnational Projects, Postcolonial Predicaments, and Deterritorialized Nation-States.* Utrecht: Gordon and Breach Publishers.

Baucic, I. 1972. *The Effects of Emigration from Yugoslavia and the Problem of Returning Emigrant Workers*. The Hague: Martinus Nijhoff.

Bauer, Thomas, Pedro T. Pereira, Michael Vogler, and Klaus F. Zimmermann. 2002. "Portuguese Migrants in the German Labor Market: Selection and Performance." *International Migration Review* 36: 467–91.

Baxter, M. Rachel Sousa, Susan A. Pacheco, and Beth Pereira Wolfson. 1985. *The Portuguese in Rhode Island: A History*. Providence: Rhode Island Heritage Commission.

Beals, Ralph. 1953. "Social Stratification in Latin America." *American Journal of Sociology* 58 (4): 327–39.

Behar, Ruth. 1993. *Translated Woman: Crossing the Border with Esperanza's Story*. Boston: Beacon Press.

Bell, Rudolph. 1979. *Fate and Honor, Family and Village: Demographic and Cultural Change in Rural Italy since 1800*. Chicago: University of Chicago Press.

Berger, Joseph. 2002. "American Dream Is Ghana Home." *The New York Times*, August 21.

Bertaux-Wiame, Isabelle. 1982. "The Life History Approach to the Study of Internal Migration: How Women and Men Came to Paris Between the Wars." Pp. 186–99 in *Our Common History: The Transformation of Europe*, eds. Paul Thompson and Natasha Burchardt. Atlantic Highlands, N.J.: Humanities Press.

Bever, Sandra Weinstein. 1999. *Migration, Household Economy and Gender: A Comparative Study of Households in a Rural Yucatec Maya Community*. Ph.D. dissertation, Department of Anthropology, Southern Methodist University.

Bhachu, Parminder. 1985. *Twice Migrants: East African Sikh Settlers in Britain*. London: Tavistock.

———. 1988. "Apni Marzi Kardhi Home and Work: Sikh Women in Britain." Pp. 76–102 in *Enterprising Women: Ethnicity, Economy and Gender Relations*, eds. Sallie Westwood and Parminder Bhachu. London: Routledge.

Blackman. Margaret. 1982. *During My Time: Florence Edenshaw Davidson, a Haida Woman*. Seattle: University of Washington Press.

Blanshard, Paul. 1962. *Freedom and Catholic Power in Spain and Portugal*. Boston: Beacon Press.

Bloemraad, Irene. 2002. "The North American Naturalization Gap: An Institutional Approach to Citizenship Acquisition in the United States and Canada." *International Migration Review* 36: 193–228.

———. 2003. "Institutions, Ethnic Leaders, and the Political Incorporation of Immigrants: A Comparison of Canada and the United States." In *Host Societies and the Reception of Immigrants*, ed. Jeffrey Reitz. San Diego: Center for Comparative Immigration Studies.

Body-Gendrot, Sophie, and Marco Martiniello. 2000. *Minorities in European Cities: The Dynamics of Social Integration and Social Exclusion at the Neighbourhood Level*. New York: St. Martins Press.

Bogue, Donald. 1969. *Principles of Demography*. New York: John Wiley.

Boissevain, Jeremy. 1965. *Saints and Fireworks: Religion and Politics in Rural Malta*. London: School of Economics Monographs in Social Anthropology, No. 30. London: Athlone.

———. 1979. "Toward a Social Anthropology of the Mediterranean." *Current Anthropology* 20: 81–93.

Boissevain, Jeremy, and Hanneke Grotenbreg. 1986. "Culture, Structure and Ethnic Enterprise: The Surinamese of Amsterdam." *Ethnic and Racial Studies* 9: 1–22.

———. 1989. "Entrepreneurs and the Law: Self-Employed Surinames in Amsterdam." Pp. 223–51 in *History and Power in the Study of Law: New Directions in Legal Anthropology*, eds. June Starr and Jane Collier. Ithaca: Cornell University Press.

Boissevain, Jeremy, and J. Clyde Mitchell. 1973. *Network Analysis: Studies in Human Interaction*. The Hague: Mouton.

Bonacich, Edna. 1973. "A Theory of Middleman Minorities." *American Sociological Review* 38: 583–94.

Borges, Marcelo. 2000. "Migration Systems in Southern Portugal: Regional and Transatlantic Circuits of Labor Migration in the Algarve (Eighteenth–Twentieth Centuries)." *International Review of Social History* 45: 171–208.

Botelho, Abel. 1936. *Amor Criollo*. Porto: Leilo e Irmão Editores.

Bott, Elizabeth. 1957. *Family and Social Network*. London: Tavistock.

Bovenkerk, J. 1974. *The Sociology of Return Migration*. The Hague: Mouton.

Brandes, Stanley. 1975. *Migration, Kinship and Community: Tradition and Transition in a Spanish Village*. New York: Academic Press.

Braudel, Fernand. 1992. *The Structure of Everyday Life: The Limits of the Possible*. Berkeley: University of California Press.

Breton, Raymond. 1964. "Institutional Completeness of Ethnic Communities and the Personal Relations of Immigrants." *American Journal of Sociology* 70: 193–205.

Brettell, Caroline B. 1977a. "Annotated Bibliography, Nineteenth and Twentieth Century Portuguese Emigration." *Portuguese Studies Newsletter* 3 (Fall–Winter 1977–78): 7–18.

———. 1977b. "Ethnicity and Entrepreneurs: Portuguese Immigrants in a Canadian City." Pp. 169–80 in *Ethnic Encounters: Identities and Contexts*, eds. George L. Hicks and Philip E. Leis. North Scituate, Mass.: Duxbury Press.

———. 1978. *Hope and Nostalgia: The Migration of Portuguese Women to Paris*. Ph.D. dissertation. Department of Anthropology, Brown University.

———. 1979. "Emigrar para Voltar: A Portuguese Ideology of Return Migration." *Papers in Anthropology* 20: 1–20.

———. 1981. "Is the Ethnic Community Inevitable? A Comparison of the Settlement Patterns of Portuguese Immigrants in Toronto and Paris." *Journal of Ethnic Studies* 9 (3): 1–17.

———. 1984. "Emigration and Underdevelopment: The Causes and Consequences of Portuguese Emigration to France in Historical and Cross-Cultural Perspective." Pp. 65–81 in *Portugal in Development: Emigration, Industrialization, and the European Community*, Thomas Bruneau et al., eds. Ottawa: University of Ottawa Press.

———. 1985. "Male Migrants and Unwed Mothers: Illegitimacy in a Northwestern Portuguese Parish." *Anthropology* 9: 87–110.

———. 1986. *Men Who Migrate, Women Who Wait: Population and History*. Princeton: Princeton University.

———. 1990a. "The Priest and His People: The Contractual Basis for Religious Practice in Portugal." Pp. 55–75 in *Religious Orthodoxy and Popular Faith in European Society*, ed. Ellen Badone. Princeton: Princeton University Press.

———. 1990b. "Leaving, Remaining and Returning: Some Thoughts on the Multifaceted Portuguese Migratory System." Pp. 61–80 in *Portuguese Migration in Global Perspective*, ed. David Higgs. Toronto: The Multicultural History Society of Ontario.

———. 1991. "Kinship and Contract: Property Transmission and Family Relations in Northwestern Portugal." *Comparative Studies in Society and History* 33: 443–65.

———. 1995. Reprint. *We Have Already Cried Many Tears: The Stories of Three Portuguese Migrant Women*. Prospect Heights, Ill.: Waveland Press. Original edition, Cambridge: Schenkman, 1982.

———. 2000. "Theorizing Migration in Anthropology: The Social Construction of Networks, Identities, Communities, and Globalscapes." Pp. 97–135 in *Migration Theory: Talking Across Disciplines*, eds. Caroline B. Brettell and James F. Hollifield. New York: Routledge.

———. 2002a. "Migration." Pp. 229–47 in *Family Life in the Long Nineteenth Century, 1789–1913*, eds. David I. Kertzer and Marzio Barbagli. New Haven: Yale University Press.

———. 2002b. "Gendered Lives: Personal Time, Family Time, Historical Time." *Current Anthropology* 43: S45–S61

———. 2002c. "The Individual/Agent and Culture/Structure in the History of the Social Sciences." *Social Science History* 26: 430–45.

———. 2003. "Bringing the City Back In: Cities as Contexts for Immigrant Incorporation." In *American Arrivals: Anthropology Engages the New Immigration*, ed. Nancy Foner. Santa Fe: School of American Research, forthcoming.

Brettell, Caroline B., and Colette Callier-Boisvert. 1977. "Portuguese Immigrants in France: Familial and Social Networks and the Structuring of Community." *Studi Emigrazione/Etudes Migrations* 14: 149–203.

Brettell, Caroline B., and Patricia A. deBerjeois. 1992. "Anthropology and the Study of Immigrant Women." Pp. 41–63 in *Seeking Common Ground: Multidisciplinary Studies of Immigrant Women in the United States*, ed. Donna Gabaccia. Westport, Conn.: Greenwood Press.

Brettell, Caroline B., and James F. Hollifield. 2000. *Migration Theory: Talking Across Disciplines*. New York: Routledge.

Brettell, Richard R., and Caroline B. Brettell. 1983. *Painters and Peasants in the Nineteenth Century*. Geneva: Skira Publications.

Brito, Joaquím Pais de. 1982. "O Estado Novo e a Aldeia mais Portuguessa de Portugal." In *O Fascismo em Portugal*. Lisbon: Regra do Jogo.

Brown, Karen McCarthy. 1991. *Mama Lola: A Vodou Priestess in Brooklyn*. Berkeley: University of California Press.

———. 1999. "Staying Grounded in a High-Rise Building: Ecological Dissonance and Ritual Accommodation in Haitian Vodou." Pp. 79–102 in *Gods of the City*, ed. Robert A. Orsi. Bloomington: Indiana University Press.

Bruneau, Thomas C., Victor M. P. da Rosa, and Alex Macleod, eds. 1984. *Portugal in Development: Emigration, Industrialization, and the European Community*. Ottawa: University of Ottawa Press.

Brydon, Lynne. 1987. "Who Moves? Women and Migration in West Africa in the 1980s." Pp. 165–180 in *Migrants, Workers, and the Social Order*, ed. Jeremy Eades. London: Tavistock.

Bryon, Margaret. 1999. "The Caribbean-Born Population in 1990s Britain: Who Will Return?" *Journal of Ethnic and Migration Studies* 25: 285–301.

———. 2000. "Return Migration to the Eastern Caribbean: Comparative Experiences and Policy Implications." *Social and Economic Studies* 49: 155–88.

Bryon, Margaret, and Stephani Condon. 1996. "A Comparative Study of Caribbean Return Migration from Britain and France: Towards a Context-Dependent Explanation." *Transactions of the Institute of British Geographers* 21: 91–104.

Buechler, Hans C., and Judith-Maria Buechler. 1981. *Carmen: The Autobiography of a Spanish Galician Woman*. Cambridge: Schenkman.

Buechler, Judith M., ed. 1976. "Women in the Migratory Process." *Anthropological Quarterly* 49 (1) (special issue).

Bueno, Lourdes. 1997. "Dominican Women's Experiences of Return Migration: The Life Stories of Five Women." Pp. 61–90 in *Caribbean Circuits: New Directions in the Study of Caribbean Migration*, ed. Patricia Pessar. New York: Center for Migration Studies.

Buescu, M. L. C. 1961. *Monsanto, etnografia e linguagem*. Lisbon: Centro de Estudos Filológicos.

Buijs, Gina, ed. 1996. *Migrant Women: Crossing Boundaries and Changing Identities*. Oxford: Berg Publishers.

Bun, Chan Kwok, and Ong Jin Hui. 1995. "The Many Faces of Immigrant Entrepreneurship." Pp. 523–31 in *The Cambridge Survey of World Migration*, ed. Robin Cohen. Cambridge: Cambridge University Press.

Burns, Allan F. 1993. *Maya in Exile: Guatemalans in Florida*. Philadelphia: Temple University Press.

Butterworth, Douglas. 1962. "A Study of the Urbanization Among Mixtec Migrants from Tilaltongo in Mexico City." *America Indígena* 22: 257–74.

Callier, Colette. 1966. "Soajo, une Communauté Feminine de l'Alto Minho." *Bulletin des Études Portuguaises* 27: 237–78.

Callier-Boisvert, Colette. 1968. "Remarques sur le Systéme de Parenté et sur la Famille au Portugal." *L'Homme* 8: 88–103.

Cancian, Frank. 1965. *Economics and Prestige in a Maya Community*. Stanford: Stanford University Press.

Cardosa, Padre Luis. 1767. *Catálogo Alfabético de Todas as Frequesias dos Reinos de Portugal*. Lisbon.

Carqueja, Bento. 1916. *O Povo Portugûes*. Porto: Livraria Chardron.

Carter, Donald. 1997. *States of Grace: Senegalese in Italy and the New European Migration*. Minneapolis: University of Minnesota Press.

Casanovas, Francisco de. 1937. *Le Peuple Portugais et ses Caracteristiques Sociales*. Lisbon: Sociedade Industrial de Tipográfia.

Castello Branco, Camillo. 1966. *O Senhor do Paço de Ninães*. Lisbon: Parceria.

Castles, Stephen, and G. Kosack. 1973. *Immigrant Workers and the Class Structure in Western Europe*. London: Oxford University Press.

Castles, Stephen, and Mark Miller. 1993. *The Age of Migration. International Population Movements in the Modern World*. New York: Guilford Press.

Cerase, Francisco P. 1974. "Expectations and Reality: A Case Study of Return Migration from the United States to Southern Italy." *International Migration Review* 8: 245–63.

Cerqueira, Silas. 1973. "L'Église Catholique et la Dictature Corporatiste Portugaise." *Revue Francaise de Science Populaire* 23: 473–514.

Cesar, Guilhermino. 1969. *0 Brasileiro na Ficção Portuguesa*. Lisboa: Parceria A.M. Pereira Lda.

Chai, Alice Yun. 1987a. "Adaptive Strategies of Recent Korean Immigrant Women in Hawaii." Pp. 65–100 in *Beyond the Public/Domestic Dichotomy: Contemporary Perspectives on Women's Public Lives*, ed. Janet Shristanian. New York: Greenwood Press.

———. 1987b. "Freed from the Elders but Locked into Labor: Korean Immigrant Women in Hawaii." *Women's Studies* 13: 223–33.

Chan, Janet, and Yuet-Wah Cheung. 1985. "Ethnic Resources and Business Enterprise: A Study of Chinese Business in Toronto." *Human Organization* 44: 142–54.

Chang, Grace. 1997. "The Global Trade in Filipina Workers." Pp. 132–52 in *Dragon Ladies: Asian American Feminists Breathe Fire*, ed. Sonia Shah. Boston: South End Press.

———. 2000. *Disposable Domestics: Immigrant Women Workers in the Global Economy*. Boston: South End Press.

Chant, Sylvia. 1992. "Migration at the Margins: Gender, Poverty and Population Movement on the Costa Rican Periphery." Pp. 49–72 in *Gender and Migration in Developing Countries*, ed. Sylvia Chant. New York: Belhaven Press.

Chant, Sylvia, and Sarah A. Radcliffe. 1992. "Migration and Development: The Importance of Gender." Pp. 1–29 in *Gender and Migration in Developing Countries*, ed. Sylvia Chant. New York: Belhaven Press.

Chantal, Suzanne. 1962. *La Vie Quotidienne au Portugal Après les Tremblements de Terre de Lisbonne en 1755*. Paris: Hachette.

Chapin, Frances W. 1989. *Tides of Migration: A Study of Migration Decision-Making and Social Progress in São Miguel, Azores*. New York: AMS Press.

———. 1992. "Channels for Change: Emigrant Tourists and the Class Structure of Azorean Migration." *Human Organization* 51: 44–52.

Charlton, Sue Ellen M. 1984. *Women in Third World Development*. Boulder: Westview Press.

Chavez, Leo. 1988. "Settlers and Sojourners: The Case of Mexicans in the United States." *Human Organization* 47: 95–107.

———. 1992. *Shadowed Lives: Undocumented Immigrants in American Society*. Fort Worth: Holt, Rinehart and Winston.

Chavira-Prado, Alicia. 1992. "Work, Health, and the Family: Gender Structure and Women's Status in an Undocumented Migrant Population." *Human Organization* 51: 53–64.

Cheng, Lucie, and Yen Espiritu. 1989. "Korean Businesses in Black and Hispanic Neighborhoods: A Study of Intergroup Relations." *Sociological Perspectives* 32: 521–34.

Chevannes, Barry, and Heather Ricketts. 1997. "Return Migration and Small Business Development in Jamaica." Pp. 161–195 in *Caribbean Circuits: New Directions in the Study of Caribbean Migration,* ed. Patricia Pessar. New York: Center for Migration Studies.

Chin, Christine. 1997. "Walls of Silence and Late Twentieth Century Representations of the Foreign Female Domestic Worker: The Case of Filipina and Indonesian Female Servants in Malaysia." *International Migration Review* 31: 353–85.

Chin, Tung Pok, with Winifred C. Chin. 2000. *Paper Son: One Man's Story.* Philadelphia: Temple University Press.

Chinas, Beverly. 1973. *The Isthmus Zapotecs: Women's Roles in Cultural Context.* New York: Holt, Rinehart and Winston.

Choy, Catherine Ceniza. 2000. "Exported to Care: A Transnational History of Filipino Nurse Migration to the United States." Pp. 113–33 in *Immigration Research for a New Century: Multidisciplinary Perspectives,* eds. Nancy Foner, Rubén G.Rumbaut, and Steven J. Gold. New York: Russell Sage.

Cinel, Dino. 1991. *The National Integration of Italian Return Migration, 1870–1929.* Cambridge: Cambridge University Press.

Cohen, Abner. 1969. *Custom and Politics in Urban Africa.* Berkeley: University of California Press.

———. 1974. *Two-Dimensional Man.* Berkeley: University of California Press.

Cole, Sally. 1998. "Reconstituting Households, Retelling Culture: Emigration and Portuguese Fisheries Workers." Pp. 13–32 in *Transgressing Borders: Critical Perspectives on Gender, Household and Culture,* eds. S. Ilcan and L. Phillips. Westport, Conn.: Bergin-Garvey.

Colen, Shellee. 1990. "Housekeeping for the Green Card: West Indian Household Workers, the State, and Stratified Reproduction in New York." Pp. 89–118 in *At Work in Homes: Household Workers in World Perspective,* American Ethnological Society Monograph 3, eds. Roger Sanjek and Shellee Colen. Washington, D.C.: American Anthropological Association.

Collier, Jane Fishburne. 1997. *From Duty to Desire: Remaking Families in a Spanish Village.* Princeton: Princeton University Press.

Comissão de Coordenação da Região Centro. 1984. *Emigração e Retorno na Região Centro.* Coimbra: Comissão de Cordenação da Região Centro.

Commission on Bilingualism and Biculturalism. 1969. *The Cultural Contribution of the Other Ethnic Groups.* Ottawa: Information Canada.

Condon, Stephanie, and P. Ogden. 1996. "Questions of Emigration, Circulation and Return: Mobility between the Caribbean and France." *International Journal of Population Geography* 2: 35–50.

Constable, Nicole. 1997. *Maid to Order in Hong Kong: Stories of Filipina Workers.* Ithaca: Cornell University Press.

———. 1999. "At Home but Not at Home: Filipina Narratives of Ambivalent Returns." *Cultural Anthropology* 14: 203–28.

Cortesão, Jaime. 1942. *O Que o Povo Canta em Portugal.* Rio de Janeiro: Livros de Portugal Lda.

Costa, Afonso. 1911. *Estudos de Economia Nacional: O Problema da Emigração.* Lisbon: Imprensa Nacional.

Costa, Antonio da. 1874. *No Minho.* Lisbon: Imprensa Nacional.

Costa, Padre António Carvalho da. 1868. *Corografia Portuguesa e Descripcam Topográfica (1706–1712).* 2d ed. Braga: D. Gouveia.

Costa, Custódio José da. 1935. *A Vida em Verso do Autor do Romance: Mistérios de Uma Donzela.* 2nd ed. Povoa de Lanhoso: Tipografía Maria da Fonte.

Crapanzano, Vincent. 1984. "Life Histories." *American Anthropologist* 86: 953–60.

Crespo, José de Almeida. 1951. *Romarias e Feiras Minhotas.* Braga.

Crissman, Lawrence W. 1967. "The Segmentary Structure of Urban Overseas Chinese Communities." *Man* 2: 185–204.

Cronin, Constance. 1970. *The Sting of Change: Sicilians in Sicily and Australia.* Chicago: University of Chicago Press.

Cruz, António. 1970. *Geografia e Economia da Província do Minho nos Fins do Século XVII.* Porto: Centro de Estudos Humanisticos, Universidade de Porto.

Curry-Rodriguez, Julia E. 1988. "Labor Migration and Familial Responsibilities: Experiences of Mexican Women." Pp. 47–63 in *Mexicanas at Work in the United States,* Mexican American Studies Monograph 5, ed. Margarita B. Melville. Houston: University of Houston.

Cutileiro, Jose. 1971. *A Portuguese Rural Society.* Oxford: Oxford University Press.

Dahya, Badr. 1973. "Transients or Settlers." *Race* 14: 241–77.

———. 1974. "The Nature of Pakistani Ethnicity in Industrial Cities in Britain." Pp. 77–118 in *Urban Ethnicity,* ed. Abner Cohen. London: Tavistock.

Das Gupta, Monisha. 1997. "What Is Indian About You? A Gendered, Transnational Approach to Ethnicity." *Gender and Society* 11: 572–96.

Davis, Kingsley. 1963. "The Theory of Change and Response in Modern Demographic History." *Population Index* 29 (4): 345–66.

Descamps, Paul. 1935. *Portugal: La Vie Sociale Actuelle.* Paris: Firmin-Didot.

Deshen, Shlomo, and Moshe Shokeid. 1974. *The Predicament of Homecoming: Cultural and Social Life of North African Immigrants in Israel.* Ithaca: Cornell University Press.

Diner, Hasia. 1983. *Erin's Daughters in America: Irish Women in the Nineteenth Century.* Baltimore: Johns Hopkins University Press.

———. 2000. *Lower East Side Memories: A Jewish Place in America.* Princeton: Princeton University Press.

Dinis, Júlio. 1868. *A Morgadinha dos Canaviais.* Lisbon.

———. 1962. *Os Fidalgos da Casa Mourisca.* Porto: Livraria Civilização.

———. 1963. *As Pupilas do Senhor Reitor.* Porto: Livraria Civilização.

Documentos Sobre a Emigração Portuguesa. 1873. Ministério dos Negócios Estrangeiros. Lisboa: Imprensa Nacional.

Dolan, Jay. 1975. *The Immigrant Church.* Baltimore: Johns Hopkins University Press.

Dollard, John. 1949. Reprint. *Criteria for the Life History.* New York: Peter Smith. Original edition, New Haven: Yale University Press, 1935.

Donato, Katherine M. 1992. "Understanding U.S. Immigration: Why Some Countries Send Women and Others Send Men." Pp. 159–84 in *Seeking Common Ground: Multidisciplinary Studies of Immigrant Women in the United States*, ed. Donna Gabaccia. Westport, Conn.: Greenwood Press.

Driedger, Leo, and Glenn Church. 1974. "Residential Segregation and Institutional Completeness: A Comparison of Ethnic Minorities." *Canadian Review of Sociology and Anthropology* 2: 36–52.

Du Bois, Cora. 1944. *People of Alor*. Minneapolis: University of Minnesota Press.

Dunn, Ashley. 1995. "In Newark, Immigration Without Fear." *New York Times*, January 17.

Dunn, Stephen, and Ethel Dunn. 1967. *The Peasants of Central Russia*. New York: Holt, Rinehart and Winston.

Durham, William H. 1989. "Conflict, Migration, and Ethnicity: A Summary." Pp. 138–45 in *Conflict, Migration and the Expression of Ethnicity*, eds. Nancie Gonzalez and Carolyn S. McCommon. Boulder, Colo.: Westview Press.

Du Toit, Brian. 1975. "A Decision-Making Model for the Study of Migration." Pp. 49–74 in *Migration and Urbanization: Models and Adaptive Strategies*, eds. Brian Du Toit and Helen I. Safa. The Hague: Mouton.

———. 1990. "People on the Move: Rural-Urban Migration with Special Reference to the Third World: Theoretical and Empirical Perspectives." *Human Organization* 49: 305–19.

Dyk, Walter. 1938. *Son of Old Man Hat: A Navaho Autobiography*. New York: Harcourt.

Eastmond, Marita. 1996. "Reconstructing Life: Chilean Refugee Women and the Dilemmas of Exile." Pp. 35–54 in *Migrant Women: Crossing Boundaries and Changing Identities*, ed. Gina Buijs. Oxford: Berg Publishers.

Eça de Queiroz, José Maria. 1886. "Introduction." In Luiz de Magalhães, *0 Brasileiro Soares*. Porto: Livraria Chardon.

Engel, Barbara. 1986. "The Woman's Side: Male Outmigration and the Family Economy in Kostroma Province." *Slavic Review* 45: 257–71.

Epstein, A. L. 1961. "The Network and Urban Social Organization." *Rhodes Livingstone Institute Journal* 29: 29–62.

Espiritu, Yen Le. 1999. "Gender and Labor in Asian Immigrant Families." *American Behavioral Scientist* 42: 628–47.

Ets, Marie Hall. 1999. *Rosa: The Life of an Italian Immigrant*. Madison: University of Wisconsin Press. Original edition, Minneapolis: University of Minnesota Press, 1970.

Evans, M. D. R. 1989. "Immigrant Entrepreneurship: Effects of Ethnic Market Size and Isolated Labor Pool." *American Sociological Review* 54: 950–62.

Ewen, Elizabeth. 1985. *Immigrant Women in the Land of Dollars, 1820–1929*. New York: Monthly Review Press.

Faist, Thomas. 1997. "The Crucial Meso Level." Pp. 187–217 in *International Migration, Immobility and Development*, eds. Tomas Hammr, Grete Brochmann, Kristoff Tamas, and Thomas Faist. New York: Berg Publishers.

Faria, Manuel Severim de. 1974. "Dos Remedios para a Falta da Gente." In *Antologia dos Economistas Portuguesas (Século XVII)*, ed António Sergio. Lisbon: Biblioteca Nacional. Original edition, 1655.

Fawcett, James T., and Robert W. Gardner. 1994. "Asian Immigrant Entrepreneurs and Non-Entrepreneurs: A Comparative Study of Recent Korean and Filipino Immigrants." *Population and Environment* 15 (3): 211–38.

Feijó, Rui Graca, and João Arriscado Nunes. 1986. "Household Composition and Social Differentiation: Northwestern Portugal in the Nineteenth Century." *Sociologia Ruralis* 26: 249–67.

Feldman-Bianco, Bela. 1992. "Multiple Layers of Time and Space: The Construction of Class, Ethnicity and Nationalism Among Portuguese Immigrants." Pp. 145–74 in *Towards a Transnational Perspective on Migration: Race, Class, Ethnicity and Nationalism Reconsidered*, eds. Nina Glick Schiller, Linda Basch, and Cristina Blanc Szanton. New York: Annals of the New York Academy of Sciences.

———. 2001. "Brazilians in Portugal, Portuguese in Brazil: Constructions of Sameness and Difference." *Identities* 8: 133–76.

Fernandez-Kelly, Maria Patricia. 1983. *For We Are Sold, I and My People: Women and Industry in Mexico's Frontier*. Albany: SUNY Press.

———. 1990. "Delicate Transactions: Gender, Home, and Employment among Hispanic Women." Pp. 183–95 in *Uncertain Terms: Negotiating Gender in American Culture*, eds. Faye Ginsburg and Anna Lowenhaupt Tsing. Boston: Beacon Press.

Ferreira de Castro, José Maria. 1928. 4th ed. *Emigrantes*. Lisbon: Guimarães and Co.

Fielding, Tony. 1992. "Migration and Culture." Pp. 201–12 in *Migration Processes and Patterns*, vol. 1, eds. Tony Champion and Tony Fielding. London: Belhaven Press.

Figueiredo, Antonio. 1975. *Portugal: Fifty Years of Dictatorship*. London: Penguin.

Fjellman, Stephen M., and Hugh Gladwin. 1985. "Haitian Family Patterns of Migration to South Florida." *Human Organization* 44: 301–12.

Foner, Nancy. 1979. *Jamaica Farewell*. London: Routledge and Kegan Paul.

———. 1987. "New Immigrants and Changing Patterns in New York City." Pp. 1–33 in *New Immigrants in New York*, ed. Nancy Foner. New York: Columbia University Press.

———. 1997. "What's New About Transnationalism? New York Immigrants Today and at the Turn of the Century." *Diaspora* 6: 355–76.

———. 2000a. "Anthropology and the Study of Immigration." Pp. 49–53 in *Immigration Research for a New Century: Multidisciplinary Perspectives*, eds. Nancy Foner, Rubén G. Rumbaut, and Steven J. Gold. New York: Russell Sage.

———. 2000b. *From Ellis Island to JFK: New York's Two Great Waves of Immigration*. New Haven: Yale University Press.

———. 2001a. *New York's New Immigrants*. New York: Columbia University Press.

———. 2001b. *Islands in the City: West Indian Migration to New York*. Berkeley: University of California Press.

Fong, Eric, and Emi Ooka. 2002. "The Social Consequences of Participating in the Ethnic Economy." *International Migration Review* 36: 125–46.

Foster, George M. 1967. *Tzintzuntzan: Mexican Peasants in a Changing World*. Boston: Little Brown.

———. 1972. "The Anatomy of Envy." *Current Anthropology* 13: 165–02.

Frank, Andre Gundre. 1967. *Capitalism and Underdevelopment in Latin America*. New York: Monthly Review Press.

Frank, Geyla. 1996. "Life History." Pp. 705–08 in *Encyclopedia of Cultural Anthropology*. New York: Henry Holt.

Freeman, Susan. 1970. *Neighbors*. Chicago: University of Chicago Press.

———. 1978. "Faith and Fashion in Spanish Religion." *Peasant Studies* 7: 101–23.

Freire, A. Braamcamp. 1905. "Povoação de Entre Douro e Minho no Século XVI." *Arquivo Histórico Portugûes* 3: 241–73.

Freitas do Amaral, Diogo. 1983. "Uma Carta do Prof. Diogo Freitas do Amaral." P. 167 in *Os Portugueses no Mundo*, ed. Manuel Alves. Lisbon: Edição de O dia.

Frey, William. 2000. *Melting Pot Suburbs: A Census 2000 Study of Suburban Diversity*. Washington, D.C.: Brookings Institution Press.

Friedl, Ernestine. 1967. "The Position of Women: Appearance and Reality." *Anthropological Quarterly* 40: 97–108.

Friedman-Kasaba, Kathie. 1996. *Memories of Migration: Gender, Ethnicity and Work in the Lives of Jewish and Italian Women in New York, 1870–1924*. Albany: SUNY Press.

Frisken, Frances, L. S. Bourne, Gunter Gad, and Robert A. Murdie. 2000. "Social Sustainability. The Toronto Experience." Pp. 68–97 in *The Social Sustainability of Cities: Diversity and the Management of Change*, eds. Mario Polese and Richard Stren. Toronto: University of Toronto Press.

Fryer, Peter, and Patricia McGowan. 1963. *Le Portugal de Salazar*. Paris: Ruedo Ibérico.

Fuchs, Lawrence H. 1968. *American Ethnic Politics*. New York: Harper and Row.

Gabaccia, Donna. 1992. *Seeking Common Ground: Multidisciplinary Studies of Immigrant Women in the United States*. Westport, Conn.: Greenwood Press.

———. 1994. *From the Other Side: Women, Gender, & Immigrant Life in the U.S. 1820–1990*. Bloomington: Indiana University Press.

Gans, Herbert. 1962. *The Urban Villagers*. Glencoe, Ill.: The Free Press.

———. 2000. "Filling in Some Holes: Six Areas of Needed Immigration Research." Pp. 76–89 in *Immigration Research for a New Century: Multidisciplinary Perspectives*, eds. Nancy Foner, Rubén G. Rumbaut, and Steven J. Gold. New York: Russell Sage.

Geertz, Clifford. 1960. "The Changing Role of a Cultural Broker: The Javanese Kijaji." *Comparative Studies in Society and History* 2: 228–49.

———. 1966. "Religion as a Cultural System." Pp. 1–46 in *Anthropological Approaches to the Study of Religion*, ed. Michael Banton. London: Tavistock.

Georges, Eugenia. 1990. *The Making of a Transnational Community: Migration, Development, and Cultural Change in the Dominican Republic*. New York: Columbia University Press.

———. 1992. "Gender, Class, and Migration in the Dominican Republic: Women's Experiences in a Transnational Community." Pp. 81–99 in *Towards a Transnational Perspective on Migration: Race, Class, Ethnicity, and Nationalism Reconsidered*, eds. Nina Glick Schiller, Linda Basch, and Christina Szanton Blanc. New York: Annals of the New York Academy of Sciences.

Gerstle, Gary, and John Mollenkopf, eds. 2001. *E Pluribus Unum? Contemporary and Historical Perspectives on Immigrant Political Incorporation*. New York: Russell Sage Foundation.

Gewertz, Deborah, and Frederick Errington. 1991. "We Think, Therefore They Are? On Occidentalizing the World." *Anthropological Quarterly* 64: 80–91.

Giddens, Anthony. 1984. *The Constitution of Society.* Cambridge: Polity Press.

Gilad, Lisa. 1989. *Ginger and Salt: Yemeni Jewish Women in an Israeli Town.* Boulder, Colo.: Westview Press.

Giles, Wenona. 1991. "Class, Gender, and Race Struggles in a Portuguese Neighborhood in London." *International Journal of Urban and Regional Research* 15: 432–41.

———. 1992. "Gender Inequality and Resistance: The Case of Portuguese Women in London." *Anthropological Quarterly* 65: 67–79.

———. 2002. *Portuguese Women in Toronto: Gender, Immigration, and Nationalism.* Toronto: University of Toronto Press.

Giner, Salvador. 1971. "Spain." Pp. 125–61 in *Contemporary Europe: Class, Status, and Power,* eds. Margaret S. Archer and Salvador Giner. London: Wiedenfeld and Nicolson.

Ginsburg, Faye. 1987. "Procreation Stories: Reproduction, Nurturance, and Procreation in the Life Narratives of Abortion Activists." *American Ethnologist* 14 (40): 623–36.

Giovannini, Maureen. 1981. "Women: A Dominant Symbol within the Cultural System of a Sicilian Town." *Man* 16: 408–26.

Girard, Alain, ed. 1954. "Français et Immigrés." Paris: Institut National d' Études Demographiques, Travaux et Documents, Cahier 20.

Glader, Paul. 2002. "Community's Success Is Concrete: Portuguese Immigrants Build on Strong Foundation." *Washington Post*, August 22, p. PW1, www. washingtonpost.com/wp-dyn/articles/A42519-200Aug20.html.

Glazer, Nathan, and Daniel P. Moynihan. 1963. *Beyond the Melting Pot: The Negroes, Puerto Ricans, Jews, Italians and Irish of New York City.* Cambridge: MIT Press.

Glick Schiller, Nina. 1997. "The Situation of Transnational Studies." *Identities* 4: 155–66.

———. 1999. "Transmigrants and Nation-States; Something Old and Something New in the U.S. Immigrant Experience." Pp. 94–119 in *Handbook of International Migration: The American Experience,* eds. Charles Hirschman, Philip Kasinitz, and Josh DeWind. New York: Russell Sage.

Glick Schiller, Nina, Linda Basch, and Cristina Szanton Blanc, eds. 1992a. *Towards a Transnational Perspective on Migration: Race, Class, Ethnicity, and Nationalism Reconsidered.* New York: New York Academy of Sciences.

———. 1992b. "Transnationalism: A New Analytical Framework for Understanding Migration." Pp. 1–24 in *Towards a Transnational Perspective on Migration: Race, Class, Ethnicity, and Nationalism Reconsidered,* eds. Nina Glick Schiller, Linda Basch, and Christina Szanton Blanc. New York: Annals of the New York Academy of Sciences.

———. 1995. "From Immigrant to Transmigrant: Theorizing Transitional Migration." *Anthropological Quarterly* 68: 48–63.

Glick Schiller, Nina, and Georges Eugene Fouron. 2001. *Georges Woke Up Laughing: Long-Distance Nationalism and the Search for Home.* Durham: Duke University Press.

Gluckman, Max. 1968. "Psychological, Sociological and Anthropological Explanations of Witchcraft and Gossip: A Clarification." *Man* 3: 20–34.

Gmelch, George. 1980. "Return Migration." *Annual Review of Anthropology* 9: 135–159.

———. 1983. "Who Returns and Why: Return Migration Behavior in Two Atlantic Societies." *Human Organization* 42: 46–54.

———. 1987. "Work, Innovation and Investment: The Impact of Return Migration in Barbados." *Human Organization* 46: 131–41.

———. 1992. *Double Passage: The Lives of Caribbean Migrants Abroad and Back Home.* Ann Arbor: University of Michigan Press.

Gmelch, George, and Sharon Bohn Gmelch. 1995. "Gender and Migration: The Readjustment of Women Migrants in Barbados, Ireland, and Newfoundland." *Human Organization* 54: 470–73.

Gmelch, George, and Walter P. Zenner. 1996. *Urban Life: Readings in Urban Anthropology.* 3d ed. Prospect Heights, Ill.: Waveland Press.

Gmelch, Sharon. 1991. *Nan: The Life of an Irish Travelling Woman.* Prospect Heights, Ill.: Waveland Press.

Gober, Patricia. 2000. "Immigration and North American Cities." *Urban Geography* 21: 83–90.

Gold, Steven J. 1995. *From the Workers' State to the Gold State: Jews from the Former Soviet Union in California.* Boston: Allyn and Bacon.

Goldey, Patricia. 1981. "Emigração e Estrutura Familiar: Estudo de um Caso no Minho." *Estudos Contemporâneos* 2/3: 111–28.

Gonçalves, Flavio. 1952. "Procissões de Mordomas." *Douro Litoral* 2: 80–86.

Gonçalves, Gabriel. 1935. "A Capela do Senhor do Cruzeiro." *Arquivo do Alto Minho* 4: 165–72.

González, Nancie Solien. 1961. "Family Organization in Five Types of Migratory Wage Labor." *American Anthropologist* 63 (6): 1264–80.

———. 1969. *Black Carib Household Structure: A Study of Migration and Modernization.* Seattle: University of Washington Press.

———. 1970. "Toward a Definition of Matrifocality." Pp. 231–43 in *Afro-American Anthropology,* eds. Norman E. Whitten, Jr. and John F. Szwed. New York: Free Press.

———. 1992. *Dollar, Dove and Eagle: One Hundred Years of Palestinian Migration to Honduras.* Ann Arbor: University of Michigan Press.

Goodson-Lawes, J. 1993. "Feminine Authority and Migration: The Case of One Family from Mexico." *Urban Anthropology* 22: 277–97.

Gottschalk, Louis, Clyde Kluckhohn, and Robert Angell, eds. 1945. *The Use of Personal Documents in History, Anthropology and Sociology.* New York: Social Science Research Council Bulletin.

Grasmuck, S., and Patricia Pessar. 1991. *Between Two Islands: Dominican International Migration.* Berkeley: University of California Press.

Graves, Nancy B., and Theodore D. Graves. 1974. "Adaptive Strategies in Urban Migration." *Annual Review of Anthropology* 3: 117–51.

Greeley, Andrew. 1971. *Why Can't They Be Like Us: America's White Ethnic Groups.* New York: Dutton.

Green, Nancy L. 1990. "L'histoire Comparative et Le Champ des Études Migra-toires." *Annales ESC,* no. 6 (novembre-décembre): 1335–50.

Gregory, David. 1976. "Migration and Demographic Change in Andalucia." Pp. 63–96 in *The Changing Faces of Rural Spain*, eds. Joseph Aceves and William Douglass. New York: Schenkman.

Grieco, Margaret. 1995. "Transported Lives: Urban Social Networks and Labour Circulation." Pp. 189–212 in *The Urban Context: Ethnicity, Social Networks and Situational Analysis*, eds. Alisdair Rogers and Steven Vertovec. Oxford: Berg Publishers.

Griffith, David C. 1985. "Women, Remittances, and Reproduction." *American Ethnologist* 12: 676–90.

Grillo, R. D. 1980. *"Nation" and "State" in Europe: Anthropological Perspectives*. New York: Academic Press.

Grimes, Kimberly M. 1998. *Crossing Borders: Changing Social Identities in Southern Mexico.* Tucson: University of Arizona Press.

Groves, Julian McAllister, and Kimberly A. Chang. 1999. "Romancing Resistance and Resisting Romance: Ethnography and the Construction of Power in the Filipina Domestic Worker Community in Hong Kong." *Journal of Contemporary Ethnography* 28: 235–65.

Guarnizo, Luis Eduardo. 1997a. "The Emergence of a Transnational Social Formation and the Mirage of Return Migration Among Dominican Transmigrants." *Identities* 4: 281–322.

———. 1997b. "Going Home: Class, Gender and Household Transformation Among Dominican Return Migrants." Pp. 13–60 in *Caribbean Circuits: New Directions in the Study of Caribbean Migration,* eds. Patricia Pessar. New York: Center for Migration Studies.

———. 2001. "On the Political Participation of Transnational Migrants: Old Practices and New Trends." Pp. 213–63 in *E Pluribus Unum? Contemporary and Historical Perspectives on Immigrant Political Incorporation*, eds. Gary Gerstle and John Mollenkopf. New York: Russell Sage.

Guarnizo, Luis, and Luz Maria Diaz. 1999. "Transnational Migration: A View from Colombia." *Ethnic and Racial Studies* 22: 397–421.

Guarnizo, Luis Eduardo, and Michael Peter Smith. 1998. "The Locations of Transnationalism." Pp. 3–34 in *Transnationalism From Below*, eds. Michael Peter Smith and Luis Eduardo Guarnizo. New Brunswick, N.J.: Transaction Books.

Gupta, Akhil, and James Ferguson. 1997. "Culture, Power, Place: Ethnography at the End of an Era." Pp. 1–29 in *Culture, Power, Place: Explorations in Critical Anthropology,* eds. Akhil Gupta and James Ferguson. Durham: Duke University Press.

Gutkind, Peter C. W. 1965. "African Urbanism, Mobility and the Social Network." *International Journal of Comparative Sociology* 6: 48–60.

Hagan, Jacqueline. 1998. "Social Networks, Gender and Immigrant Incorporation: Resources and Constraints." *American Sociological Review* 63: 55–67.

Halter, Marilyn. 1993. *Between Race and Ethnicity: Cape Verdean American Immigrants, 1860–1965.* Urbana: University of Illinois Press.

Hammam, Mona. 1986. "Capitalist Development, Family Division of Labor, and Migration in the Middle East." Pp. 158–73 in *Women's Work: Development and*

Division of Labor by Gender, eds. Eleanor Leacock, Helen I. Safa. South Hadley, Mass.: Bergin and Garvey.

Hammel, Eugene A., and Peter Laslett. 1974. "Comparing Household Structure over Time and Between Cultures." *Comparative Studies in Society and History* 16: 73–109.

Hart, Dianne Walta. 1997. *Undocumented in L.A.: An Immigrant's Story.* Wilmington: Scholarly Resources.

Hawkins, Freda. 1988. *Canada and Immigration: Public Policy and Public Concern.* Montreal: McGill-Queens University Press.

Heath, Dwight B. 1973. "New Patrons for Old: Changing Patron-Client Relationships in the Bolivian Yungas." *Ethnology* 12: 75–98.

Helweg, Arthur W. 1979. *Sikhs in England.* Oxford: Oxford University Press.

Herculano, Alexandre. 1873. "A Emigração." Pp. 105–282 in *Opúsculos,* 4th ed. Lisbon: Livaría Bertrand.

Herzfeld, Michael. 1985. *The Poetics of Manhood: Contest and Identity in a Cretan Mountain Village.* Princeton: Princeton University Press.

———. 1986. "Within and Without: The Category of 'Female' in the Ethnography of Modern Greece." Pp. 215–34 in *Gender and Power in Rural Greece,* ed. Jill Dubisch. Princeton, N.J.: Princeton University Press.

Hirsch, Jennifer S. 1999. "En el Norte la Mujer Manda: Gender, Generation, and Geography in a Mexican Transnational Community." *American Behavioral Scientist* 42: 1332–49.

Ho, Christine G. T. 1993. "The Internationalization of Kinship and the Feminization of Caribbean Migration: The Case of Afro-Trinidadian Immigrants in Los Angeles." *Human Organization* 52: 32–40.

Hobsbawn, Eric. 1969. *Bandits.* New York: Dell.

Hoffman-Nowotny, H. J. 1978. "European Migration After WW II." Pp. 85–105 in *Human Migration,* eds. W. H. McNeill and R. S. Adams. Bloomington: University of Indiana Press.

Holmes, Douglas. 1989. *Cultural Disenchantments: Worker Peasantries in Northeast Italy.* Princeton: Princeton University Press.

Holtzman, Jon D. 2000. "Dialing 911 in Nuer: Gender Transformations and Domestic Violence in a Midwestern Sudanese Refugee Community." Pp. 390–408 in *Immigration Research for a New Century: Multidisciplinary Perspectives,* eds. Nancy Foner, Rubén G. Rumbaut, and Steven J. Gold. New York: Russell Sage.

Hondagneu-Sotelo, Pierrette. 1992. "Overcoming Patriarchal Constraints: The Reconstruction of Gender Relations among Mexican Immigrant Men and Women." *Gender and Society* 6: 393–415.

———. 1994. *Gendered Transitions: Mexican Experiences of Immigration.* Berkeley: University of California Press.

———. 2001. *Doméstica: Immigrant Workers Cleaning and Caring in the Shadows of Affluence.* Berkeley: University of California Press.

Houstoun, M. F., R. G. Kramer, and J. M. Barrett. 1984. "Female Predominance of Immigration to the United States since 1930: A First Look." *International Migration Review* 18: 908–63.

Hudson, Ray, and Jim Lewis. 1985. *Uneven Development in Southern Europe: Studies of Accumulation, Class, Migration and the State.* London: Methuen.

Kasinitz, P., and J. Freidenberg-Hjerbstein. 1987. "The Puerto Rican Parade and West Indian Carnival: Public Celebrations in New York City." Pp. 327–49 in *Caribbean Life in New York City: Sociocultural Dimensions*, eds. Constance Sutton and Elsa Chaney. New York: Center for Migration Studies.

Kayser, Bernard. 1972. *Cyclically Determined Homeward Flows of Migrant Workers*. Paris: OECD.

Kearney, Michael. 1995. "The Local and the Global: The Anthropology of Globalization and Transnationalism." *Annual Review of Anthropology* 24: 547–65.

Kearney, Michael, and Carole Nagengast. 1989. *Anthropological Perspectives on Transnational Communities in Rural California*. Davis, Calif.: California Institute for Rural Studies.

Keefe, Eugene, David P. Coffin, Sallie M. Hicks, William A. Mussen Jr., Robert Rinehart, and William J. Simon. 1977. *Area Handbook of Portugal*. Washington: American University Foreign Area Studies.

Kelson, Gregory A., and Debra L. DeLaet. 1999. *Gender and Immigration*. New York: New York University Press.

Kempadoo, Kamala, and Jo Doezema, eds. 1998. *Global Sex Workers: Rights, Resistance, and Redefinition*. New York: Routledge.

Kemper, Robert V. 1977. *Migration and Adaptation: Tzintzuntzan Peasants in Mexico City*. Beverly Hills, Calif.: Sage Publications.

Kendall, Laurel. 1988. *The Life and Hard Times of a Korean Shaman: Of Tales and the Telling of Tales*. Honolulu: University of Hawaii Press.

Kenna, Margaret E. 1992. "Mattresses and Migrants: A Patron Saint's Festival on a Small Greek Island Over Two Decades." Pp. 155–72 in *Revitalizing European Rituals*, ed. Jeremy Boissevain. London: Routledge.

Kenny, Michael. 1960. "Patterns of Patronage in Spain." *Anthropological Quarterly* 33: 14–23.

———. 1976. "Twentieth-Century Spanish Expatriate Ties with the Homeland." Pp. 97–121 in *The Changing Faces of Rural Spain*, eds. Joseph Aceves and William Douglass. New York: Schenkman.

Kertzer, David L. 1984. *Family Life in Central Italy, 1880–1910*. New Brunswick, N.J.: Rutgers University Press.

Khandelwal, Madhulika S. 2002. *Becoming American, Being Indian: An Immigrant Community in New York City*. Ithaca: Cornell University Press.

Kibria, Nazli. 1993. *Family Tightrope: The Changing Lives of Vietnamese Americans*. Princeton: Princeton University Press.

Kikemura, Akemi. 1981. *Through Harsh Winters: The Life of a Japanese Immigrant Woman*. Novato, Calif.: Chandler & Sharp Publishers.

King, Russell. 1978. "Return Migration: Review of Some Cases from Southern Europe." *Mediterranean Studies* 1: 3–30.

King, Russell, Jill Mortimer, Allan Strachen, and Anna Trono. 1985. "Return Migration and Rural Economic Change: A South Italian Case Study." Pp. 101–22 in *Uneven Development in Southern Europe: Studies of Accumulation, Class, Migration and the State*, eds. Ray Hudson and Jim Lewis. London: Methuen.

Krickus, Richard. 1976. *Pursuing the American Dream: White Ethnics and the New Populism*. Bloomington: Indiana University Press.

Klaver, Jeanine. 1997. *From the Land of the Sun to the City of Angels: The Migration Process of Zapotec Indians from Oaxaca, Mexico, to Los Angeles, California*. Amsterdam: The Dutch Geographical Society.

Klimt, Andrea C. 1989. "Disorderly Meetings: Arguments about Gender in a Migratory Context." Paper presented at the International Conference Group on Portugal, Durham, N.H., September 21–24.

———. 1992. *Temporary and Permanent Lives: The Construction of Identity among Portuguese Migrants in Germany*. Ph.D. dissertation, Department of Anthropology, Stanford University.

———. 2000a. "European Spaces: Portuguese Migrants' Notions of Home and Belonging." *Diaspora* 9: 259–85.

———. 2000b. "Enacting National Selves: Authenticity, Adventure, and Disaffection in the Portuguese Diaspora." *Identities* 6: 513–50.

Kluckhohn, Clyde. 1945. "The Personal Document in Anthropological Science." Pp. 79–173 in *The Use of Personal Documents in History, Anthropology and Sociology*, eds. Louis Gottschalk, Clyde Kluckhohn, and Robert Angell. New York: Social Science Research Council Bulletin no. 53.

Knörr, Jacqueline, and Barbara Meier, eds. 2000. *Women and Migration: Anthropological Perspectives*. New York: St. Martin's Press.

Koebel, William. 1909. *Portugal: Its Land and People*. London: A. Constable.

Kofman, Eleonore. 1999. "Female 'Birds of Passage' a Decade Later: Gender and Immigration in the European Union." *International Migration Review* 33: 269–99.

Kramer, Jane. 1976. "Migrant Workers in Europe." *The New Yorker*, March 22, 43–84.

Krauss, Clifford. 2002. "Green Tea Flavors the Land of the Maple Leaf." *New York Times*, March 21, p. A2.

Kurien, Prema. 1999. "Gendered Ethnicity: Creating a Hindu Indian Identity in the United States." *American Behavioral Scientist* 42: 648–70.

Kwong, Peter. 1996. *The New Chinatown*. New York: Hill and Wang.

———. 1997. "Manufacturing Ethnicity." *Critique of Anthropology* 17: 365–87.

———. 1998. *Forbidden Workers: Illegal Chinese Immigrants and American Labor*. New York: New Press.

Laguerre, Michel S. 1998. *Diasporic Citizenship: Haitian Americans in Transnational America*. New York: St. Martin's Press.

Lamas, Maria. 1948. *As Mulheres do Meu País*. Lisbon: Editora Actualis.

Lamb, Sarah. 2001. "Being a Widow and Other Life Stories: The Interplay Between Lives and Words." *Anthropology and Humanism* 26: 16–34.

Lamphere, Louise. 1985. "Bringing the Family to Work: Women's Culture on the Shop Floor." *Feminist Studies* 11: 519–55.

———. 1986a. "From Working Daughters to Working Mothers: Production and Reproduction in an Industrial Community." *American Ethnologist* 13: 118–30.

———. 1986b. "Working Mothers and Family Strategies: Portuguese and Colombian Women in a New England Community." Pp. 266–83 in *International Migration: The Female Experience*, eds. Rita J. Simon and Caroline B. Brettell. Totowa, N.J.: Rowman and Allenheld.

———. 1987. *From Working Daughters to Working Mothers: Immigrant Women in a New England Community*. Ithaca: Cornell University Press.

Lamphere, Louise, Filomena M. Silva, and John P. Sousa. 1980. "Kin Networks and Strategies of Working-Class Portuguese Families in a New England Town." Pp. 219–49 in *The Versatility of Kinship*, eds. Linda Cordell and Stephen Beckerman. New York: Academic Press.

Langness, L. L. 1965. *The Life History in Anthropological Science*. New York: Holt, Rinehart and Winston.

Langness, L. L., and Geyla Frank. 1985. *Lives: An Anthropological Approach to Biography*. Novato, Calif.: Chandler and Sharp.

Lee, R. H. 1960. *The Chinese in the USA*. Hong Kong: Hong Kong University Press.

Lee, W. R. 1977. "Bastardy and the Socioeconomic Structure of Southern Germany." *Journal of Interdisciplinary History* 7: 403–25.

Leeds, Anthony. 1987. "Work, Labor, and Their Recompenses: Portuguese Life Strategies Involving Migration." Pp. 9–60 in *Migrants in Europe: The Role of Family, Labor and Politics*, eds. Hans C. Buechler and Judith-Maria Buechler. Westport, Conn.: Greenwood Press.

Leeds, Elizabeth. 1984. *Labor Export, Development and the State: The Political Economy of Portuguese Emigration*. Ph.D. dissertation, Department of Political Science, Massachusetts Institute of Technology.

Leite, J. Costa. 1987. "Emigração Portuguesa: a lei e os números (1855–1914)." *Análise Social* 23: 463–80.

Leite de Vasconcellos, Joaquím de. 1958. *Etnografia Portuguesa*, vol. 4. Lisbon: Imprensa Nacional.

Lessinger, Johanna. 1995. *From the Ganges to the Hudson: Indian Immigrants in New York City*. Boston: Allyn and Bacon.

Levine, Robert. 1966. "Sex Roles and Economic Change in Africa." *Ethnology* 5: 186–93.

Levine, Sarah. 1979. *Mothers and Wives: Gusii Women of East Africa*. Chicago: University of Chicago Press.

Levitt, Peggy. 1998a. "Local-Level Global Religion: The Case of U.S.–Dominican Migration." *Journal for the Scientific Study of Religion* 37: 74–89.

———. 1998b. "Social Remittances: Migration-Driven Local-Level Forms of Cultural Diffusion." *International Migration Review* 32: 926–48.

———. 2000. "Migrants Participate Across Borders: Toward an Understanding of Forms and Consequences." Pp. 459–79 in *Immigration Research for a New Century*, eds. Nancy Foner, Rubén Rumbaut, and Steven J. Gold. New York: Russell Sage.

———. 2001a. *The Transnational Villagers*. Berkeley: University of California Press.

———. 2001b. "Transnational Migration; Taking Stock and Future Directions." *Global Networks* 3: 195–216.

Lewis, Oscar. 1959. *Five Families: Mexican Case Studies in the Culture of Poverty*. New York: Basic Books.

———. 1961. *The Children of Sanchez*. New York: Random House.

———. 1966. *La Vida*. New York: Random House.

Li, Wei. 1998. "Anatomy of a New Ethnic Settlement: The Chinese *Ethnoburb* in Los Angeles." *Urban Studies* 35: 479–501.

Lianos, Thomas. 1976. "Flows of Greek Outmigration and Return Migration." *International Migrations* 13: 119–33.

Lieberson, Stanley. 1963. *Ethnic Patterns in American Cities*. Glencoe, Ill.: The Free Press.

Light, Ivan, and Parminder Bhachu. 1993. *Immigration and Entrepreneurship: Culture, Capital, and Ethnic Networks*. New Brunswick, N.J.: Transaction Publishers.

Lin, Jennifer. 2000. "Sex Trade Ensnares Female Immigrants in the U.S." *Detroit Free Press*, November 16, www.frep.com/news/nw/zprost16_20001116.htm.

Lison-Tolosana, Carmelo. 1976. "The Ethics of Inheritance." Pp. 305–15 in *Mediterranean Family Structures*, ed. J. G. Peristiany. Cambridge: Cambridge University Press.

Litt, Edgar. 1970. *Beyond Pluralism: Ethnic Politics in America*. New York: Scott Foresman.

Little, Kenneth. 1957. "The Role of Voluntary Associations in West African Urbanization." *American Anthropologist* 59: 579–96.

Livi Bacci, Massimo. 1972. *The Demographic and Social Pattern of Emigration from the Southern European Countries*. Florence: Dipartimento Statistico Matematico dell' Universita di Firenze.

Lockwood, Victoria S. 1990. "Development and Return Migration to Rural French Polynesia." *International Migration Review* 24: 347–71.

Loewen, James W. 1971. *The Mississippi Chinese*. Cambridge: Harvard University Press.

Logan, John, Richard Alba, and T. L. McNulty. 1994. "Ethnic Economies in Metropolitan Regions: Miami and Beyond." *Social Forces* 72: 691–724.

Lomonaco, Barbara. 1993. *Empty Nests and Anxious Lives: Migration, Gender, and the Cultural Construction of Distress in a Greek Island Community*. Ph.D. dissertation, Department of Anthropology, Southern Methodist University.

Lopreato, Joseph. 1965. "How Would You Like to Be a Peasant?" *Human Organization* 24: 298–307.

———. 1967. *Peasants No More: Social Class and Social Change in an Underdeveloped Society*. San Francisco: Chandler.

Louie, Miriam Ching Yoon. 2001. *Sweatshop Warriors: Immigrant Women Workers Take on the Global Factory*. Cambridge: South End Press.

Lubkemann, Stephen C. 2003. "Race, Class, and Kin in the Negotiation of 'Internal Strangerhood' among Portuguese Retornados, 1975–2000." Pp. 75–94 in *Europe's Invisible Migrants*, ed. Andrea L. Smith. Amsterdam: Amsterdam University Press.

Lucassen, Jan, and Leo Lucassen, eds. 1997. *Migration, Migration History, History: Old Paradigms and New Perspectives*. Bern: Peter Lang.

Lucassen, Leo. 2002. "Old and New Migrants in the Twentieth Century: A European Perspective." *Journal of American Ethnic History* 21: 85–101.

Macedo, Duarte Ribeiro de. 1675. *Discurso Sobre a Introdução dos Artes no Reino*. Lisbon.

Magalhães, Luiz de. 1886. *O Brasileiro Soares*. Porto: Livraria Chardon.

Mahler, Sarah J. 1995. *American Dreaming: Immigrant Life on the Margins*. Princeton: Princeton University Press.

———. 1998. "Theoretical and Empirical Contributions Toward a Research Agenda for Transnationalism." Pp. 64–100 in *Transnationalism From Below*, eds.

Michael Peter Smith and Luis Eduardo Guarnizo. New Brunswick, N.J.: Transaction Books.
———. 1999. "Engendering Transnational Migration: A Case of Salvadorans." *American Behavioral Scientist* 42: 690–719.
———. 2001. "Transnational Relationships: The Struggle to Communicate Across Borders." *Identities* 7: 583–619.
Malheiros, Jorge. 2002. "Portugal Seeks Balance of Emigration, Immigration." *Migration Information Source,* www.migrationinformation.org/Profiles/display.cfm?id+77.
Mandelbaum, David G. 1973. "The Study of Life History: Gandhi." *Current Anthropology* 14: 177–96.
Mangin, William. 1970. *Peasants in Cities: Readings in the Anthropology of Urbanization.* Boston: Houghton Mifflin.
Manique, Luiz de Pina. 1970. *A Populacão de Portugal em 1798. 0 Censo de Pina Manique.* Paris: Fundacão Calouste Gulbenkian.
Manning, Robert. 1998. "Multicultural Washington, D.C.: The Changing Social and Economic Landscape of a Past Industrial Metropolis." *Ethnic and Racial Studies* 21: 328–54.
Marcus, George, and Michael Fischer. 1986. *Anthropology as Cultural Critique.* Chicago: University of Chicago Press.
Margolis, Maxine. 1990. "From Mistress to Servant: Downward Mobility among Brazilian Immigrants in New York City." *Urban Anthropology* 19: 215–30.
———. 1994. *Little Brazil: An Ethnography of Brazilian Immigrants in New York City.* Princeton: Princeton University Press.
Martin, Phillip, and Jonas Widgren. 2002. "International Migration: Facing the Challenge." *Population Bulletin* 57 (1): 3–40.
Martins, Herminio. 1971. "Portugal." Pp. 60–89 in *Contemporary Europe: Class, Status, and Power,* eds. Margaret S. Archer and Salvador Giner. London: Wiedenfeld and Nicolson.
Martins, J. P. de Oliveira. 1885. *Política e Economia Nacional de Portugal.* Lisbon: Magalhães e Moniz.
———. 1956. Reprint. *Fomento Rural e Emigração.* Lisbon: Guimarães & Ca. Editores. Original edition, 1887–1892.
Massey, Douglas, Rafael Alarcon, Jorge Durand, and Humberto Gonzalez. 1987. *Return to Aztlan: The Social Process of International Migration from Western Mexico.* Berkeley: University of California Press.
Massey, Douglas S., Joaquin Arango, Graeme Hugo, Ali Kouaouci, Adela Pellegrino, and J. Edward Taylor. 1993. "Theories of International Migration: A Review and Appraisal." *Population and Development Review* 19: 431–66.
———. 1994. "An Evaluation of International Migration Theory: The North American Case." *Population and Development Review* 20: 699–751.
———. 1998. *Worlds in Motion: Understanding International Migration at the End of the Millennium.* Oxford: Clarendon Press.
Massey, Douglas S., and E. Parrado. 1994. "Migradollars: The Remittances and Savings of Mexican Migrants to the U.S.A." *Population Research and Policy Review* 13: 3–30.

Mayer, Philip. 1961. *Townsmen or Tribesmen*. Cape Town: Oxford University Press.

McAlister, Elizabeth. 1998. "The Madonna of 115th Street Revisited: Vodou and Haitian Catholicism in the Age of Transnationalism." Pp. 123–60 in *Gatherings in Diaspora: Religious Communities and the New Immigration*, eds. R. Stephen Warner and Judith G. Wittner. Philadelphia: Temple University Press.

Meintel, Deirdre. 1987. "The New Double Workday of Immigrant Workers in Quebec." *Women's Studies* 13: 273–93.

———. 2002. "Cape Verdean Transnationalism, Old and New." *Anthropologica* 44: 25–42.

Meintel, Deidre, Micheline Labelle, Genevieve Turcotte, and Marianne Kempineers. 1984. "Migration, Wage Labor, and Domestic Relationships: Immigrant Women in Montreal." *Anthropologica* 26: 135–69.

Melville, Margarita. 1988. *Mexicanas at Work in the United States*. Houston: University of Houston, Mexican American Studies Program.

Menjívar, Cecilia. 1999. "The Intersection of Work and Gender: Central American Women and Employment in California." *American Behavioral Scientist* 42: 601–27.

———. 2000. *Fragmented Ties: Salvadoran Immigrant Networks in America*. Berkeley: University of California Press.

Menjívar, Cecilia, Julie Da Vanzo, Lisa Greenwell, and R. Burciaga Valdez. 1998. "Remittance Behavior Among Salvadoran and Filipino Immigrants in Los Angeles." *International Migration Review* 32: 97–126

Michaels, Anne. 1998. *Fugitive Pieces*. New York: Alfred A. Knopf.

Miller, Randall M., and Thomas D. Marzik, eds. 1977. *Immigrants and Religion in Urban America*. Philadelphia: Temple University Press.

Millett, David. 1971. "The Orthodox Church: Ukranian, Greek and Syrian." Pp. 47–57 in *Immigrant Groups*, ed. Jean L. Elliott. Scarborough, N.J.: Prentice Hall.

Mills, Mary Beth. 1997. "Contesting the Margins of Modernity: Women, Migration and Consumption in Thailand." *American Ethnologist* 24: 37–61.

———. 1998. "Gendered Encounters with Modernity: Labor Migrants and Marriage Choices in Contemporary Thailand." *Identities* 5: 301–34.

Minces, Juliette. 1973. *Les Travailleurs Étrangers en France*. Paris: Seuil.

Mintz, Sidney. 1960. *Worker in the Cane: A Puerto Rican Life History*. New Haven: Yale University Press.

———. 1989. "The Sensation of Moving, While Standing Still." *American Ethnologist* 16: 786–96.

———. 1998. "The Localization of Anthropological Practice." *Critique of Anthropology* 18 (2): 117–33.

Mitchell, J. Clyde, ed. 1969. *Social Networks in Urban Situations*. Manchester: Manchester University Press.

———. 1974. "Social Networks." *Annual Review of Anthropology* 3: 279–99.

Mollenkopf, John Hull. 1999. "Urban Political Conflicts and Alliances: New York and Los Angeles Compared." Pp. 412–22 in *The Handbook of International Migration: The American Experience*, eds. Charles Hirschman, Philip Kasinitz, and Josh DeWind. New York: Russell Sage.

Momsen, Janet. 1992. "Gender Selectivity in Caribbean Migration." Pp. 73–90 in *Gender and Migration in Developing Countries*, ed. Sylvia Chant. London: Belhaven Press.

Moore, Barrington. 1961. *Social Origins of Dictatorship and Democracy: Lord and Peasant in the Making of the Modern World.* Boston: Beacon Press.

Moore, Henrietta. 1994. *A Passion for Difference.* Bloomington: Indiana University Press.

Morawska, Eva. 1990. "The Sociology and Historiography of Immigration." Pp. 187–240 in *Immigration Reconsidered: History, Sociology and Politics*, ed. Virginia Yans-Mclaughlin. New York: Oxford University Press.

———. 2001. "Immigrants, Transnationalism, and Ethnicization: A Comparison of This Great Wave and the Last." Pp. 175–212 in *E Pluribus Unum? Contemporary and Historical Perspectives on Immigrant Political Incorporation*, eds. Gary Gerstle and John Mollenkopf. New York: Russell Sage.

Morokvasic, Mirjana. 1983. "Women in Migration: Beyond the Reductionist Outlook." Pp. 13–31 in *One Way Ticket: Migration and Female Labour*, ed. Annie Phizacklea. London: Routledge and Kegan Paul.

Murphy, Robert F. 1964. "Social Change and Acculturation." *Transactions, New York Academy of Sciences* 26 (7): 845–54.

Neale, Rusty, and Virginia Neale. 1987. "As Long as You Know How to Do Housework: Portuguese-Canadian Women and the Office-Cleaning Industry in Toronto." *Resources for Feminist Research* 16: 39–41.

Nee, Victor, Jimy M. Sanders, and Scott Sernau. 1994. "Job Transitions in an Immigrant Metropolis: Ethnic Boundaries and the Mixed Economy." *American Sociological Review* 59: 849–72.

Nelson, Nici. 1992. "The Women Who Have Left and Those Who Have Stayed Behind: Rural-Urban Migration in Central and Western Kenya." Pp. 109–38 in *Gender and Migration in Developing Countries*, ed. Sylvia Chant. New York: Belhaven Press.

Noivo, Edite. 1997. *Inside Ethnic Families: Three Generations of Portuguese-Canadians.* Montreal: McGill-Queen's University Press.

Nunes, João Arriscado. 1985. "Is There One Household Formation System in Northwestern Portugal?" Unpublished paper.

Nunes, João. 1986. "On Household Composition in Northwestern Portugal: Some Critical Remarks and a Case Study." *Sociologia Ruralis* 26: 48–69.

Nunes, Rosana Barbosa. 2000. "Portuguese Immigrants in Brazil: An Overview." *Portuguese Studies Review* 8: 27–44

O'Connor, Mary. 1990. "Women's Networks and the Social Needs of Mexican Immigrants." *Urban Anthropology* 19: 81–98.

Organization for Economic Cooperation and Development. 1967. *Emigrant Workers Returning to their Home Countries.* Paris: OECD.

Ogden, Philip E., 1995. "Labour Migration to France." Pp. 289–96 in *The Cambridge Survey of World Migration*, ed. Robin Cohen. Cambridge: Cambridge University Press.

O'Neill, Tom. 2001. "Selling Girls in Kuwait: Domestic Labour Migration and Trafficking Discourse in Nepal." *Anthropologica* 43: 153–64.

Ong, Aihwa. 1987. *Spirits of Resistance and Capitalist Discipline: Factory Women in Malaysia*. Albany: SUNY Press.

Ong, Paul, and Tania Azores. 1994. "The Migration and Incorporation of Filipino Nurses." Pp. 164–95 in *The New Asian Immigration in Los Angeles and Global Restructuring*, eds. Paul Ong, Edna Bonacich, and Lucie Cheng. Philadelphia: Temple University Press.

Ortigão, Ramalho. 1944. *Costumes e Perfis*. Lisbon: Livraria Clássica Editora.

Orsi, Robert, ed. 1999. *Gods of the City*. Bloomington: Indiana University Press.

Ortner, Sherry. 1973. "On Key Symbols." *American Anthropologist* 75: 1338–46.

———. 1995. "Resistance and the Problem of Ethnographic Refusal." *Comparative Studies in Society and History* 37: 173–93.

Ovalle-Bahamón, Ricardo E. 2003. "The Wrinkles of Decolonization and Nationness: White Angolans as Retornados in Portugal." Pp. 147–68 in *Europe's Invisible Migrants*, ed. Andrea L. Smith. Amsterdam: Amsterdam University Press.

Paine, Robert. 1967. "What Is Gossip About: An Alternative Hypothesis." *Man* 2: 278–85.

———. 1971a. "A Theory of Patronage and Brokerage." Pp. 8–21 in *Patrons and Brokers in the East Arctic*. Newfoundland Social and Economic Papers 2, ed. Robert Paine. St Johns, Newfoundland: Memorial University.

———. 1971b. "Conclusions." Pp. 98–105 in *Patrons and Brokers in the East Arctic*. Newfoundland Social and Economic Papers 2, ed. Robert Paine. St Johns, Newfoundland: Memorial University.

Paine, Suzanne. 1974. *Exporting Workers: The Turkish Case*. London: Cambridge Press.

Parati, Graziella. 1997. "Looking through Non-Western Eyes: Immigrant Women's Autobiographical Narratives in Italian." Pp. 118–42 in *Writing New Identities: Gender, Nation, and Immigration in Contemporary Europe*, eds. Gisela Brinker-Gabler and Sidonie Smith. Minneapolis: University of Minnesota Press.

Parenti, Michael. 1967. "Ethnic Politics and Persistence of Ethnic Identification." *American Political Science Review* 61: 717–26.

Parkin, D. J. 1969a. *Neighbors and Nations in an African City Ward*. Berkeley: University of California Press.

———. 1969b. "Tribe as Fact and Fiction in an East African City." Pp. 273–96 in *Tradition and Transition in East Africa*, ed. P. H. Gulliver. Berkeley: University of California Press.

Parreñas, Rhacel Salazar. 2001. *Servants of Globalization: Women, Migration, and Domestic Work*. Stanford: Stanford University Press.

Parsons, Anne. 1967. "Is the Oedipus Complex Universal? A South Italian Nuclear Complex." Pp. 352–99 in *Personalities and Cultures: Readings in Psychological Anthropology*, ed. Robert Hunt. New York: Natural History Press.

Pascual, A. 1970. *El Retorno de los Emigrantes*. Barcelona: Nova Terra.

Pedraza, Silvia. 1990. "Immigration Research: A Conceptual Map." *Social Science History* 14: 43–67.

———. 1991. "Women and Migration: The Social Consequences of Gender." *Annual Review of Sociology* 17: 303–25.

Percheiro, A. Gomes. 1878. *Portugal e Brazil: emigração e colonização*. Lisbon: Tipografia Luso-Hispanhola.

Pereira, Gil. 1983. "Os Portugueses, Veículos de Cultura." Pp. 21–22 in *Os Portugueses no Mundo*, ed. Manuel Alves. Lisbon: Edição de O Dia.

Pereira, Miriam Halpern. 1981. *A Política Portuguesa de Emigração, 1850–1930*. Lisbon: A Regra do Jogo.

Perlmann, Joel, and Roger Waldinger. 1997. "Second Generation Decline? Children of Immigrants, Past and Present—A Reconsideration." *International Migration Review* 31: 893–922.

———. 1999. "Immigrants, Past and Present: A Reconsideration." Pp. 223–38 in *The Handbook of International Migration: The American Experience*, eds. Charles Hirschman, Philip Kasinitz and Josh DeWind. New York: Russell Sage.

Pessar, Patricia R. 1984. "The Linkage Between the Household and Workplace of Dominican Women in the U.S." *International Migration Review* 18: 1188–211.

———. 1995. "On the Homefront and in the Workplace: Integrating Immigrant Women into Feminist Discourse." *Anthropological Quarterly* 68: 37–47.

———, ed. 1997. *Caribbean Circuits: New Directions in the Study of Caribbean Migration*. New York: Center for Migration Studies.

———. 1999a. "Engendering Migration Studies: The Case of New Immigrants to the United States." *American Behavioral Scientist* 42: 577–600.

———. 1999b. "The Role of Gender, Households and Social Networks in the Migration Process: A Review and Appraisal." Pp. 53–70 in *The Handbook of International Migration: The American Experience*, eds. Charles Hirschman, Philip Kasinitz, and Josh DeWind. New York: Russell Sage.

Pessar, Patricia, and Sarah Mahler. 2001. "Gendered Geographies of Power: Analyzing Gender Across Transnational Spaces." *Identities* 7: 441–59.

Pettman, J. J. 1996. "A Political Economy of Sex." Pp. 197–208 in *Globalisation: Theory and Practice*, eds. Eleanore Kofman and G. Youngs. London: Pinter.

Philpott, Stuart B. 1973. *West Indian Migration*. London: LSE Monographs in Anthropology.

Pina-Cabral, João de. 1981a. "Paved Roads and Enchanted Mooresses: The Perception of the Past among the Peasant Population of the Alto Minho." *Man* 22: 715–35.

———. 1981b. "0 Pároco Rural e o Conflito entre Visões do Mundo no Minho." *Estudos Contemporâneos* 2/3: 75–110.

———. 1984a. "Female Power and the Inequality of Wealth and Motherhood in Northwestern Portugal." Pp. 75–91 in *Women and Property—Women As Property*, ed. Renee Hirschon. London: Croom-Helm.

———. 1984b. "Comentários Críticos Sobre a Casa e a Família no Alto Minho Rural." *Análise Social* 20: 263–84.

———. 1986. *Sons of Adam, Daughters of Eve: The Peasant World View of the Alto Minho*. Oxford: Clarendon Press.

———. 1987. "Socio-Cultural Differentiation and Regional Identity in Portugal." Unpublished paper.

———. 1991. *Os Contextos da Antropologia*. Lisbon: Difusâo Editorial.

Pinkney, David. 1958. *Napoleon the Third and the Rebuilding of Paris*. Princeton, N.J.: Princeton University Press.

Pires, R. Pena, M. José Maranhão, João P. Quintela, Fernando Moniz, and Manuel Pisco. 1987. *Os Retornados: Um Estudo Sociográfico*. Lisbon: Instituto de Estudos para o Desenvolvimento.

Pires Cabral, A. M., ed. 1985. *A Emigração na Literatura Portuguesa: Uma Colectanea de Textos*. Lisbon: Serie Migrações.

Pitt-Rivers, Julian. 1954. *The People of the Sierra*. Chicago: University of Chicago Press.

Plotnicov, Leo. 1967. *Strangers to the City: Urban Man in Jos, Nigeria*. Pittsburgh: University of Pittsburgh Press.

———. 1970. "Rural-Urban Communication in Contemporary Nigeria: The Persistence of Traditional Social Institutions." *Journal of Asian and African Studies* 5: 66–82.

Poggie, John J. 1973. *Between Two Cultures: The Life of an American-Mexican*. Tucson: University of Arizona Press.

Poinard, Michel. 1983a. "Emigrantes Portugueses: O Regresso." *Análise Social* 19: 29–56.

———. 1983b. "Emigrantes Retornados de França: A Reinserção na Sociedade Portuguesa." *Análise Social* 19: 261–96.

Portes, Alejandro. 1987. "The Social Origins of the Cuban Enclave Economy of Miami." *Sociological Perspectives* 30 (4): 340–72.

Portes, Alejandro, ed. 1996. *The New Second Generation*. New York: Russell Sage.

Portes, Alejandro, and R. Manning. 1986. "The Immigrant Enclave: Theory and Empirical Examples." Pp. 47–68 in *Competitive Ethnic Relations*, eds. J. Nagel and S. Olzak. Orlando, Fla.: Academic Press.

Portes, Alejandro, and Rubén Rumbaut. 2001. *Legacies: The Story of the Immigrant Second Generation*. Berkeley: University of California Press.

Portes, Alejandro, and Min Zhou. 1993. "The New Second Generation: Segmented Assimilation and Its Variants among Post-1965 Immigrant Youth. *Annals of the American Academy of Political and Social Sciences* 530: 74–96.

Psimmenos, Iordannis. 2000. "The Making of Periphractic Spaces: The Case of Albanian Undocumented Female Migrants in the Sex Industry of Athens." Pp. 81–102 in *Gender and Migration in Southern Europe: Women on the Move*, eds. Floya Anthias and Gabriella Lazaridis. Oxford: Berg Publishers.

Radin, Paul. 1926. *Crashing Thunder: The Autobiography of a Winnebago Indian*. New York: D. Appleton.

Rapport, Nigel, and Andrew Dawson. 1998. "Home and Movement: A Polemic." Pp. 19–38 in *Migrants of Identity: Perceptions of Home in a World of Movement*, eds. Nigel Rapport and Andrew Dawson. Oxford: Berg Publishers.

Rapport, Nigel, and Joanna Overing. 2000. *Social and Cultural Anthropology: The Key Concepts*. New York: Routledge.

Rath, Jan, ed. 2002. *Unraveling the Rag Trade: Immigrant Entrepreneurship in Seven World Cities*. New York: Berg Publications

Rath, Jan, and Robert Kloosterman. 2000. "Outsiders' Business: A Critical Review of Research on Immigrant Entrepreneurship." *International Migration Review* 34: 657–81.

Ravenstein, E. G. 1885. "The Laws of Migration." *Journal of the Royal Statistical Society* 48: 167–277.

Redfield, Robert. 1930. *Tepotztlan, a Mexican Village: A Study of Folk Life*. Chicago: University of Chicago Press.

Reitz, Jeffrey G. 1998. *Warmth of the Welcome: The Social Causes of Economic Success for Immigrants in Different Nations and Cities*. Boulder: Westview Press.

Repak, Terry A. 1995. *Waiting on Washington: Central American Workers in the Nation's Capital*. Philadelphia: Temple University Press.

Rhoades, Robert. 1978. "Intra-European Return Migration and Rural Development: Lessons from the Spanish Case." *Human Organization* 37: 136–47.

———. 1979. "From Caves to Main Street: Return Migration and the Transformation of a Spanish Village." *Papers in Anthropology* 20: 57–74.

Riegelhaupt, Joyce Firstenberg. 1964. *In the Shadow of the City: Integration of a Portuguese Village*. Ph.D. dissertation, Department of Anthropology, Columbia University.

———. 1967. "Saloio Women: An Analysis of Informal and Formal Political and Economic Roles of Portuguese Peasant Women." *Anthropological Quarterly* 40: 109–26.

———. 1973. "Festas and Padres: The Organization of Religious Action in a Portuguese Parish." *American Anthropologist* 75: 835–51.

———. 1979. "Os Camponeses e a Política no Portugal de Salazar—o Estado Corporative e o 'a politicismo' nas aldeias." *Análise Social* 15: 505–23.

———. 1984. "Popular Anti-Clericalism and Religiosity in Pre-1974 Portugal." Pp. 93–116 in *Religion, Power and Protest in Local Communities*, ed. Eric R. Wolf. New York: Mouton.

Robertson, George, Mellinda Mash, Lisa Tickner, Jon Bird, Barry Curtis, and Tim Putnam, eds. 1994. *Travellers' Tales: Narratives of Home and Displacement*. London: Routledge.

Robinson, Richard. 1977. "The Religious Question and the Catholic Revival in Portugal, 1900–1930." *Journal of Contemporary History* 12: 345–62.

Rocha, Nuno. 1962. *França: A Emigração Dolorosa*. Lisbon: Editora Ulliseia, Varia 4.

Rocha-Trindade, Maria Beatriz. 1973. *Immigrés Portugais*. Lisbon: Instituto Superior de Ciencias Sociais e Política Ultramarina.

———. 1984. "O Diálogo Instituido." *Nova Renascença* 4: 229–45.

———. 1990. "Portuguese Migration to Brazil in the Nineteenth and Twentieth Centuries: An Example of International Cultural Exchanges." Pp. 7–28 in *Portuguese Migration in Global Perspective*, ed. David Higgs. Toronto: Multicultural History Society of Ontario.

———. 1995. "The Repatriation of Portuguese From Africa." Pp. 337–41 in *The Cambridge Survey of World Migration*, ed. Robin Cohen. Cambridge: Cambridge University Press.

Rocha-Trindade, Maria Beatriz, and R. Raveau, eds. 1998. *Présence Portugaise en France*. Lisbon: Universidade Aberta.

Rogers, Susan. 1975. "Female Forms of Power and the Myth of Male Dominance: A Model of Female/Male Interaction in Peasant Society." *American Ethnologist* 2: 727–56.

———. 1987. "Good to Think: The 'Peasant' in Contemporary France." *Anthropological Quarterly* 60: 56–63.

Rollwagen, Jack. 1975. "Introduction: The City as Context: A Symposium." *Urban Anthropology* 4: 1–4.

Roseberry, William. 1988. "Political Economy." *Annual Review of Anthropology* 17: 161–85.

Ross, Marc, and Thomas Weisner. 1977. "Rural-Urban Migrant Networks in Kenya." *American Ethnologist* 4: 359–72.

Rouse, Roger. 1989. *Mexican Migration to the United States: Family Relations in the Development of a Transnational Migrant Circuit.* Doctoral dissertation, Department of Anthropology, Stanford University.

Rowland, Robert. 1981. "Ancora e Montaria, 1827: Duas Freguesias do Noroeste Segundo os Livros de Registo das Companhias de Ordenanças." *Estudos Contemporâneos* 2/3: 199–242.

———. 1984. "Sistemas Familiares e Padrões Demográficos em Portugal: Questões Para uma Investigacão Comparada." *Ler História* 3: 13–32.

———. 1985. "Demographic Patterns and Rural Society in Portugal." *Sociologia Ruralis* 26: 36–47.

Royal Commission on Bilingualism and Biculturalism. 1970. *The Cultural Contribution of Other Ethnic Groups.* Ottawa: Information Canada.

Sá Carneiro, Francisco. 1983. "Os Portugueses no Mundo: Ontem e Hoje." Pp. 25–27 in *Os Portugueses no Mundo*, ed. Manuel Alves. Lisbon: Edição de O dia.

Safa, Helen I. 1975. "Introduction." Pp. 1–13 in *Migration and Development: Implications for Ethnic Identity and Political Conflict*, eds. Helen I. Safa and Brian du Toit. The Hague: Mouton.

Salzinger, Leslie. 1991. "A Maid by Any Other Name: The Transformation of 'Dirty Work' by Central American Immigrants." Pp. 139–60 in *Ethnography Unbound: Power and Resistance in the Modern Metropolis*, eds. Michael Burawoy, et al. Berkeley: University of California Press.

Sampaio, Bruno. 1898. *O Brasil Mental.* Lisbon: Livraria Chardron.

Sanchis, Pierre. 1976. *Arraial, La Fête d'un Peuple: Les Pèlerinages Populaires au Portugal.* Paris: Écoles de Hautes Études en Sciences Sociales.

Sanjek, Roger, and Shellee Colen, eds. 1990. *At Work in Homes: Household Workers in World Perspective.* Washington, D.C.: American Ethnological Society.

Saunders, George. 1981. "Men and Women in Southern Europe: A Review of Some Aspects of Cultural Complexity." *Journal of Psychoanalytic Anthropology* 4: 435–66.

Schaafsma, Juliette. 2000. "Current Patterns of Male Seasonal Migration and its Effects on Mafa Women." Pp. 40–62 in *Women and Migration: Anthropological Perspectives*, eds. Jacqueline Knörr and Barbara Meier. New York: St. Martins Press.

Schmitters, Philippe. 1976. "The Social Origins, Economic Bases and Political Imperatives of Authoritarian Rule in Portugal." Paper presented to the Conference Group on Modern Portugal, Toronto.

Schnappers, Dominique. 1974. "Centralisme et federalisme culturels: les immigrés italiens en France et aux Etats Unis." *Annales* 29: 1141–59.

Schneider, Peter, Jane Schneider, and Edward Hansen. 1971. "Modernization and Development: The Role of Groups in the European Mediterranean." *Comparative Studies in Society and History* 14: 328–49.

Schwartz, Barry. 1987. *George Washington: The Making of an American Symbol.* New York: Free Press.

Scott, James. 1985. *Weapons of the Weak: Everyday Forms of Peasant Resistance*. New Haven: Yale University Press.

Segalen, Martine. 1984. "Nuclear Is Not Independent: Organization of the Household in the Pays Bigouden Sud in the Nineteenth and Twentieth Centuries." Pp. 163–86 in *Households*, eds. Robert McC. Netting, Richard R. Wilk, and Eric J. Arnould. Los Angeles: University of California Press.

Segura, Denise A. 1989. "Chicanas and Immigrant Women at Work: The Impact of Class, Race and Gender on Occupational Mobility." *Gender and Society* 3: 37–52.

Serrão, Joel. 1974. *Emigração Portuguesa*. Lisbon: Collecção Horizonte 12.

———. 1976. *Testemunhos Sobre a Emigração Portuguesa*. Lisbon: Livros Horizonte.

Seton-Watson, Hugh. 1977. *Nations and States: An Enquiry into the Origins of Nations and the Politics of Nationalism*. Boulder: Westview Press.

Shostak, Marjorie. 1981. *Nisa: The Life and Words of a !Kung Woman*. Cambridge: Harvard University Press.

Silva, Manuela, Rogério Roque Amaro, Guy Clausse, Custódio Conim, Madalena Matos, Manuel Pisco, and Luís Miguel Seruya. 1984. *Retorno, Emigração e Desenvolvimento Regional em Portugal*. Lisbon: Instituto de Estudos para o Desenvolvimento.

Silva, Philip T., Jr. 1976. "The Position of 'New' Immigrants in the Fall River Textile Industry." *International Migration Review* 10: 221–32.

Silverman, Sydel. 1965. "Patronage and Community-Nation Relationships in Central Italy." *Ethnology* 4: 172–89.

———. 1975. *Three Bells of Civilization*. New York: Columbia University Press.

Simmel, Georg. 1955. *The Sociology of Georg Simmel*. Glencoe, Ill.: Free Press.

Simmons, Leo W. 1979. *Sun Chief: The Autobiography of a Hopi Indian*. New Haven: Yale University Press. Original edition, 1942.

Simões, Nuno. 1934. *O Brasíl e a Emigração Portuguesa*. Coimbra: Imprensa da Universidade.

Simon, Rita J. 1992. "Sociology and Immigrant Women." Pp. 23–40 in *Seeking Common Ground: Multidisciplinary Studies of Immigrant Women in the United States*, ed. Donna Gabaccia. Westport, Conn.: Greenwood Press.

———, ed. 2000. *Sexual Trafficking: An International Horror Story*. Washington, D.C.: Women's Freedom Network.

Simon, Rita James, and Caroline B. Brettell, eds. 1986. *International Migration: The Female Experience*. Totowa, N.J.: Rowman and Allenheld.

Singer, Audrey, and Amelia Brown. 2001. "Washington, D.C." Pp. 974–82 in *Encyclopedia of American Immigration*, ed. James Ciment. Armonk, N.Y.: M.E. Sharpe.

Sjoberg, G. 1964. "The Rural-Urban Dimension in Pre-Industrial, Transitional and Industrial Societies." Pp. 127–60 in *Handbook of Modern Sociology*, ed. R. F. L. Faris. Chicago: Rand McNally.

Smith, Andrea L., ed. 2003. *Europe's Invisible Migrants*. Amsterdam: Amsterdam University Press.

Smith, Michael Peter, and Luis Eduardo Guarnizo, eds. 1998. *Transnationalism From Below*. New Brunswick, N.J.: Transaction Books.

Smith, Robert C. 1998. "Transnational Localities: Community, Technology and the Politics of Membership within the Context of Mexico and U.S. Migration."

Pp. 196–238 in *Transnationalism From Below*, eds. Michael Peter Smith and Luis Eduardo Guarnizo. New Brunswick, N.J.: Transaction Books.

Solé, Carlota. 1995. "Portugal and Spain: From Exporters to Importers of Labour." Pp. 316–20 in *The Cambridge Survey of World Migration*, ed. Robin Cohen. Cambridge: Cambridge University Press.

Sone, Monica. 1953. *Nisei Daughter*. Seattle: University of Washington Press.

Sousa, D. Agostinho. 1943. *Pastoral Sobre Festas*. Porto.

Sousa Ferreira, Eduardo. 1976. *Origens e Formas da Emigração*. Lisbon: Iniciativas Editoriais.

Sousa Ferreira, Eduardo, and Guy Clausse, eds. 1986. *Closing the Migratory Cycle: The Case of Portugal*. Saarbrücken: Verlag Breitenback Publishers.

Sousa Franco, Antonio de. 1974. *A Emigração para a Europa no Conjunto da Emigração Portuguesa*. Lisbon: Mundo em Movimento 1.

Stack, Carol. 1996. *Call to Home: African Americans Reclaim the Rural South*. New York: Basic Books.

Stalker, Peter. 2000. *Workers without Frontiers: The Impact of Globalization on International Migration*. Boulder: Lynne Rienner.

Statistics Canada. 1991. *Census of Canada 1991*. Ottawa: Ministry of Supply and Services.

Stepick, Alex. 1998. *Pride against Prejudice: Haitians in the United States*. Boston: Allyn and Bacon.

Summerfield, Hazel. 1996. "Patterns of Adaptation: Somali and Bangladeshi Women in Britain." Pp. 83–98 in *Migrant Women: Crossing Boundaries and Changing Identities*, ed. Gina Buijs. Oxford: Berg Publishers.

Suttles, Wayne. 1960. "Affinal Ties, Subsistence, and Prestige among the Coast Salish." *American Anthropologist* 62: 296–305.

Sweet, Louise. 1967. "The Women of Ain ad Adyr." *Anthropological Quarterly* 40: 167–83.

Taft, Donald R. 1923. *Two Portuguese Communities in New England*. New York: Columbia University Press.

Tapinos, Georges. 1975. *L'immigration Étrangère en France*. Paris: INED.

Teixeira, Carlos. 1995. "The Portuguese in Toronto: A Community on the Move." *Portuguese Studies Review* 4: 57–75.

Thomas, W. I., and Florian Znaniecki. 1927. *The Polish Peasant in Europe and America*. New York: Alfred A. Knopf.

Thomas-Hope, E. 1985. "Return Migration and Implications for Caribbean Development." Pp. 157–73 in *Migration and Development in the Caribbean*, ed. R. A. Pastor. Boulder: Westview Press.

———. 1986. "Transients and Settlers: Varieties of Caribbean Migrants and the Socioeconomic Implications of their Return." *International Migration* 24: 559–70.

Tilly, Charles. 1978. "Migrations in Modern European History." Pp. 48–72 in *Human Migration Patterns and Policies*, eds. William McNeill and Ruth Adams. Bloomington: Indiana University Press.

Truong, Thanh-Dam. 2000. "Gender, International Migration and Social Reproduction: Implications for Theory, Policy, Research and Networking." Pp. 27–90 in *Gender and Migration*, eds. Katie Willis and Brenda Yeoh. Cheltenham: Edward Elgar Publishing.

Turner, Victor. 1967. *The Forest of Symbols: Aspects of Ndembu Ritual*. Ithaca: Cornell University Press.

Tyner, James A. 1999. "The Global Context of Gendered Labor Migration from the Philippines to the United States." *American Behavioral Scientist* 42: 671–89.

Ui, Shiri. 1991. "Unlikely Heroes: The Evolution of Female Leadership in a Cambodian Ethnic Enclave." Pp. 161–77 in *Ethnography Unbound: Power and Resistance in the Modern Metropolis*, eds. Michael Burawoy et al. Berkeley: University of California Press.

Underhill, Ruth. 1985. *Papago Woman*. Prospect Heights, Ill.: Waveland Press. Original edition, 1936.

United Nations. 1995. *International Migration Policies and the Status of Female Migrants*. Proceedings of the United Nations Expert Group Meeting on International Migration Policies and the Status of Female Migrants, Aan Miniato, Italy, March 28–31, 1990. New York: United Nations.

Vallee, Frank G. 1971. "Regionalism and Ethnicity: the French Canadian Case." Pp. 151–59 in *Immigrant Groups*, ed. Jean Elliott. Scarborough, N.J.: Prentice Hall.

Vecoli, Rudolph. 1999. "Foreword, 1970 edition." Pp. v–xi in *Rosa: The Life of an Italian Immigrant*, ed. Maria Hall Ets. Madison: University of Wisconsin Press.

Waldinger, Roger, ed. 2001. *Strangers at the Gates: New Immigrants in Urban America*. Berkeley: University of California Press.

Wall, Karin. 1984. "Mulheres que Partem e Mulheres que Ficam: Uma Primeira Análise da Funcão Social e Economica das Mulheres no Processo Migratório." *Ler História* 3: 53–63.

Walton, J. 1985. "The Third 'New' International Division of Labour." Pp. 3–16 in *Capital and Labour in the Urbanized World*, ed. J. Walton. London: Sage.

Warner, R. Stephen, and Judith G. Wittner, eds. 1998. *Gatherings in Diaspora: Religious Communities and the New Immigration*. Philadelphia: Temple University Press.

Watson, James L. 1975. *Emigration and the Chinese Lineage: The Mans in Hong Kong and London*. Berkeley: University of California Press.

Watson, Lawrence C., and Maria-Barbara Watson-Franke. 1985. *Interpreting Life Histories: An Anthropological Inquiry*. New Brunswick, N.J.: Rutgers University Press.

Weatherford, D. 1986. *Foreign and Female: Immigrant Women in America, 1840–1930*. New York: Schocken Books.

Weinberg, Sydney Stahl. 1992. "The Treatment of Women in Immigration History: A Call for Change." Pp. 3–22 in *Seeking Common Ground: Multidisciplinary Studies of Immigrant Women in the United States*, ed. Donna Gabaccia. Westport, Conn.: Greenwood Press.

Werbner, Pnina. 1990. *The Migration Process: Capital, Gifts, and Offerings among British Pakistanis*. New York: Berg Publishers.

Weyland, Petra. 1993. *Inside the Third World Village*. London: Routledge.

Wheeler, Douglas. 1978. *Republican Portugal: A Political History 1910–1926*. Madison: University of Wisconsin Press.

Whiteford, Michael. 1976. *The Forgotten Ones: Colombian Countrymen in an Urban Setting*. Gainesville: The University of Florida Press.

Whyte, William Foote. 1943. *Street Corner Society: The Social Structure of an Italian Slum*. Chicago: University of Chicago Press.

Williams, Jerry. 1982. *And Yet They Come: Portuguese Immigration from the Azores to the United States*. New York: Center for Migration Studies.

———. 1990. "Azorean Migration Patterns in the United States." Pp. 145–57 in *Portuguese Migration in Global Perspective*, ed. David Higgs. Toronto: Multicultural History Society of Ontario.

Willis, Katie, and Brenda Yeoh, eds. 2000. *Gender and Migration*. Cheltenham: Edward Elgar Publishing.

Wilson, Tamar Diana. 1994. "What Determines Where Transnational Labor Migrants Go? Modifications in Migration Theories." *Human Organization* 53: 269–78.

Wolf, Diane L. 1990. "Linking Women's Labor with the Global Economy: Factory Workers and Their Families in Rural Java." Pp. 25–47 in *Women Workers and Global Restructuring*, ed. Kathryn Ward. Ithaca, N.Y.: IRL Press.

Wolf, Eric. 1956. "Aspects of Group Relations in a Complex Society: Mexico." *American Anthropologist* 58: 1065–1078.

———. 1957. "Closed Corporate Peasant Communities in Mesoamerica and Central Java." *Southwestern Journal of Anthropology* 13 (1): 1–18.

Wolfinger, Raymond. 1965. "The Development and Persistence of Ethnic Voting." *American Political Science Review* 59: 896–908.

Wrench, John, and John Solomos. 1993. *Racism and Migration in Western Europe*. Oxford: Berg Publishers.

Wyman, Mark. 1993. *Round-Trip to America: The Immigrants Return to Europe, 1880–1930*. Ithaca, N.Y.: Cornell University Press.

Yoon, In-Jin. 1991. "The Changing Significance of Ethnic and Class Resources in Immigrant Businesses: The Case of Korean Immigrant Businesses in Chicago." *International Migration Review* 25: 303–31.

Young, Scott. 1957. "New Canadians: Payday Road Gang Heyday." *Toronto Globe and Mail*, June 4.

Yuan, D. 1970. "Voluntary Segregation: A Study of New York Chinatown." Pp. 134–44 in *Minority Responses*, ed. Minako Kurokawa. New York: Random House.

Zelinsky, Wilbur, and Barrett A. Lee. 1998. "Heterolocalism: An Alternative Model of the Sociospatial Behaviour of Immigrant Ethnic Communities." *International Journal of Population Geography* 4: 281–98.

Zetter, Roger. 1999. "Reconceptualizing the Myth of Return: Continuity and Transition amongst the Greek-Cypriot Refugees of 1974." *Journal of Refugee Studies* 12: 1–22.

Zhou, Min. 1992. *Chinatown: The Socioeconomic Potential of an Urban Enclave*. Philadelphia: Temple University Press.

———. 1999. "Segmented Assimilation: Issues, Controversies, and Recent Research on the New Second Generation." Pp. 196–211 in *The Handbook of International Migration: The American Experience*, eds. Charles Hirschman, Philip Kasinitz, and Josh DeWind. New York: Russell Sage.

Zimmer, C., and H. Aldrich. 1987. "Resource Mobilization through Ethnic Networks, Kinship and Friendship Ties of Shopkeepers in England." *Sociological Perspectives* 30: 422–45.

Index

About the Author

Caroline Brettell is professor and chair of the department of anthropology at Southern Methodist University. For five years (1989–1994) she served as director of the women's studies program at Southern Methodist University. She has her Ph.D. in anthropology from Brown University (1978). Prior to joining the SMU faculty in 1988, she was a research associate in the Family and Community History Center at the Newberry Library in Chicago.

She is a specialist on migration and on Portuguese culture and society. In the area of migration, she has focused particularly on the study of immigrant women in a comparative context. Her work in Portugal has focused not only on the topic of migration but also on religion, gender issues, property and inheritance, kinship, and cultural change. As an active member of the Social Science History Association, an organization for which she served as president in 2000–2001, she has a special interest in the relationships between anthropology and history.